≝ ACCESS TO JUSTICE ≝

⹀ ACCESS TO JUSTICE ⹀

Deborah L. Rhode

OXFORD
UNIVERSITY PRESS

2004

OXFORD
UNIVERSITY PRESS

Oxford New York
Auckland Bangkok Buenos Aires Cape Town Chennai
Dar es Salaam Delhi Hong Kong Istanbul Karachi Kolkata
Kuala Lumpur Madrid Melbourne Mexico City Mumbai Nairobi
Sao Paulo Shanghai Taipei Tokyo Toronto

Published by Oxford University Press, Inc.
198 Madison Avenue, New York, New York 10016

www.oup.com

Oxford is a registered trademark of Oxford University Press

Library of Congress Cataloging-in-Publication Data
Rhode, Deborah L.
Access to justice / by Deborah L. Rhode.
    p. cm.
ISBN 978-0-19-530648-4
1. Legal aid—United States. 2. Legal assistance to the poor—United States.
3. Justice, Administration of—United States. I. Title.
KF336 .R48 2004
344.7303′258—dc22   2003023136

Cover image:
James Dow, American, born 1942
Grady County Courthouse, Jury Box, Cairo, Georgia, 1976, printed 1983
Photograph, gelatin silver print
Image: 19.6 × 25.0 cm (7 $\frac{11}{16}$ × 9 $\frac{13}{16}$ in.)
Sheet: 21.34 × 27.94 cm (8 $\frac{3}{8}$ × 11 in.)
Museum of Fine Arts, Boston
Gift of Richard S. and Jeanne L. Press in honor of Stephen D. Paine
1998.657

Printed in the United States of America
on acid-free paper

For Dedi Felman

⌐ ACKNOWLEDGMENT ⌐

In a book on justice, it is a daunting challenge to do justice gracefully to all who have given so generously of their time and talents. Many students provided valuable research assistance, particularly Eric Beckenhauer, Nathan Doty, Avlana Eisenberg, Carolyn Janiak, Jonathan Sanders, and Angie Schwartz. I also benefitted immeasurably from a Stanford statistician, Elizabeth Cameron, and the superb staff of the Stanford Law Library, particularly David Bridgeman, Paul Lomio, Sonia Moss, and Erika Wayne. Colleagues from both the academic and legal services community gave exceptionally insightful comments: Cynthia Adcock, Barbara Babcock, Gary Blasi, Stephen Bright, John Donahue, Pauline Grayson, Deborah Hensler, Alan Houseman, Esther Lardent, Lawrence Marshall and Alan Morrison. Special gratitude goes to Lawrence Friedman, who lent his vast store of knowledge to the entire book. I owe similar debts to my assistant, Mary Tye, who prepared the manuscript with extraordinary skill and endless good humor. Funding for the empirical survey described in chapter 7 came from the generous efforts of my Stanford colleagues, Joseph Grundfest and David Mills, and from the Roberts Program in Law and Social Governance.

The book is dedicated to my editor at Oxford University Press, Dedi Felman. She saw from the outset what it could and should be, and guided its progress with exceptional wisdom and judgment. My greatest debt, however, on this and every project, is to my husband Ralph Cavanagh. More than a quarter century ago, as law students, we coauthored a study involving access to justice. And it has been his vision, values, and support that have sustained me in all the work that has followed.

CONTENTS

⇉ ACCESS TO JUSTICE ⇇

≝ 1 ≝

EQUAL JUSTICE UNDER LAW

The Gap between Principle and Practice

"Equal justice under law" is one of America's most proudly proclaimed and widely violated legal principles. It embellishes courthouse entrances, ceremonial occasions, and constitutional decisions. But it comes nowhere close to describing the legal system in practice. Millions of Americans lack any access to justice, let alone equal access. According to most estimates, about four-fifths of the civil legal needs of the poor, and two- to three-fifths of the needs of middle-income individuals, remain unmet. Government legal aid and criminal defense budgets are capped at ludicrous levels, which make effective assistance of counsel a statistical impossibility for most low-income litigants. We tolerate a system in which money often matters more than merit, and equal protection principles are routinely subverted in practice.[1]

This is not, of course, the only legal context in which rhetoric outruns reality. But it is one of the most disturbing, given the fundamental rights at issue. A commitment to equal justice is central to the legitimacy of democratic processes. And many nations come far closer than our own to realizing this ideal in practice. It is a shameful irony that the country with the world's most lawyers has one of the least adequate systems for legal assistance. It is more shameful still that the inequities attract so little concern. Over the last two decades, national spending on legal aid has been cut by a third, and increasing restrictions have been placed on the clients and causes that government-funded programs can represent. Groups that are the most politically vulnerable are now the most legally vulnerable as well. Federally funded programs may not take cases involving the "unworthy" poor, defined expansively to in-

3

clude prisoners, undocumented aliens, women seeking abortions, and school desegregation plaintiffs.[2]

Although indigent criminal defendants are theoretically entitled to effective assistance of counsel, few actually receive it. Over 90 percent of cases are resolved by guilty pleas, generally without any factual investigation. Court-appointed lawyers' preparation is often minimal, sometimes taking less time than the average American spends showering before work. In the small minority of cases that go to trial, convictions have been upheld where defense counsel were asleep, on drugs, suffering from mental illness, or parking their cars during key parts of the prosecution's case.[3]

What perpetuates the problem is the lack of public recognition that there is a serious problem. Although most Americans agree that the wealthy have advantages in the justice system, about four-fifths believe that it is still the "best in the world." About the same number also believe, incorrectly, that the poor are entitled to counsel in civil cases. Only a third of Americans think that low-income individuals would have difficulty finding legal assistance, a perception wildly out of touch with reality. Fewer than 1 percent of lawyers are in legal aid practice, which works out to about one lawyer for every 1,400 poor or near-poor persons in the United States.[4]

The criminal justice system reflects an even wider gap between public perceptions and daily realities. Americans generally believe that the process coddles criminals, whose lawyers routinely get them off on technicalities. Such assumptions come largely from movies, television, and the highly publicized trials in which zealous advocacy is the norm. Counsel for O. J. Simpson and the Oklahoma bombers left no stones unturned. But they were charging by the stone. Most defense counsel cannot, and no media glare is available to encourage adequate preparation. Few Americans have any clear appreciation of what passes for justice among the have-nots. And those who do are not necessarily motivated to respond. The groups most in need of legal assistance have the least access to political leverage that could secure it. A common attitude, expressed with uncommon candor by one chair of a state legislative budget committee, is that he did not really "care whether indigents [were] represented or not."[5]

This book is about why all of us *should* care about access to justice. It is not only the poor who are priced out of the current system. Millions of Americans, including those of moderate income, suffer untold misery because legal protections that are available in principle are inaccessible in practice. Domestic violence victims cannot obtain protective orders, elderly medical patients cannot collect health benefits, disabled children are denied educational services, defrauded consumers lack affordable remedies. . . . The list is long and the costs incalculable. Moreover, those who attempt to navigate the system unassisted confront unnecessary obstacles at every turn. In most family, housing, bankruptcy, and small claims courts, the majority of litigants lack legal representation. Yet the system has been designed by and for lawyers, and too little effort has been made to ensure that it is fair or even comprehensible to the average claimant.

The chapters that follow chronicle the shameful gap between our rhetorical commitments and daily practices concerning access to justice. This opening essay gives an overview of our current pathologies and essential prescriptions. Discussion then turns to a different diagnosis of the problem: the widespread view that America has too much law and lawyering, rather than too little. Yet while some of the public's concerns about frivolous litigation and excessive expense have ample basis, most of the prevailing wisdom about litigiousness rests on flawed premises and points to misconceived solutions. What should be of greatest concern are not excessive lawsuits but inaccessible rights and remedies. This is the focus of the chapters that follow. Discussion begins with a historical perspective on our current plight. Subsequent chapters look at particular dimensions of the problem: the obstacles to self-help and low-cost services for middle Americans; the glaring shortfall in civil and criminal legal assistance for the poor; and the limitations of the bar's preferred responses—government-funded aid and charitable "pro bono" contributions by lawyers. Drawing on the recommendations set forth in these chapters, a concluding essay offers a roadmap of crucial reforms. The basic conclusion is straightforward. Given the increasing centrality of law in American life, we can no longer afford a system that most citizens cannot themselves afford.

Defining the Goal: Access for Whom? For What? How Much? And Who Should Decide?

In theory, "equal justice under law" is difficult to oppose. In practice, however, it begins to unravel at key points, beginning with what we mean by "justice." In most discussions, "equal justice" implies equal access to the justice system. The underlying assumption is that social justice is available through procedural justice. But that, of course, is a dubious proposition. Those who receive their "day in court" do not always feel that "justice has been done," and with reason. The role that money plays in legal, legislative, and judicial selection processes often skews the law in predictable directions. Even those who win in court can lose in life. Formal rights can be prohibitively expensive to enforce, successful plaintiffs can be informally blacklisted, and legislatures may overturn legal rulings that lack political support.[6]

These difficulties are seldom acknowledged in discussions of access to justice, which assume that more is better, and that the trick is how to achieve it. But even from a purely procedural standpoint, that assumption leaves a host of conceptual complexities unaddressed. What constitutes a "legal need"? A vast array of conflicts and concerns could give rise to legal action. How much claiming and blaming is our society prepared to subsidize? Does access to law also require access to legal assistance, and if so, how much is enough? For what, for whom, from whom? Should government support go to only the officially poor or to all those who cannot realistically afford lawyers? Under what circumstances do individuals need full-blown representation by attorneys, as opposed to other less expensive forms of assistance? How do legal needs compare with other claims on our collective resources? And, most important, who should decide?

The complexities are compounded if we also think seriously about what would make justice truly "equal." Equal to what? Although there is broad agreement that the quality of justice should not depend on the ability to pay, there is little corresponding consensus on an alternative. How do we deal with disparities in incentives, resources, and legal ability? True equality in legal assistance would presumably require not only massive public expenditures but also the restriction of private expenditures. And, as R. H. Tawney once noted about equal opportunity generally, it is not clear what would alarm proponents most, "the denial of the principle or the attempt to apply it." If cost were no constraint, what would prevent excessive resort to expensive procedural processes? Our ideal world is surely not one in which all disputes are fully adjudicated, but can we develop more equitable limiting principles than ability to pay?[7]

These questions cannot be resolved in the abstract, and subsequent chapters explore their implications in light of particular policy issues. However, a few general observations can help put such concerns into broader context. By virtually any measure, our nation falls well short of providing even minimal, let alone equal, access to justice for Americans of limited means. Unlike most other industrialized nations, the United States recognizes no right to legal assistance for civil matters and courts have exercised their discretion to appoint counsel in only a narrow category of cases. Legislative budgets have been equally restrictive. The federal government, which provides about two-thirds of the funding for civil legal aid, now spends only about $8 per year for those living in poverty. Less than 1 percent of the nation's total expenditures on lawyers goes to help the seventh of the population that is poor enough to qualify for legal assistance. The inadequacies in criminal defense for indigents are of similar magnitude. On average, court-appointed lawyers receive only about an eighth of the resources available to prosecutors. Moreover, millions of Americans who are above poverty thresholds are also priced out of the legal process for the vast majority of their legal concerns.[8]

These inequities are particularly appalling for a nation that considers itself a global leader in human rights. Equal justice may be an implausible aspiration, but more accessible legal institutions are within our reach. Many nations with comparable justice systems and far fewer lawyers than the United States do much better at making basic rights available. These countries typically provide more sources of low-cost legal assistance, and more substantial government subsidies for low-income residents. For example, according to the most recent comparative research available, the United States allocates only about a sixteenth per capita of what Great Britain budgets for civil legal assistance, a sixth of what New Zealand provides, and a third of what some Canadian provinces guarantee. The following chapters leave no doubt that realistic reforms in our nation's delivery of legal services could go a long way to insuring that more Americans can assert their most fundamental rights. To make that possible, the public needs a clearer sense of its own stake in the reform agenda.[9]

The Increasing Role of Law and the Rationale for Legal Assistance

As commentators since Alexis de Tocqueville have noted, law and lawyers occupy a distinctively central role in American society. The importance that we attach to legal institutions has deep ideological and structural roots. It is not surprising that a nation founded by individuals escaping from governmental persecution should be wary of state power and protective of individual rights. Cross-national studies find that Americans are less willing than citizens of other nations to trust a centralized government to address social problems and to meet social welfare needs. This distrust is reflected and reinforced by political institutions that give courts a crucial role in constraining state power, safeguarding individual rights, and shaping public policy. The United States relies on legal institutions to protect fundamental values such as freedom of speech, due process, and equal opportunity that are central to our cultural heritage and constitutional traditions. This nation also finds privately financed lawsuits to be a fiscally attractive way of enforcing statutory requirements without spending taxpayer dollars on legal costs. Much of this country's environmental, health, safety, consumer, and antidiscrimination regulation occurs through litigation.[10]

Moreover, despite policymakers' frequent laments about legalization, the role and reach of law is increasing, a trend that reflects broader global forces. As patterns of life become more complex and interdependent, the need for legal regulation becomes correspondingly greater. In Western industrialized countries, improvements in the standard of living have also led to increased expectations about the functions of law in maintaining that standard. Throughout the last half century, many societies have come to expect what legal historian Lawrence Friedman labels "total justice." Unsafe conditions, abusive marriages, discriminatory conduct, and inadequacies in social services that were once accepted as a matter of course now prompt demands for legal remedies and for assistance in obtaining them. More and more of our everyday life is hedged about by law. Family, work, and commercial relationships are subject to a growing array of legal obligations and protections. As law becomes increasingly crucial and complex, access to legal services also becomes increasingly critical.[11]

The Right to Legal Assistance

That need for legal assistance has not been entirely lost on judicial and legislative decision makers, but neither have they taken the steps necessary to insure it. In 1932 the U.S. Supreme Court offered the common sense observation that an individual's "right to be heard [in legal proceedings] would be, in many cases, of little avail if it did not comprehend the right to be heard by counsel." In the years that followed, judges gradually built on that recognition to find a constitutional right to lawyers for indigent criminal defendants. However, courts have largely failed to extend guarantees of legal assistance to civil contexts, even where crucial interests are at issue. In the leading decision on point, *Lassiter v. Department of Social Services*, the Supreme Court interpreted the due process clause to require appointment of counsel in civil cases only if the proceeding would otherwise prove fundamentally unfair. In making that determination, courts must consider three basic factors: "the private interests at stake, the government's interest, and the risk that [lack of counsel] will lead to an erroneous decision."[12]

Although that standard is not unreasonable on its face, courts have applied it in such restrictive fashion that counsel is almost never required in civil cases. The *Lassiter* decision itself is a representative example. There, an incarcerated woman lost parental rights after a hearing at which she had no attorney. In the majority's view, such legal assistance would not have made a "determinative difference," given the state's strong factual case and the absence of "troublesome points of law." Lower courts have proven similarly reluctant to guarantee lawyers or to ensure their compensation, even in contexts where their aid would clearly be critical.[13]

This reluctance is problematic on several grounds. Some civil proceedings implicate interests as significant as those involved in many minor criminal proceedings where counsel is required. It is, for example, a cruel irony that in cases involving protective orders for victims of domestic violence, defendants who face little risk of significant sanctions are entitled to lawyers, while victims whose lives are in jeopardy are not. The rationale for subsidized representation seems particularly strong in cases like *Lassiter*, where fundamental interests are at issue, legal standards are imprecise and subjective, proceedings are formal and adversarial, and resources between the parties are grossly imbalanced. Under such circumstances, opportunities for legal assistance are crucial to the legitimacy of the justice system. As the Supreme Court has recognized in other contexts, the "right to sue and defend" is a right "conservative of all other rights, and lies at the foundation of an orderly government." Providing representation necessary to make those rights meaningful fosters values central to the rule of law and social justice. For many individuals, legal aid is equally critical in legislative and administrative contexts. Such assistance is the only way that millions of Americans can participate in these governance processes. Not only does access to legal services help prevent erroneous decisions, it also affirms a respect for human dignity and procedural fairness that are core democratic ideals.[14]

Courts' reluctance to extend the right to legal assistance has more to do with pragmatic than principled considerations. As law professor Geoffrey Hazard has noted, no "politically sober judge, however anguished by injustice unfolding before her eyes," could welcome the battles involved in trying to establish some broadly enforceable right to counsel. Given legislatures' repeated refusal to fund legal assistance at anything close to realistic levels, courts are understandably wary about stepping into the breach.[15]

Political Opposition to Legal Services

Political opposition to guaranteed legal services builds on several long-standing concerns, reviewed in greater detail in chapters 3 and 4. The first is that much of the assistance that poverty lawyers provide may in fact worsen the plight of the poor. One commonly cited example involves representation of "deadbeat" tenants or consumers. Landlords and merchants forced to litigate such matters allegedly pass on their costs in increased rents or prices to other, equally impoverished but more deserving individuals who manage to honor their financial obligations. A further objection is that even if some legal services do help the poor, it is inefficient to provide those services in kind rather than through cash transfers. Any broad-based entitlement to legal aid assertedly would encourage over-investments in law, as opposed to other purchases that the poor might value more, such as food, medicine, education, or housing. Critics note that poor people with unmet legal needs rarely spend their discretionary income on lawyers. And it is by no means clear that clients, if given the choice, would invest in the kinds of impact litigation that legal services attorneys often prefer.[16]

These claims raise several difficulties that do not emerge clearly in public debate. To begin with, the value of legal assistance cannot be gauged only by what the poor are willing and able to pay. Those who cannot meet their most basic subsistence needs also cannot make many purchases that would prove cost-effective in the longer term. That is part of what traps them in poverty. Yet even for those individuals, legal services may be a highly efficient use of resources. A few hours of legal work can result in benefits far exceeding their costs. Reviews of legal services programs reveal countless examples, such as brain-damaged children and elderly citizens on fixed incomes who receive essential medical treatment, or impoverished nursing mothers who gain protection from dangerous pesticides. For many forms of legal assistance, it would be difficult, if not impossible, to attach a precise dollar value, but the benefits may be enormous and enduring. Government-subsidized assistance makes it possible for millions of poor people to leave violent marriages, avoid homelessness, and obtain crucial health, education, and vocational services.[17]

Moreover, law is a public good. Protecting legal rights often has value beyond what those rights are worth to any single client. As chapter 5 notes, holding employers of farm workers accountable for unsafe field conditions, making landlords liable for violations of housing codes, or imposing penalties for consumer fraud can provide an essential deterrent against future abuse. Contrary to critics' claims, it is by no means clear that the costs of defending such lawsuits will all be passed on to other poor people, or that those costs are excessive in light of the deterrent value that they serve. Understaffed legal services offices have little reason to spend scarce resources litigating meritless cases that critics endlessly invoke. This is not to suggest that society in general or the poor in particular would benefit if every potential claim were fully litigated. But neither is ability to pay an effective way of screening out frivolous cases. America's gross inequalities in access to justice are an embarrassment to a nation that considers its legal system a model for the civilized world.[18]

The Inadequacy of Legal Assistance

A half century ago, the Supreme Court observed that "[t]here can be no equal justice where the kind of trial a man gets depends on the amount of money he has." Both criminal and civil proceedings bear daily witness to the truth of that observation. Yet our nation's judicial and legislative decision makers have repeatedly failed to address it.[19]

Criminal Defense

In criminal cases, over three-quarters of defendants facing felony charges are poor enough to qualify for court-appointed counsel. Legal assistance for these defendants takes three main forms: competitive contracts, individual case assignments, and public defender programs. As with Tolstoy's unhappy families, each of these systems breeds unhappiness in its own way.

Under competitive bidding systems, lawyers offer to provide representation for all, or a specified percentage of a jurisdiction's criminal cases, in exchange for a fixed price, irrespective of the number or complexity of matters involved. Such systems discourage effective assistance by selecting attorneys who are willing to accept a high volume of defendants at low cost. Annual caseloads can climb as high as 900 felony matters or several thousand misdemeanors. Rarely can these lawyers afford to do adequate investigation, file necessary motions, or take a matter to trial. "Meet 'em, greet 'em and plead 'em" is standard practice among contract attorneys. In one all too typical example, a lawyer who agreed to handle a county's entire criminal caseload for $25,000 filed only three motions in five years.[20]

Similar disincentives for effective representation occur under other systems. Some assign private practitioners on a case-by-case basis. These lawyers receive minimal flat fees or hourly rates, coupled with a ceiling on total compensation. Limits of $1,000 are common for felony cases, and some states allow less than half that amount. Teenagers selling sodas on the beach make higher rates than these attorneys. Low ceilings apply even for defendants facing the death penalty, and attorneys subject to such compensation caps have ended up with hourly rates below $4. For most court-appointed lawyers, thorough preparation is a quick route to financial ruin. Analogous problems often arise in the remaining jurisdictions, which rely on public defender offices. Although the quality of representation in some of these offices is quite high, others operate with crushing caseloads.[21]

Under all of these systems, the vast majority of court-appointed counsel lack sufficient resources to hire the experts and investigators who are often essential to an effective defense. The same is true for defendants who retain their own counsel. Most of these individuals are just over the line of indigence and cannot afford substantial legal expenses. Their lawyers typically charge a flat fee, payable in advance, which creates obvious disincentives to prepare thoroughly or proceed to trial.[22]

Many defense counsel also face nonfinancial pressures to curtail their representation. A quick plea spares lawyers the strain and potential humiliation of an unsuccessful trial. Such bargains also preserve good working relationships with judges and prosecutors, who confront their own, often overwhelming caseload demands. Indeed, a reputation for thorough representation on behalf of the accused is unlikely to work to counsel's advantage among the judiciary who control appointments. Judges coping with already unmanageable caseloads have been reluctant to appoint "obstructionist" lawyers who routinely raise technical defenses or demand lengthy trials. Taken together, these financial and nonfinancial pressures help explain why over 90 percent of defendants plead guilty, generally before their counsel does any factual investigation.[23]

The problem is compounded by the lack of accountability for inadequate performance. As chapter 6 indicates, neither market forces nor judicial and bar oversight structures provide a significant check on shoddy representation. Defendants typically lack sufficient information to second guess lawyers' plea recommendations and trial strategies. Even if clients doubt the adequacy of their counsel, they can seldom do much about it. Indigent defendants have no right to select their attorneys, and court-appointed lawyers do not depend for their livelihood on the satisfaction of clients.

Nor is "mere negligence" enough to trigger bar disciplinary action, establish malpractice liability, or overturn convictions based on ineffective assistance of counsel. Convicted criminals are generally unsympathetic litigants. To establish their lawyer's civil liability, they must also establish their own innocence. To obtain a reversal of a conviction, they must show specific errors falling below "prevailing professional norms" and a "reasonable probability" that "but for counsel's unprofessional errors, the results would have been different." That burden is almost impossible to meet. In one representative survey, over 99 percent of ineffective assistance claims were unsuccessful. Tolerance for ineptitude and inexperience runs even to capital cases. Defendants have been executed despite their lawyers' lack of any prior trial experience, ignorance of all relevant death penalty precedents, or failure to present any mitigating evidence. As one expert puts it, too many capital cases end up in the hands of lawyers who have "never tried a case before and never should again."[24]

Civil Contexts

Many low-income civil litigants fare no better. As noted earlier, legal services offices can handle less than a fifth of the needs of eligible clients and often are able to offer only brief advice, not the full range of assistance that is necessary. In some jurisdictions, poor people must wait over two years before seeing a lawyer for matters like divorce that are not considered emergencies, and other offices exclude such cases entirely. Legal aid programs that accept federal funds may not accept entire categories of clients who have nowhere else to go, such as prisoners or undocumented immigrants. Unrealistic income eligibility ceilings also exclude many individuals just over the poverty line who also cannot afford counsel. The result is that millions of Americans are locked out of law entirely.

Millions more attempt to represent themselves in a system stacked against them.[25]

Self-Representation and Nonlawyer Assistance

The last quarter century has witnessed a rapid growth in self-representation and in related materials and businesses. Kits, manuals, interactive computer programs, on-line information, form processing services, and courthouse facilitators have emerged to assist those priced out of the market for lawyers. But especially for the individuals who need help most, those of limited income and education, such forms of assistance fall far short. Much of the difficulty lies with judicial and bar leaders who have resisted access to law without lawyers. On issues like procedural simplification and lay services, the legal profession has often contributed more to the problem than the solution.

Procedural Hurdles

In courts that handle housing, bankruptcy, small claims, and family matters, parties without lawyers are less the exception than the rule. Cases in which at least one side is unrepresented are far more common than those in which both sides have counsel. In some jurisdictions, over four-fifths of these matters involve self-represented "pro se" litigants. Yet a majority of surveyed courts have no formal pro se assistance services, such as facilitators who can advise parties, or interactive computer kiosks that can help them complete legal forms. Many of the services that are available are unusable by those who need help most: low-income litigants with limited computer competence and English language skills.[26]

All too often, parties without lawyers confront procedures of excessive and bewildering complexity, and forms with archaic jargon left over from medieval England. Court clerks and mediators are instructed not to give legal "advice," since that would constitute "unauthorized practice of law." Even courts that have pro se facilitators caution them against answering any "should" questions, such as "which form should I file?" The result is that many parties with valid claims are unable to advance them. Pro se litigants in family and housing courts achieve less favorable results than litigants with lawyers who raise similar issues.[27]

Some courts are openly hostile to unrepresented parties, whom they view as tying up the system or attempting to gain tactical advantages.

Even the most sympathetic judges often have been unwilling to push for reforms that will antagonize lawyers whose economic interests are threatened by pro se assistance. Particularly for elected judges, support from the organized bar is critical to their reputation, election campaigns, and advancement. And encouraging parties to dispense with lawyers wins few friends in the circles that matter most.[28]

The Lawyer's Monopoly

Similar considerations have worked against other efforts to broaden access to nonlawyer providers of legal services. Almost all of the scholarly experts and commissions that have studied the issue have recommended increased opportunities for such lay assistance. Almost all of the major decisions by judges and bar associations have ignored those recommendations. Nonlawyers who engage in law-related activities are subject to criminal prohibitions that are inconsistently interpreted, unevenly enforced, and inappropriately applied. The dominant approach is to prohibit individuals who are not members of the state bar from providing personalized legal advice. For example, independent paralegals generally may type documents but may not answer even simple legal questions or correct obvious errors. The American Bar Association has recently taken actions to strengthen enforcement of these prohibitions, and many state and local bars have launched similar efforts. Yet research concerning nonlawyer specialists in other countries and in American administrative tribunals suggests that these individuals are generally at least as qualified as lawyers to provide assistance on routine matters where legal needs are greatest. As chapter 4 indicates, concerns about unqualified or unethical lay assistance could be addressed through more narrowly drawn prohibitions and licensing structures for nonlawyer providers.[29]

Unrepresented Parties

A profession truly committed to access to justice would not only support such reforms, it would also rethink the rules governing lawyers' dealings with unrepresented parties. In response to massive opposition from attorneys, the ABA rejected a proposed ethical standard that would have prevented lawyers from "unfairly exploiting" pro se litigants' ignorance of the law and from "procur[ing] an unconscionable result." According to opponents, "parties 'too cheap to hire a lawyer' should not be 'coddled' by special treatment." Under the rule ultimately approved, lawyers' sole responsibilities are to avoid implying that they are disinterested, to refrain from giving advice that is not disinterested, and to make "reasonable efforts" to correct misunderstandings concerning their role. Such minimal obligations have proven totally inadequate to curb overreaching behavior. Counsel for more powerful litigants in landlord–tenant, consumer, and family law disputes have often misled weaker unrepresented parties into waiving important rights and accepting inadequate settlements. Since these individuals typically do not know, cannot prove, or cannot afford lawsuits to prove that they were misinformed by opposing counsel, such conduct has rarely resulted in any disciplinary sanctions or legal remedies.[30]

Inadequate Resources

Further problems arise in the small number of civil cases where courts or legislatures have mandated appointment of counsel for indigent litigants. As in criminal matters, ludicrously inadequate compensation discourages effective representation. Even where legal assistance is adequate, court time is not. Overcrowded caseloads lead to rubber stamp review in matters that most affect ordinary Americans. Judges who spend weeks presiding over minor commercial disputes may have less than five minutes available to decide the future of an abused or neglected child. Equal justice is what we put on courthouse doors, not what happens inside them.[31]

The Limitations of Lawyers' Pro Bono Service

A final context in which rhetoric outruns reality involves lawyers' charitable "pro bono publico" service. Bar ethical codes and judicial decisions have long maintained that lawyers have a responsibility to assist those who cannot afford counsel. Leaders of the profession have endlessly applauded the "quiet heroism" of their colleagues in discharging that responsibility. A constant refrain in bar publications is that "no other profession . . . is as charitable with its time and money."[32]

Such claims suggest more about the profession's capacity for self-delusion than self-sacrifice. As chapters 3 and 7 indicate, pro bono assistance has never addressed more than a tiny fraction of the public's needs for assistance, and neither courts nor bar associations have been willing to require significant public service contributions. The scope of judicial power to compel lawyers to provide unpaid legal assistance remains unsettled, largely because the power has so rarely been exercised. The Supreme Court has never definitively resolved the issue, although some of its language and summary rulings imply that the judiciary has inherent authority to require such assistance at least in criminal cases. Lower court decisions are mixed, but most have upheld mandatory court appointments as long as the required amount of service is not "unreasonable." Yet in the face of strong resistance and inadequate performance by many lawyers, courts have been reluctant to exercise their appointment power. They have been even less willing to adopt ethical rules requiring a minimum amount of pro bono service. State codes of conduct include only aspirational standards, which typically call for twenty to fifty hours a year of unpaid assistance (or the financial equivalent) primarily to persons of limited means or other charitable causes.[33]

How many lawyers meet these aspirational standards and how much service they actually provide to the poor is impossible to determine with any precision. Information is spotty because only three states mandate reporting of contribution levels, and because many lawyers take liberties with the definition of "pro bono" and include any uncompensated or undercompensated work. However, the best available research suggests that the American legal profession averages less than half an hour a week and under half a dollar a day in pro bono contributions, little of which goes to the poor. Most goes to assist family, friends, and charitable causes that largely benefit middle and upper income groups. Fewer than 10 percent of lawyers accept referrals from legal aid or bar-sponsored poverty-related programs. Pro bono participation by the profession's most affluent members reflects a particularly dispiriting distance between the bar's idealized image and actual practices. Only a third of the nation's large law firms have committed themselves to meet the ABA's Pro Bono Challenge, which requires contributions equivalent to 3 to 5 percent of gross revenues, and fewer still meet that goal. Lawyers at the nation's one hundred most financially successful firms have typically averaged eight minutes per day on pro bono service.[34]

Mandatory Pro Bono Service

Efforts to increase the profession's public service commitments have met with both moral and practical objections that are reviewed at greater length in chapter 7. As a matter of principle, many attorneys believe that compulsory charity is a contradiction in terms and that requiring service would infringe their own rights. From their perspective, if equal justice is a societal value, then society as a whole should bear its cost. The poor have fundamental needs for food and medical care, but we do not demand that grocers or doctors donate their help in meeting those needs. Why should lawyers' responsibilities be greater?[35]

There are several problems with this claim, beginning with its assumption that pro bono service is "charity." Lawyers have special powers and privileges that entail special obligations. Attorneys in this nation have a much more extensive and exclusive right to provide crucial services than attorneys in other countries or members of other professions. The American bar has jealously guarded those prerogatives, and its success in restricting lay competition has helped to price legal assistance out of reach for many consumers. Under these circumstances, it is not unreasonable to expect lawyers to make some pro bono contributions in return for their privileged status. The standards set forth in bar ethical codes calling for under an hour a week of service hardly justify the overblown descriptions that many lawyers attach: "latent fascism," "economic slavery," and "involuntary servitude."[36]

Critics, however, raise a further, more pragmatic objection to pro bono obligations. From their perspective, having reluctant dilettantes dabble in poverty law is an expensive and often ineffective way of providing services of unverifiable quality. But the question is always, "compared to what?" For many low-income groups, some assistance will be better than none, which is their current alternative. And as chapter 7 indicates, concerns of cost-effectiveness could be readily addressed by two strategies: offering a broad range of service opportunities coupled with educational programs and support structures; and allowing lawyers unwilling or unqualified to provide direct service the option of substituting cash assistance to legal aid providers.[37]

Moreover, critics often overlook or undervalue the extent to which pro bono activities serve professional as well as societal interests. For many lawyers, public service offers ways to gain additional skills, trial experience, and community contacts. Such career development opportunities, in the context of causes to which attorneys are committed, are often their most rewarding professional experiences. Public interest work can reconnect many lawyers to the social justice concerns that sent them to law school in the first instance. And exposing all members of the bar to how the justice system functions, or fails to function, for the have-nots may also broaden support for reform.[38]

A similar point could be made about increasing pro bono service by law students. Fewer than 10 percent of law schools now require such service, and most students graduate without pro bono legal experience. Issues concerning access to justice and public service have been missing or marginal in core law school curricula, and bar accreditation standards have failed to make such concerns an educational priority. These oversights represent a missed opportunity for both the profession and the public. Pro bono programs can offer students, no less than lawyers, invaluable skills training and a window on what passes for justice among low-income communities. If we want lawyers to see public service as a professional responsibility, that message must start in law school.[39]

An Agenda for Reform

No issue presents a more dispiriting distance between America's core principles and actual practices than access to justice. But rather than addressing the tension, we retreat into platitudes. We embrace equal justice as a social ideal, but fail to make even minimal access a social priority. The reasons reflect both ignorance and self-interest. Most Americans are not well informed about access to justice. Nor do they have adequate incentives to mobilize for reform. Unlike health care, which is a crucial and continuing need, the demand for legal assistance is much more episodic and more readily met, however imperfectly, by self-help. So too, the obstacles to reform are especially formidable, given the organized bar's incentives and capacity for resistance. No other occupation enjoys such prominence in all three branches of government, and it has traditionally been well-positioned to block changes that might benefit the public at the profession's expense.

Yet a number of forces are now coalescing to improve the prospects for reform. First, unmet needs are growing. As noted earlier, federal funding for civil legal aid has been cut by almost a third in real dollars over the last two decades, and most cash-strapped states and localities have been unable to make up the difference. Nor have their criminal defense budgets kept pace with escalating demands. The injustices resulting from shoddy representation have also attracted greater notice among the press and public, partly as a result of the increasing numbers of defendants who are exonerated by DNA evidence. Moreover, the growing market in self-help materials, fueled by escalating technological innovation, has encouraged more individuals to represent themselves, and to demand more accessible dispute resolution services. In the face of such pressures, almost all states have created new access to justice organizations and initiatives. A growing constituency within the legal profession also has come to recognize the need for greater support of these efforts. Bar leaders are increasingly aware that if they do not become more responsive to public needs, others will. Unless lawyers develop the necessary reforms, reforms will be forced upon them.

The chapters that follow identify concerns that should guide this agenda for change. Despite the conceptual difficulties in defining what precisely we mean by access to justice and how much is enough, several core principles should command broad agreement.

- First, equal access to justice may be an unattainable ideal, but adequate access should be a social priority. To that end, courts, bar associations, law schools, legal aid providers, and community organizations must work together to coordinate comprehensive systems for the resolution of disputes and the delivery of legal services.
- Second, these systems should maximize individuals' opportunities to address law-related problems themselves, without expensive representation by attorneys.
- Third, those who need legal services, but cannot realistically afford them, should have access to competent assistance. Opportunities for help should be available for all individuals of limited means, not just the "worthy poor" now eligible for federally funded civil legal aid.

Law without Lawyers

Legal needs fall across a spectrum, ranging from basic information to full-service representation by attorneys. Reforms that minimized the need for costly representation could enable many individuals to more effectively address their law-related problems. Strategies include: increased simplification of the law; readily accessible self-help materials and document preparation assistance; better protection of unrepresented parties; greater access to nonlawyer providers; and expanded opportunities for informal dispute resolution. All jurisdictions should have comprehensive pro se assistance programs and less restrictive rules governing unauthorized lay practice. An appropriate regulatory structure should take account of the ability of nonlawyer specialists to provide adequate assistance, the risks of injury if they do not, and the ability of consumers to evaluate providers' qualifications and to remedy problems resulting from ineffective performance. Sweeping prohibitions on lay practitioners should be replaced with licensing and certification systems that impose competence qualifications, ethical standards, and effective malpractice remedies.[40]

Alternative Dispute Resolution

Americans would also benefit from more effective channels for informal dispute resolution, not only in courthouses but also in neighborhood, workplace, and commercial settings. Considerable evidence suggests that well-designed employee and consumer grievance procedures benefit both business and individual participants, and that most people prefer to resolve disputes through informal, out-of-court processes. Promoting fair internal remedies will generally prove more cost-effective than relying on less accessible judicial intervention. So too, alternative dispute resolution procedures for certain civil and minor criminal matters can often enable participants to craft outcomes that better address their underlying problems than more formal adversarial processes.[41]

Legal Services

Finally, effective legal assistance must be available to all who need but cannot realistically afford it. What constitutes "effective," "need," and "affordability" are, of course, somewhat subjective determinations. But by almost any standard, our current system falls far short. Both judicial and legislative decision makers must do more to ensure competent performance of lawyers in criminal cases and opportunities for legal representation in civil cases. Courts should strengthen standards governing malpractice and ineffective assistance of counsel, and require states to allocate sufficient resources for indigent defense. In civil contexts, the judiciary should be more willing to appoint lawyers and to strike down funding restrictions that prevent adequate representation.

Other eligibility restrictions also require rethinking. Most European nations guarantee legal assistance for a much broader category of individuals than those entitled to legal aid in the American system. In these countries, eligiblity criteria include: Does the claim have a reasonable possibility of success? What would be the benefits of legal assistance or the harms if it is unavailable? Would a reasonable lawyer, advising a reasonable client, suggest that the client use his or her own money to pursue the issue? In assessing financial eligibility, these systems typically operate with sliding scales. Such an approach permits at least partial coverage for a broader range of clients than American legal aid offices, which serve only those below or just over the poverty line. Other nations' more liberal eligibility structures avoid a major limitation of the United States model, which excludes many individuals with urgent problems and no realistic means of addressing them.[42]

Expanding coverage in this country will, to be sure, pose substantial challenges. In a political climate that has been reducing entitlements for the poor, any proposal for increased legal assistance will face an uphill battle. But an aid structure that included a wider spectrum of the public would have broader appeal than the current program, which benefits only low-income communities. Moreover, subsidies for an expanded system could come from a variety of sources likely to command greater support than general funds. Examples include: a small progressive tax on law-related revenues; a surcharge on court filing fees based on the amount in controversy; increased opportunities for fee awards to prevailing parties; and pro bono requirements for lawyers that could be satisfied by a minimum amount of annual service, such as fifty hours, or the financial equivalent. In a nation that spends over $90 billion every year on private legal fees, a modest 2 percent tax would substantially increase the capacity of civil legal aid programs. So would more significant pro bono contributions by close to a million attorneys.[43]

Defining the Challenge

It is a national disgrace that civil legal aid programs now reflect less than 1 percent of the nation's legal expenditures and that a majority of Americans have a justice system that they cannot afford to use. It is a professional disgrace that pro bono service occupies less than 1 percent of lawyers' working hours and that the organized bar has so often put its own economic interests ahead of the public's. We can and must do better.

To be sure, this country has come a considerable distance since 1919, when Reginald Heber Smith published his landmark account of *Justice and the Poor*. At that time, most indigent criminal defendants had no right to counsel and the entire nation had only about sixty full-time legal aid attorneys with a combined budget of less than $200,000. Yet despite our substantial progress, we are nowhere close to the goal that Smith envisioned, which is also engraved on the entrance of the U.S. Supreme Court: "Equal Justice under Law." That should remain our aspiration. And it should not just decorate our courthouse doors; it should guide what happens inside them.

LITIGATION AND ITS DISCONTENTS

Too Much Law for Those Who Can Afford It,
Too Little for Everyone Else

When most Americans think about access to law, their primary impression is that the country has too much, not too little. Part of the reason is the media's delight in profiling loony litigation. America faces no shortage in supply. There are cases that seem too big for courts, cases that seem too small, and cases that should never have been cases at all. At one end of the spectrum are the megasuits that amble along for decades, wreaking financial havoc on all but the lawyers. At the other end of the spectrum are the trivial pursuits: football fans who sue referees; beauty contestants who sue each other; prison inmates who want chunky rather than smooth peanut butter; mothers who ask a court to resolve a playground shoving match between their three-year-olds; fathers unhappy about their fifteen-year-old's position on high school athletic team or their fifth-grader's failure to make the cheerleading squad; and a purchaser of cracker jacks who demands damages for a missing prize.[1]

Each year in teaching professional ethics, I focus a class session on litigiousness and begin with highlights from such cases. I describe the facts and offer a prize to any student who correctly guesses the outcomes. Few come close. The following are representative examples of the disagreement among judges, juries, and the public generally about what constitutes a frivolous lawsuit.

- The purchaser of a porn video *Belle of the Ball* sued the store in which he bought it on grounds that the featured "actress" graced the screen for only ten of seventy-five minutes. Alleged damages included the cost of medication to treat an asthma attack "brought on by the stress and strain of being ripped off."

- A student who spent eleven fruitless years in search of "the perfect state of life" promised by Maharaishi International University finally sued the school for fraudulent misrepresentations. Although the university had promised that he would learn to fly, the plaintiff had only learned to "hop with legs folded in the lotus position." And contrary to the school's claims, chanting in the method prescribed did not reverse the aging process or enable him to "self-levitate."
- A customer of Sizzler whose steak arrived well done, not medium well done, voiced dissatisfaction not only about the meat but also about the table, the salad, and other aspects of the meal. When adequate remedies were not forthcoming, he called the police from his cell phone "to get the situation corrected." The officer who arrived instead told the customer to pay up and get out, or face arrest. The lawsuit that followed sought damages from the restaurant owner, the police department, and the chief of police.
- A McDonald's drive-in customer wedged a chocolate milkshake between his legs as he headed back to the road. In reaching for French fries on the seat beside him, he inadvertently squeezed his legs. When the cold milkshake fell into his lap, the startled driver ploughed into the car in front of him. He subsequently sued McDonald's for failure to warn him of the risks of eating and driving.
- A high school student sued the date who stood her up for the school prom, seeking the cost of her shoes, hairdo, flowers, and court filing fee.
- A woman who dried a poodle in her microwave sued the manufacturer for failure to warn her of the unhappy result.[2]

Most of my students are dismayed to discover that the non-levitating student received a six-figure damages award, that only one of the lawyers involved was sanctioned for bringing a frivolous lawsuit (counsel for the Sizzler's plaintiff), and that the attorney in the McDonald's suit was commended for a "creative and imaginative" claim. As to whether the prom date's recovery of $82 constituted a misuse of the justice system, opinion divides, largely along gender lines. The existence of these cases, and the varying outcomes and reactions that they evoke, are emblematic of broader controversies about how much blaming and claiming belongs in the justice system.

Legal Hypochondria: Argument by Anecdote

Americans are in widespread agreement that the nation has too much frivolous litigation, but as these examples suggest, there is also broad disagreement about what falls into that category. Over four-fifths of the public, and about four-fifths of surveyed jurors, think that too many meritless cases are filed. But assessments of merit often vary widely. In a multiplaintiff asbestos case in Texas, five different juries, after hearing exactly the same facts, reached substantially different results. The inconsistencies also show up in judicial determinations of what cases are sufficiently frivolous to warrant sanctions. One representative study asked three hundred federal judges to consider ten hypothetical claims based on reported decisions. In six of the cases, the judges divided almost evenly on whether to award sanctions.[3]

Frivolous Cases

Complaints about frivolous litigation, and disputes about how to define and control it, are by no means a recent phenomenon. For over three centuries, Americans have fulminated against the bar's "cursed hungry caterpillars" and "plagues of locusts" tormenting the nation with "epidemics" of unwarranted litigation and "sapping the vitality" from the free enterprise system. The basis for this diagnosis is largely anecdotal. It draws heavily on what commentators label "news as vaudeville": the aberrant, amusing "fuzz and wuzz" of court proceedings like those noted above. Such cases receive disproportionate attention and for obvious reasons. In an increasingly competitive media market, the line between news and entertainment increasingly blurs. Serious coverage of the legal system struggles to survive among livelier rivals: talk radio, tabloid trash, and docudramas. As a result, factual content often is dumbed down and spruced up in ways that preempt informed debate. The public gets anecdotal glimpses of atypical cases without a sense of their overall significance.[4]

The problem is exacerbated by political polemics and business-sponsored media campaigns that take considerable poetic license. According to then California Governor Pete Wilson, the "lawyer's briefcase has become a weapon of terror." In his 1992 presidential debates, George H. W. Bush maintained that "Americans were suing each other too much and caring for each other too little." His son continued the theme a decade later in calling for tort reforms to curb "wasteful" litigation. Without apparent irony, a president who owed his election to a lawsuit lamented that: "We're a litigious society; everybody is suing, it seems like. There are too many lawsuits in America. . . ." Their effect, according to Bush, is to "terrorize small business owners" and drive doctors out of practice. And, he pointed out, "no one has ever been healed by a frivolous lawsuit." Advertising campaigns sponsored by business and insurance interests offer variations on the same theme. Some campaigns feature public parks and recreational facilities shut down because of liability concerns; other television ads show vaccines withdrawn from the market and pregnant women unable to find maternity care. A bumper sticker accompanying one campaign reads: "Go Ahead Hit Me. (I need the money)." The demons in these morality plays are, of course, "fat cat" attorneys who are "living in the lap of luxury" at the expense of taxpayers and consumers. The Manhattan Institute's Report and Website, Trial Lawyers, Inc., chronicles abuses. Books sell widely with titles like *The Case against Lawyers* and *The Rule of Lawyers: How the New Litigation Elite Threatens America's Rule of Law.* Their message is simple. Attorneys are "making out like bandits," while bankrupting businesses, clogging the courts with "inane conflicts," and pricing insurance out of reach for millions.[5]

The bar responds in kind. The Association of Trial Lawyers of America (ATLA) periodically launches major advertising efforts to educate voters and juries about the "true" villains and victims in personal injury litigation. In the world that ATLA commercials portray, only attorneys stand between the ordinary citizen and the "corporate wolves" at the door: swindlers, polluters, and manufacturers of unsafe products. Recent public relations efforts to halt malpractice reforms feature a disabled child in a wheelchair who will never walk again because of a "careless medical error." In another advertisement, a woman recounts having both breasts removed after a false diagnosis of cancer. "Who do you trust to say what's fair?" an unseen narrator asks rhetorically. "The jury, or corporations and their politicians? Don't let them put profits over people."[6]

These sound bites distort the reality they claim to describe. As one tort expert notes, "editorial writers, policy analysts, and legislators typically pick one of these competing [accounts], pair it with a few highly salient (and invariably unrepresentative) anecdotes, and then offer their preferred policy initiative as the solution du jour. . . . Those involved in this series of kabuki-like performances demonstrate little interest in determining which of these competing realities is true. . . ." The result is that reform strategies are proceeding without an informed understanding of procedural pathologies, their underlying causes, and the complex trade-offs that solutions will require.[7]

The first difficulty is that critics' accounts of "hyperlexis" prove neither that America has exceptional levels of legal hypochondria, nor that frivolous claims occupy a substantial amount of judicial time. Courts in many cultures provide outlets for petty grievances and develop strategies for sanctioning or summarily dismissing clearly meritless cases. The United States' current collection of loony litigants might look less alarming if the public had a fuller historical and cross-cultural picture. The 9,000 slander suits that once confronted Belgrade courts surely dwarf any American counterparts.[8]

Moreover, what qualifies as a frivolous claim generally depends on the eye of the beholder. Although some cases like those described earlier meet almost anyone's definition, the line between vindictiveness and vindication is often difficult to draw. Sexual harassment lawsuits were once routinely dismissed as "petty slights of the hypersensitive," beneath judicial notice. Yet only through these "petty" claims have Americans finally begun to recognize the real price of such abuse. Sexual harassment costs the average Fortune 500 company an estimated $6 million annually in turnover, worker absences, and lost productivity. Thousands of employees and students suffer major psychological and sometimes financial harm from unprovoked abuse.[9]

So too, many favorite illustrations of trivial claims and outrageous verdicts rely on misleading factual accounts. A textbook illustration involves a multimillion dollar punitive damages award against McDonald's for serving coffee at scalding temperatures. To most Americans, this case served as an all-purpose indictment of the legal profession and legal process; an avaricious lawyer paraded a petty incident before an out-of-control jury and extracted an absurd recovery. Politicians, pundits, and industry leaders replayed endless variations on the theme summarized by the national Chamber of Commerce: "Is it fair to get a couple of million dollars from a restaurant just because you spilled hot coffee on yourself?"[10]

On closer examination, the question no longer looks rhetorical. The plaintiff, a seventy-nine-year-old woman, suffered acutely painful third degree burns from 180 degree coffee. She spent eight days in the hospital and returned again for skin grafts. Only after McDonald's refused to reimburse her medical expenses did she bring suit. At trial, jurors learned of 700 other burn cases involving McDonald's coffee during the preceding decade. Although medical experts had warned that such high temperatures were causing serious injuries, the corporation's safety consultant had viewed the number of complaints as "trivial." The jury's verdict of $2.3 million was not an arbitrary choice. Its punitive damages award represented two days of coffee sales revenues, and the judge reduced the judgment to $640,000. To avoid an appeal, the plaintiff then settled the case for a smaller undisclosed amount. McDonald's put up warning signs and other fast-food chains adopted similar measures. While evaluations of this final result may vary, it was not the patently "ridiculous" travesty that critics described.[11]

Nor is the McDonald's claim an isolated case. Examples of litigiousness that are "deficient in drama" sometimes "have drama grafted on." All too often, facts fall by the wayside to make a better story, and the public misses what the real story should be. When unrepresentative anecdotes substitute for analysis, they camouflage broader trends. Stories are easier to sell than statistics, so descriptions of what the American Tort Reform Association terms "lawsuit abuse" tend to be long on folklore and short on facts. The problem is compounded by cognitive biases. Because vivid incidents are especially easy to recall, our tendency is to overestimate how frequently they occur. Drama displaces data, and Americans end up with a misdiagnosis of both the problem and the prescription.[12]

Litigation Rules

A case in point is the perennially popular assertion that the United States is experiencing an escalating epidemic of litigation and has become "the world's most litigious nation." Scholars have been debunking this claim so often that it is startling how much bunk survives. Current litigation rates in the United States are not exceptionally high, either in comparison with prior eras or with many other Western industrial nations not known for contentiousness. Americans were more likely to sue a century ago than they are now. Court filings in the United States now are in the same range, when adjusted for population, as those in Canada, Australia, New Zealand, England, and Denmark. It is true, as subsequent discussion suggests, that Americans resort to litigation more often than other nations to solve social problems. But whether or when this is undesirable is far more complicated than critics generally assume. The question is always, compared to what?[13]

In any event, litigation rates are no measure of abusive litigation. Uncontested divorces account for much of the recent growth in civil caseloads. Yet the higher frequency of marital breakdowns appears less a reflection of increased litigiousness than of increased expectations for marital satisfaction and decreased tolerance of domestic violence. Nor do such cases constitute a major drain on judicial resources: one representative survey clocked the average uncontested divorce hearing at four minutes. Although business leaders are the sharpest critics of "hyper-lexis," the disputes between businesses are the largest and fastest growing category of civil litigation. Tort cases that trigger the most critiques, such as personal injury litigation and defective product claims, are declining. Federal class action fees and settlement costs have remained stable over the last decade. Improvements in product safety, increased use of alternative dispute resolution, and tort reforms that make lawsuits less profitable have all played a role in curbing litigation.[14]

The Malpractice Problem

What are, however, rising are the size of tort awards and malpractice premiums, and these trends are a major source of business, professional, and consumer concern. For example, in product liability litigation, the median award, not including punitive damages, has tripled over the last decade. Medical malpractice recoveries have also increased at more modest rates. Malpractice premiums in some regions and some specialties have grown dramatically; the median increase has ranged between 15 to 30 percent, and some doctors have paid as high as 112 percent. It is, however, unlikely that the average increases are the product of abusive litigation or runaway jury verdicts. Indeed, the most commonly cited reason for the growing size of awards is that medical costs have increased at about the same rate as recoveries and plaintiffs' lawyers are more selective in the litigation that they bring; only cases with reasonably strong evidence of liability and substantial damages are worth litigating. Punitive damages, the most common target of critics, occur in only about 4 percent of cases that plaintiffs win in court, and only about 2 percent of malpractice claims result in victories at trial. Contrary to common wisdom, juries are no more likely than judges to be swayed by sympathy for injured victims and to award punitive damages.[15]

So too, the average increase in malpractice premiums is not exceptional in relation to health care costs and reflects a number of factors that bear no relation to the merits of the suits filed. First, the average increase in doctors' premiums over the last quarter century has been between 11 and 12 percent, and is about the same as recent increases in health insurance premiums for individual consumers and their employers. Moreover, according to most experts, the spikes in costs for physicians in some areas are largely attributable to factors other than litigation, for example, poor investment revenues for insurance companies, the loss of a few major providers, and the need to compensate for price wars in the 1990s, when greater competition kept premiums low. How much effect large damage awards have on malpractice policy costs is subject to debate. Some evidence suggests that caps on awards have not significantly affected malpractice policy costs, while other research finds a modest impact. States like California that have curtailed premiums have done so by regulating the insurance industry, not by limiting lawsuit recoveries. That is not to deny the hardships resulting from malpractice premium increases, nor to discount other problems in the tort system. But it is to suggest that the nature and causes of those problems are rather different than conventional wisdom assumes.[16]

Redefining the Problem: Inefficiency, Inconsistency, and Inequity

Undercompensation of Victims

Although excessive litigation is the pathology dominating public discussion and policy agendas, systematic research reveals that the more serious flaws involve undercompensation of victims and, as noted below, overcompensation of lawyers. For example, the most systematic research finds that only about 10 percent of accident victims file claims and only 2 to 3 percent bring lawsuits. So too, a review of some 30,000 New York hospital records disclosed that only about 12 percent of patients who sustained injuries from negligent medical care brought malpractice actions and only half of those received compensation. Other research on medical malpractice cases has found that plaintiffs on average recovered just over half their costs, and those with the most severe injuries ended up with only a third. Similar patterns of undercompensation hold for victims of unsafe products and of automobile and airline accidents. The tort liability system reimburses only about 4 percent of victims' direct costs of accidental injuries.[17]

Part of the reason lies in the highly expensive adversarial system on which Americans rely to compensate most injuries. This nation turns to courts for needs that other countries meet through less costly administrative measures and social services. For example, accident victims in many Western industrialized societies can seek assistance from agency-run compensation structures or guaranteed health insurance and no-fault wage replacement systems, rather than from personal injury litigation. Litigation American-style is too expensive for claims involving modest economic damages and medical costs. Recent tort reforms capping pain and suffering awards have made lawsuits even less feasible for the vast majority of injuries. Cases worth less than $150,000 are typically priced out of the court system.[18]

Expenses

The expense of legal proceedings is not, of course, lost on the public. Over four-fifths of surveyed Americans believe that litigation is too slow and too costly, and about three-quarters believe that it is damaging the country's economy. About half of surveyed corporate leaders think that product liability suits have a major impact on their company's international competitiveness. Yet while concerns about expense are eminently justifiable, the fears about economic productivity are less well grounded. Precise cost assessments are lacking, but Brookings Institution research estimates that tort liability could represent no more than 2 percent of the total expense of United States goods and services, an amount "highly unlikely" to have a substantial effect on American competitiveness. Other estimates suggest that businesses' total liability for all legal claims, including torts, is about 25 cents for every 100 dollars in revenue. Given those modest costs, it is not surprising that corporate risk managers have reported relatively little adverse effect from liability on larger economic indicators such as gross revenues or market share. In managers' experience, the major impact of tort claims has been to improve product safety and warning efforts.[19]

A related concern about the expense of litigation is that undue risks of liability and excessive insurance premiums cause businesses not to distribute valuable products and force doctors to shift their practice location, change their specialty, or order unnecessary medical tests. Critics claim that Americans are guided less by the rule of law than the fear of law. Here again, concern is warranted, but the extent of the problem is often overstated. The exodus of doctors appears confined to certain geographic areas and a few fields like obstetrics. On the average, only about 3 percent of doctors' revenue goes to cover malpractice premiums, an amount not self-evidently excessive or likely to cause major career changes.

Most research has not found a systematic relationship between insurance premium increases and withdrawals from practice. Studies of "defensive medicine" suggest that liability risks have led to both desirable and excessive precautions. Whether the costs are justified involves complex value trade-offs that popular debate generally ignores or obscures. A review by the federal government's Office of Technology Assessment concluded that "a relatively small proportion of all diagnostic procedures, certainly less than 8 percent overall—is performed primarily due to conscious concern about malpractice liability risk." Many experts also believe that the frequency of unnecessary procedures has been declining still further as a result of cost constraints imposed by managed care. While product withdrawals have sometimes been a major problem, as in the case of vaccines for childhood illnesses, in other instances, litigation has resulted in the removal of major safety risks. Obvious examples include the tragedies prevented from toxic shock syndrome, flammable pajamas, and dalkon shields.[20]

Exaggerated portraits of litigation expenses also compound the problem that critics describe. Systematic overestimation of liability costs encourages unnecessary tests or product removals. And media coverage that disproportionately focuses on huge damage awards encourages such skewed perceptions. Cases reported by the press have verdicts between four and twenty times larger than the average. Because the news needs to be new, exceptional awards attract disproportionate coverage. They are also easier for reporters to identify, because plaintiffs' lawyers have an obvious interest in publicizing large victories rather than humiliating losses or modest settlements. Moreover, cases involving exceptional recoveries or frivolous claims tend to be especially memorable. The combined effect of selective reporting and selective recall leads to misperceptions of the likelihood of large recoveries, particularly in tort contexts. Even relatively well-informed individuals, including lawyers, legislators, and insurance adjusters, have highly inflated perceptions of the frequency of litigation, as well as the size and likelihood of plaintiffs' verdicts.[21]

Overcompensation of Lawyers

Research on the litigation system reveals significant problems, but they are not the ones highlighted in popular debate and policy agendas. The most serious concerns involve inefficiency and inconsistency. Litigation is an extremely expensive way to compensate victims. Plaintiffs' attorneys collect an estimated $30 to $40 billion annually in legal fees—money that could otherwise help prevent or compensate injuries. In cases of automobile accidents, almost 50 percent of the payments by insurance companies end up in the hands of lawyers for both sides rather than victims. In other tort cases, the transaction costs are even higher, averaging close to 60 percent. And in mass tort litigation involving asbestos, two-thirds of insurance expenditures have gone to lawyers and experts. Those costs are not inevitable. Other countries do better by relying more heavily on official investigations and nonlitigious dispute resolution procedures to resolve accident claims. In Japan, for example, experts estimate that legal fees consume only about 2 percent of compensation payments. Few victims find it necessary even to hire lawyers. The Netherlands' no-fault system for reimbursing asbestos victims similarly manages to avoid the excessive transaction costs of American litigation. These systems may, of course, create other problems of undercompensation. But undercompensation is also common in our own system, which prices modest claims out of the system entirely and imposes excessive transaction costs on those that remain.[22]

The problems are compounded in class action cases where the real parties in interest are the lawyers. In some cases, class members' injuries are trivial, but the costs of trial are sufficient to lead to settlements that provide generous counsel fees for plaintiffs' attorneys and minimal compensation for clients. That prospect is particularly inviting if the remedy can be structured so that most plaintiffs will not claim damages to which they are theoretically entitled. The most notorious example is the coupon settlement, in which prevailing parties receive a discount against future purchases of the defendants' products. Often, the amounts are too trivial to justify efforts to collect them. In one all too typical case, only two of 96,754 coupons were ever redeemed, a rate of .002 percent. In other cases involving big-ticket items like cars or trucks, few plaintiffs would be likely to make another purchase within the redemption period. Because attorneys fees for prevailing parties are generally based on the damages officially awarded, not those actually claimed, lawyers may be well compensated by coupon settlements that are little more than sales promotions for defendants' own products.[23]

Such strategies received the treatment that they deserved in columnist Dave Barry's account of the "Adhesive Denture Menace." This national peril arose after a manufacturer recalled certain adhesives containing traces of benzene, a potential carcinogen. Without evidence of any actual injuries, vigilant attorneys brought suit on behalf of purchasers unaware of their "victimhood." The settlement gave several hundred known buyers $7, and some 2,800 undocumented buyers the opportunity to fill out forms and receive a package of discount coupons. Lawyers' fees and expenses totaled almost a million dollars. As Barry acknowledged, this may seem like "a lot of money. . . . [But] it cannot be easy, taking a case wherein it appears to the naked untrained layperson eye that nobody has suffered any observable harm, and using legal skills, turning it into a financial transaction that involves thousands of people and a million dollars! Plus coupons!"[24]

However, the value of these cases cannot be measured solely in economic terms. Their function is also deterrence. Class actions serve to discourage misconduct where none of the injured parties suffers large enough individual damages to justify legal challenge. Generous awards in successful cases also help compensate attorneys for cases that are not. The same is true of tort litigation more generally. Some plaintiffs' lawyers incur large risks in subsidizing lawsuits that serve crucial public interests. An entrepreneurial bar has often been able to penalize those responsible for hazardous products, fraudulent, negligent, or discriminatory practices, and violations of legal rights in a wide range of other contexts. Litigation has kicked in where politicians and government regulators have feared to tread, and we have a safer and more just society as a consequence. Moreover, it does not appear that most plaintiffs' attorneys earn excessive returns for bringing such actions. Outside the large metropolitan areas where high-stakes litigation centers, the average earnings of contingent fee attorneys are not significantly greater than those of counsel who bill hourly.[25]

Yet while the problem of excessive fees is frequently overstated, it clearly needs addressing. In too many cases, windfall recoveries for lawyers far exceed a reasonable return, or the incentive necessary to bring socially useful lawsuits. The cost of such excessive fees does not fall only on businesses with deep pockets. The result may be to increase prices or reduce the funds available for compensating seriously injured plaintiffs. The *American Lawyer* magazine had it right in a story about one class attorney who represented some 80,000 clients with the same basic claims for leaky plumbing. Despite the relatively minimal work required, he sought over $100 million in fees and expenses, totaling about two-thirds of the class settlement fund. The story's headline came to the point: "Greedy, Greedy, Greedy."[26]

Errors and Inconsistencies

Not only is the American adversary system excessively expensive, it is also inaccurate and inconsistent. Two major studies of medical malpractice cases found that while most victims of substandard care did not file claims or recover any compensation, more than 80 percent of those who did bring suit had not received deficient care. Almost half nonetheless recovered damages because the expenses of trial and risks of a large verdict made modest settlements an attractive alternative for insurers. So too, studies of other personal injury claims reveal high levels of fraud, which is estimated to cost insurance companies between $80 and $120 billion annually.[27]

In the cases that go to trial, results are often idiosyncratic and not well related to the extent of the plaintiff's injury and the defendant's culpability. Which side has the most effective lawyers, whether the case is filed in a "plaintiff-friendly" region, and whether the defendant appears to have a deep pocket. For example, in one study of two decades of Chicago jury awards, plaintiffs who fell in buildings owned by a corporation recovered significantly higher damages than those who fell on government property, and three times as much as those who fell in a private residence. The willingness of trial lawyers and insurance interests to make substantial campaign contributions to judges known for their sympathies in tort cases has a corrosive effect on the fact and appearance of justice. In mass tort cases, much depends on when the party's injury is discovered and how quickly the claim proceeds. Many asbestos victims with serious injuries will recover less than those with minor claims because, by the time those injuries develop, most of the defendants will be bankrupt and their assets largely exhausted. Other factors contribute to the inconsistency in treatment of similar cases, such as the vagueness of criteria for determining pain and suffering awards and punitive damages, and jurors' lack of information or experience concerning the recoveries for similar claims in other cases. Many studies find a poor correlation between juries' and experts' evaluations of the same claims. Although, as noted earlier, most serious injuries are undercompensated, a few plaintiffs hit the jackpot. Awards like the $28 billion verdict for a single smoker in a tobacco case add a level of uncertainty that works against rational settlement behavior and consistent outcomes.[28]

Defenders of the tort system, typically the lawyers who are its most frequent beneficiaries, claim that any inefficiencies are outweighed by the deterrence functions that a fault-based adversarial process insures.

Yet as experts readily acknowledge, we have little systematic evidence of how much deterrence that process adds to other regulatory controls, and whether it is worth the price. Most research suggests that the deterrent effect in tort cases is muted by liability insurance and by the delays, inconsistencies, and inaccuracies of litigation. For example, studies of medical malpractice find that the chances that a physician's negligent error will lead to compensation are under 5 percent. And because doctors' malpractice premiums generally do not reflect their personal record, the economic sanctions imposed by current liability structures are often indirect and ineffectual. Physicians already have strong personal and professional reasons to avoid negligent practices, and it is not clear that an expensive fault-based compensation system adds a crucial measure of deterrence. So too, research on other tort litigation finds that the threat of lawsuits exerts a significant but vague influence on individual and organizational behavior. As experts note, because the linkage between culpability and liability is tenuous, the message is: "'Be careful or you will be sued.' Unfortunately it does not say how to be careful, or more important, how careful to be."[29]

Overreliance on Law

Moreover, the strengths of the American legal structure in compensating for political inaction carry countervailing costs. Many problems that land in courts by default could be addressed more effectively by legislative or regulatory action. Particularly in cases involving major societal interests or mass torts, delegating decision making to the least accountable branch of government raises as many problems as it resolves. The tobacco litigation is a stunning example of the inordinate health and legal costs that have resulted from political paralysis. At last count, trial lawyers were set to pocket more than $75 billion over the next quarter century. Some netted fees that worked out to $150,000 per hour. Much of that money could more productively have gone for prevention and treatment if the government had acted earlier.[30]

In short, our culture's heavy reliance on litigation, particularly in personal injury contexts, comes at a substantial price, although the major problems are not the ones that dominate public debate. American rates of litigation are neither as exceptional nor as great a drain on productivity as critics often suggest. But the system for compensating victims is inefficient, inconsistent, and inequitable. Those with serious injuries are undercompensated, similar cases do not receive similar treatment, defendants draw murky or misleading messages about the risks of liability, and the costs of dispute resolution are excessive. These are not new concerns. To understand their persistence, Americans need a more informed picture of their underlying causes and the complexities of crafting solutions.

Reassessing Causes; Rethinking Solutions

In short, the American public gets a distorted picture of both litigation-related problems and the forces that perpetuate them. The conventional wisdom is that fault lies with conniving claimants, rapacious lawyers, and a contentious culture. The most popular prescriptions follow directly from that diagnosis: make litigation less profitable and make losers pay its costs. But such superficial analyses misdescribe our problems and misdirect our responses.

As chapter 1 noted, America's heavy reliance on courts is deeply rooted in our cultural values and political traditions. Our wariness of "big government" is reflected in a constitutional structure of fragmented authority, which often makes the judicial, rather than legislative or executive branch, the ultimate decision maker. Yet a system with multiple checks and balances can often end up in policy paralysis; conflicts readily develop between state, federal, and local authorities, or between legislative and executive officials. Litigation becomes a way to bypass these logjams.[31]

Privately financed lawsuits also decrease the need to spend taxpayer dollars on enforcing legal standards and compensating victims. Personal injury litigation provides a social safety net that other nations offer through guaranteed health insurance and no-fault wage replacement systems. In addition, these suits can give government a way to minimize its own responsibility for caring for victims. The tobacco litigation is again a dramatic illustration of the fiscal appeal of this approach. Cash-strapped states had much to gain and nothing to lose by joining forces with the private bar to recover public health expenditures related to smoking. Lawyers recovered record fees in exchange for financing and orchestrating the litigation; states obtained large damage awards with no legal expenses. Similar coalitions are now challenging other industries, such as gun and lead paint manufacturers.[32]

Critics who lament American litigiousness rarely focus on these underlying forces or on the complex trade-offs that significant reform strategies would entail. Dispute resolution strategies that seem effective in other legal cultures may not transplant well to our own. A full evaluation of potential reform strategies is beyond the scope of this book. But to put the debate over access to justice in perspective, it makes sense at least to suggest better ways of thinking about litigation-related problems and appropriate policy responses. To that end, we should first focus on core principles. What are the major goals of the justice system, and how should we measure its effectiveness in achieving them?

A broad range of scholarly and popular commentary speaks to both of these questions and generates an equally broad range of views. But there is consensus on several main points. The primary objectives of a civil litigation system should be to resolve disputes, compensate victims, and deter violations of legal standards. Key criteria for assessing the performance of that system include its costs in time, money, and acrimony, and its procedural and substantive fairness. The substantive standard is, of course, the most difficult to apply. Part of the problem in developing a reform agenda is the lack of consensus on what constitutes reasonable outcomes, particularly in personal injury cases. But some measure of agreement seems likely on certain core values. One is consistency; similar cases should yield similar results. A second is the opportunity to be heard and to obtain some measure of individualized treatment. These are, to some extent, competing values. Individualized opportunities are costly and create more scope for inconsistent results. But only by explicitly addressing the trade-offs are we likely to obtain reform strategies that respond to our highest aspirations and most critical concerns.

Commonly proposed reform strategies take three main forms. One approach is to discourage litigation by making recovery more difficult both for plaintiffs and their attorneys. A second strategy is to focus on better management of legal claims. Examples include greater use of sanctions for frivolous cases and alternative forms of dispute resolution. A final option is to reduce the need for litigation by creating other compensation systems or by minimizing the problems that give rise to legal disputes.

Tort Reform

The modern tort reform movement has relied primarily on the first approach. Beginning in the 1970s, an alliance of businesses, professional associations, insurance companies, and a few nonprofit and governmental organizations began a major campaign to limit "litigation abuse." A second wave of reform occurred in the mid-1980s and another in the late 1990s. A renewed push started after the Republican election victories in 2000. Each effort brought modest success, primarily in terms of state legislation and education of judges and juries about the implications of large awards for taxpayers and consumers. The main legislative reforms have involved placing limits on punitive and noneconomic damages like pain and suffering; creating panels to screen medical malpractice cases; restricting lawyers' contingent fees; limiting venue to prevent parties from shopping for "plaintiff-friendly" jurisdictions; and altering the substantive tort law on matters such as the availability of damages from "collateral" sources or from joint defendants whose codefendants are insolvent. In the most recent campaign, additional objectives have included federal legislation to cap pain and suffering awards and to restrict class actions by measures such as increased judicial scrutiny of forum shopping, noncash benefits, and class certification decisions. Attention also has focused on more fundamental changes, such as "loser pay" proposals that would make unsuccessful litigants liable for their opponents' legal fees.[33]

Some of these reforms create as many problems as they solve. As noted earlier, the vast majority of tort victims are undercompensated, not overcompensated. Only a small minority file successful claims and those most seriously injured receive the least adequate recoveries. Limiting damages compounds these injustices. Such limitations strike hardest at those with the most severe disabilities and at individuals like low-wage workers or full-time homemakers, whose noneconomic losses are too modest to justify litigation. Moreover, the impact of such limitations on insurance costs is modest. A Congressional Budget Office study estimated that a national cap of $250,000 would reduce consumers' health insurance premiums by less than one half of 1 percent. According to some medical association estimates, the effect of similar state legislation would be to lower doctors' premiums by only about 6 percent. If, as these associations claim, America is truly facing a malpractice crisis, such responses are scarcely adequate.[34]

Requiring unsuccessful litigants to pay their adversaries' legal fees might reduce frivolous claims, but at the cost of discouraging meritorious ones as well. Those most likely to suffer would not be corporations that can absorb additional legal costs as tax-deductible business expenses. The real losers would be people of moderate means with strong but not certain claims who cannot risk subsidizing both sides of an unsuccessful suit. Supporters of fee-shifting initiatives seldom discuss this problem.

Instead, they emphasize that "loser pay" systems are the norm in other nations. But these countries typically have more comprehensive legal assistance, social welfare, and health insurance programs. Such programs reduce reliance on privately financed litigation to subsidize the costs of injuries, which also reduces the chilling effects of fee liability. American advocates of fee-shifting policies are also diplomatically silent about Florida's unsuccessful experience. After five years, the state abolished its loser-pays system in medical malpractice cases. Although the threat of additional legal fees did somewhat reduce the number of malpractice cases filed, it also increased the number that went to trial. Plaintiffs fought harder because the stakes were higher. Moreover, a significant number of losing plaintiffs had insufficient assets to pay opponents' costs, so defendants' overall expenses were also higher. Whether comparable results could be avoided under more carefully designed systems is a complex question on which experts disagree. But supporters of fee-shifting have made little effort to educate policymakers or the public about the complicated and uncertain trade-offs that their proposal would entail.[35]

Alternative Dispute Resolution

The second type of reform proposals, which attempt to improve management of legal disputes, holds more promise, but often suffers from the same limitations as discussions of litigiousness. The public gets too much sweeping rhetoric and too little careful factual analysis. Critics of the current system frequently present alternative dispute resolution (ADR) as an all-purpose prescription. It becomes *the* preferred solution for excessive expense, delay, and combativeness. Critics of ADR offer similarly sweeping assessments. In their analysis, alternative dispute resolution offers "apartheid justice"—a strategy for bypassing rather than addressing inadequacies in the current structure.[36]

To make sense of this debate, the public needs fewer categorical pronouncements and more contextual evaluation. The last two decades have witnessed a dramatic growth in the range and sophistication of ADR methods, such as arbitration, mediation, and adjudication by privately retained judges. Some recent tort reform proposals would build on this experience by creating specialized tribunals to hear malpractice or product liability cases. Current ADR methods vary considerably in structure and offer different strengths and limitations. Not all respond effectively to concerns about litigiousness. Public debate too often relies on overly simplified or idealized models. ADR advocates tend to compare a courtroom trial, with all its costs, to a more informal, participatory process, with all its virtues. From this perspective, adversarial proceedings look far less attractive than alternatives that can assist parties to identify underlying interests, explore possibilities for mutual gains, and discover strategies that may prevent or resolve future disputes.[37]

Yet as ADR critics note, 90 percent of cases now settle without the full expense of trial and many ADR processes are no less costly or contentious than traditional adjudication. For example, proceedings before privately selected arbiters, judges, or jury panels rely on conventional adversarial frameworks. Opportunities for delay and obfuscation can be comparable to those plaguing current litigation processes. Imbalances of wealth, power, and information may skew outcomes under any dispute resolution system, including ones that rely on nonadversarial approaches. Research comparing mediation and adjudication does not find consistent differences in costs, speed, or participant satisfaction.[38]

Rather, this research underscores the importance of context both in structuring and evaluating dispute resolution processes. Problems are most likely to surface in arbitration, mediation, and screening processes that are mandatory rather than voluntary or that fail to address major disparities in power and resources. For example, compulsory workplace arbitration systems that involve employers who are repeat players often systematically disadvantage employees who are not. In one study involving such cases, the odds of an employer winning were about 5 to 1. Only repeat players had incentives to investigate the records of ostensibly "neutral" decision makers to identify possible biases. Even where parties are more evenly matched, ADR is not always a desirable substitute for adjudication. Processes designed to satisfy private parties lack public accountability and may undervalue public interests. ADR methods do not require appointed or elected officials to enforce norms that are subject to democratic or judicial oversight. Informal procedures aimed at private settlements may provide insufficient development of legal precedents or inadequate deterrence of unlawful conduct.[39]

Yet the issue in evaluating legal processes should always be: Compared to what? Critics who denounce ADR as second-class justice need to consider how often first class is available, and on what terms. The deficiencies common in alternative dispute resolution are chronic in conventional adjudication as well. Private settlements are the norm, not the exception, and procedural protections that are available in theory are often missing in practice. Imbalances of wealth, power, and information skew outcomes even in cases receiving the closest judicial oversight. As the title of Professor Marc Galanter's now classic article put it, the "Haves Come Out Ahead" in most legal settings.[40]

If any single lesson emerges from the burgeoning research on dispute resolution, it is that no single method is uniformly superior. Yet the current legal process is heavily weighted in favor of a single adversarial structure, which does not always serve either participants' or societal interests. What the public needs instead is a broader range of procedural choices and the information necessary to make them; more innovation and evaluation should be priorities. Proposals along these lines are not in short supply. Many ADR experts have developed promising blueprints for "multidoor courthouses" that would "fit the forum to the fuss." These courthouses would allocate different types of cases to appropriate dispute resolution processes based on several basic criteria: the nature of the controversy; the novelty or complexity of the relevant law; the relationship between the parties; the priorities that the participants attach to various features of the dispute resolution process; and the societal interests at issue. Cases involving relatively small monetary damages and the application of settled legal precedents may not justify the expense of full-scale adjudication. In other contexts, the relationship between the parties may argue for procedures that are best able to address power disparities or to foster long-term working relationships. Specialized tribunals may be appropriate where subject-matter expertise and experience are critical to insuring reasonable and consistent treatment of similar cases. Development of special substantive rules, such as an adequate standardized formula for pain and suffering damages, could assist such tribunals in reaching more uniform awards that did not penalize low-income victims.[41]

No-Fault Compensation Systems

A related, but more fundamental, reform strategy would be to replace the litigation/ADR structure with a more streamlined no-fault compensation system. Many other countries have successfully implemented such systems in areas such as personal injury, discrimination, and administrative benefits. These processes often make lawyers unnecessary and provide effective remedies with minimal transaction costs. The United States has adopted similar systems for a few contexts, like workplace accidents and the September 11 terrorist attack. Some private institutions have also attempted to preempt litigation by creating their own no-fault reimbursement funds. For example, a small but growing number of hospitals and insurance companies have an "honesty policy" under which they inform patients of mistakes and provide compensation for lost wages and medical expenses. Experience to date suggests that these policies are highly cost-effective. Many experts have advocated analogous specialized tribunals and streamlined no-fault compensation structures for "adverse medical events." Such systems could offer a number of advantages over malpractice litigation: more timely remedies, coverage for a broader group of victims, and lower transaction costs.[42]

Whether no-fault frameworks provide adequate deterrence of negligent conduct in other personal injury contexts has been subject to considerable debate. Much may depend on the details of the system and surrounding legal culture. However, in the case of medical malpractice, some evidence suggests that no-fault frameworks could result in more frequent reporting of errors and give providers greater incentives to reduce all preventable injuries, not just those demonstrably linked to negligence. For a health care system that now causes somewhere between 44,000 to 98,000 avoidable patient deaths annually, this would be a significant benefit.[43]

A rational reform agenda would provide more experimentation with no-fault frameworks, specialized tribunals, and other ADR approaches, as well as more systematic information about their effectiveness. How well do different models serve societal goals concerning efficiency, deterrence, fairness, cost, and accessibility? Granting the risks of superficial cross-cultural comparisons, what can we learn from other countries' approach to similar legal problems? Although we need more adequate data on such questions, the research available suggests that expanding procedural options is a move in the right direction. Parties' satisfaction with the legal process is heavily dependent on assessments of its procedural fairness, and some opportunities for direct participation, not mediated through lawyers, can increase perceptions of fairness. Most individuals prefer to handle legal grievances in informal, out-of-court settings and to have more control over the process than is possible in litigation. Expanding alternative dispute resolution also introduces a measure of competition that may promote improvements. If individuals have choices, they have greater leverage in making their needs heard and in enhancing the quality of the options available.[44]

Professional Misconduct

A final cluster of reform strategies should focus on the misconduct that breeds excessive litigation and related abuses. For example, more effective disciplinary processes for doctors and lawyers could help address the roots of the problem. Some research suggests that over the last decade, 5 percent of physicians have been responsible for a third of malpractice awards and settlements. It does not, of course, follow that these doctors are responsible for a similarly disproportionate share of the vast number of medical errors that never result in claims. Nor are many of these errors the product of individual negligence. But a system that more effectively weeded out practitioners with a history of incompetence would produce substantial savings in lives and dollars. Further progress might come from changing malpractice insurance rates and health care regulation to build in more incentives for quality control. Avoidable errors can be reduced through improvements in prevention and oversight structures.[45]

Excessive Legal Fees

Courts, bar associations, and legislatures could also do more to curb excessive legal fees and frivolous cases. Closer judicial scrutiny and more stringent contingent fee standards could help insure that lawyers' charges do not exceed a reasonable return for the work performed and risk assumed. Greater efforts should focus on preventing suits with little merit from remaining financially advantageous for counsel. Courts could, for example, require that percentage fees in class actions be based on the damages that class members actually receive, not the theoretical value of unredeemed coupons. Another strategy, reflected in some state statutes and proposed legislation, is to provide more limits on the percentage formula lawyers can charge, based primarily on how far the case progresses and how time-consuming preparation becomes. So, for example, in a matter settled without filing suit, lawyers may collect only 25 percent of the recovery. In a case settled after filing, their share may not exceed a third, and in a case that goes to trial, they can collect 40 percent. Reasonable fee ceilings in cases involving very large damage awards could curb excessive windfalls in contexts like the tobacco litigation. Disciplinary agencies could also impose significant sanctions on attorneys who repeatedly file meritless suits or charge extortionate fees. In California's first such effort, the bar sought suspension of three attorneys who held small businesses hostage for payoff settlements in unfair competition cases. It should not, however, have taken some 3,000 claims, with boiler-plate pleadings and no investigation of the underlying facts, in order to trigger disciplinary action.[46]

The greatest difficulty in developing an effective litigation reform agenda is political not conceptual. We do not lack for innovative ideas and promising models from abroad. But we do lack an informed public committed to addressing the most fundamental problems and the forces that perpetuate them. Policy debates have been hijacked by special interests and skewed information. Lawyers seeking maximum fees, businesses seeking maximum profits, and physicians seeking minimum liability have invested vast efforts in pushing their own agendas. Few of the reform proposals that seem remotely plausible are likely to produce the result that most Americans want: a dispute resolution system that is efficient, equitable, and affordable. Significant progress is unlikely until more disinterested players enter the arena and give the public a better understanding of the most serious problems and plausible prescriptions. H. L. Mencken was right that "what ails the truth is that it is mainly uncomfortable and often dull." The litigiousness debate is no exception. Frivolous cases make entertaining reading but a misleading blueprint for reform.

⹀ 3 ⹀

HISTORICAL PERSPECTIVES

Legal Rights and Social Wrongs

Access to justice is a concept deeply rooted but unevenly observed in Anglo-American law. In 1215, England's Magna Carta pledged: "To no one will we sell, to no one will we refuse or delay, right or justice." Another seven centuries passed before that principle encompassed a general right to counsel in English legal proceedings. In this country, progress has occurred at a somewhat less leisurely pace, but individuals of limited means have always lacked adequate access to legal assistance and legal proceedings.

Early Understandings of Access to Justice

The historical record concerning access to justice is surprisingly spotty. It is, however, clear that for most of American history, access to law was considered a basic right but access to lawyers was not. Nor, until recently, were legal services seen as either a governmental or professional responsibility. Early state constitutions generally included some guarantee of equal access to justice or equal protection of the law, and as noted below, the Sixth Amendment of the U.S. Constitution protected defendants' right to retain their own counsel. But none of these guarantees encompassed access to legal assistance for those who could not afford it. English law, however, did offer some precedent for appointment of counsel at courts' discretion. The 1495 Statute of Henry VII authorized such appointments for the poor, and cases from the fifteenth century on made occasional references to judges' authority to assign counsel. How often they actually did so remains unclear. The same is true of analogous American provisions. For example, a 1647 Virginia act provided that when a litigant was about to lose a cause "by his weakness" as an advocate, the judge could appoint some "fitt man out of the people" to argue the case. Little information is available about the circumstances under which courts exercised that authority, and how often lawyers were expected to provide uncompensated assistance. However, most research suggests that such appointments were uncommon. Much of the reason has to do with Americans' historic distrust of lawyers and the relatively uncomplicated nature of early court proceedings.[1]

The colonial years in America were, on the whole, not friendly to the bar. Few of the early settlers were lawyers or welcomed lawyers. Several colonies prohibited pleading for hire or excluded attorneys from their courts. Public distrust stemmed from multiple causes. Colonists who had suffered legal persecution in England had an understandable animosity toward a profession that had assisted in their oppression. Many religious and political leaders did not want to share authority and viewed lawyers as likely to stir up disputes and interfere with social harmony. Merchants and planters preferred to govern their affairs directly, without expensive intermeddlers. Lawyers were also ready scapegoats for the failures of the justice system to deliver justice as participants perceived it. Popular distrust intensified after the Revolutionary War, as lawyers' role in debt collection inspired particularly vitriolic and sometimes violent protests. A profession that profited from procedural technicalities and the "ruins of the distressed" was bound to attract backlash.[2]

However, the prominent role that lawyers played in establishing and governing the new nation also enhanced their influence. The postwar period witnessed the growth of bar associations that further succeeded, at least briefly, in raising the profession's status by tightening requirements for admission. But such restrictions ill-suited the populist spirit that resurfaced during the Jacksonian period, and by the Civil War, little effort was made to limit who could offer legal services.[3]

To many Americans, lawyers seemed not only an evil but an unnecessary evil. In its first centuries, the nation's law was far less complicated than it is today. Legislative regulations, legal precedent, and legal texts were of more manageable proportions. Nonlawyers could often master enough information to argue a simple case, especially where judges of lower courts were themselves not lawyers. Individuals with some smattering of legal knowledge were also sometimes available for assistance at modest fees. Until the late nineteenth century, bar admission standards were typically lax, legal education was rudimentary, and the profession enjoyed no monopoly on legal advice. As a result, most courthouses attracted a culture of part-time practitioners, sometimes including even innkeepers or land speculators, as well as minor court officials. Men of "clever penmanship and easy volubility," might provide representation at a bargain. To be sure, this legal low life attracted its fair share of complaints, often from lawyer competitors. But many critics viewed licensed attorneys as little better. "Pettifoggers" and "shysters" among both groups were blamed for stirring up unnecessary litigation and providing incompetent assistance; some jurisdictions prohibited lay representation entirely. But where they were available, quasi-professionals also helped to keep law reasonably accessible and affordable.[4]

However, as the population grew in size and the economy became more complex, so too did the law. Statutory and common law requirements multiplied, and the corresponding growth of court systems injected additional complications of procedure and jurisdiction. It became harder to navigate the system unassisted. The influx of immigrants and the increase of an urban underclass of limited education and literacy created additional opportunities for injustice. Those who could neither afford counsel nor assert their own rights were increasingly vulnerable. By the turn of the twentieth century, their plight began attracting serious concern.[5]

The Evolution of a Right to Counsel in Criminal Proceedings

English Precedents

During the formative period of American law, English precedents offered no guarantee of counsel in criminal proceedings. Until the mid-eighteenth century, defendants generally had to conduct their own defense. The assumption was that assistance from the presiding judge would be sufficient to prevent manifest injustice. Ironically enough, in felony cases, the very legal context in which litigants had most at stake, they could not be represented by counsel, even if they could afford it. The security of the state was deemed more important than protection of individual rights. The only exception to this ban on representation involved charges of treason, which members of Parliament could imagine themselves confronting. Accordingly, a 1695 statute required courts to appoint counsel in treason proceedings on the defendants' request. But for other felonies, which potentially carried a death sentence, defendants had no right to representation. By contrast, in misdemeanor cases, where the government's interest was viewed as less weighty, defendants were allowed to retain counsel.[6]

This double standard was tolerable only because English courts, of their own volition, often permitted accused felons liberal opportunities for consultation with counsel concerning legal questions during trial. By the mid-eighteenth century, these counsel were assuming most defense functions, except closing arguments. However, it was not until 1836 that all felony defendants in England gained the right to be represented at trial, and even then, many could not afford to exercise it. Some defendants benefited from a ritual known as dock briefs. By payment of a token fee, they could enlist the service of any barrister who happened to be in court while they were in the prisoner's dock for indictment, and who did not disappear before the appointment could be made. The practice persisted because some barristers were willing to take these uncompensated cases in order to gain experience and enhance their reputation. But the need for assistance far outstripped supply. To address the gap, England's 1903 Poor Persons Defense Act authorized judges to appoint compensated counsel where, "by reason of the gravity of the charges" or other "exceptional" circumstances, justice required such an appointment. However, courts' reluctance to exercise that authority and the inadequacy of fees available continued to leave many defendants without assistance. Finally, in 1949, England's Legal Aid and Advice Act provided that doubts should be resolved in favor of appointment and established a more reasonable compensation structure.[7]

Early American Practices

The early American approach was more liberal in principle, but, by most accounts, not all that dissimilar in practice. Given their history, colonists generally had greater concerns about governmental tyranny and oppressive prosecutions than their English forebears and were therefore more willing to provide safeguards for criminal defendants, at least in capital cases. Several colonial statutes authorized appointment of counsel in such cases, and most colonies recognized defendants' right to retain their own counsel. However, early court records seldom reveal whether the accused had representation, and the few studies available indicate that the appointment power was no more frequently exercised in colonial America than in England.[8]

Drafters of the U.S. Constitution followed the prevailing approach toward legal representation. The Sixth Amendment guarantees that in all criminal prosecutions, the accused shall enjoy the right "to have the Assistance of Counsel for his defence." It appears unlikely that the framers intended this provision to include only licensed attorneys. Many jurisdictions had too few to go around, particularly after the Revolution, when attorneys sympathetic to Great Britain had left the colonies. Nothing in the history of the Sixth Amendment suggests that it was meant to foreclose courts' widespread reliance on lay advocates with some legal training. Nor does that history reveal any intent to require counsel for those unable to afford it. Such a requirement would have been a departure from settled practice and inconsistent with two statutes adopted around the same time governing federal trials. These statutes confirmed defendants' right to retain counsel and required appointment of lawyers on the request of indigents only in cases of treason or other capital crimes. On their own motion, federal courts sometimes asserted inherent authority to appoint unpaid counsel in other felony cases. Most accounts suggested that this practice of ad hoc uncompensated appointments worked tolerably well in the nineteenth and early twentieth centuries, given the modest number of federal prosecutions, the relative prestige of federal trial work, and judges' selectivity in exercising their authority.[9]

However, the problems of attracting qualified counsel were far greater in state courts, and statutory guarantees were less extensive. Although most criminal defendants could not afford lawyers, until the mid-twentieth century only about a dozen states required courts to appoint counsel in all felony cases or to advise defendants of their right to request such assistance. A smaller number required appointments only in capital cases. The rest of the states gave courts discretion to appoint a lawyer or authorized them to do so when defendants affirmatively requested assistance. No state granted a right to counsel for appeals or for habeas corpus proceedings seeking federal review of a state conviction. Although courts occasionally exercised their inherent authority to appoint a lawyer if there appeared to be strong grounds for an appeal, unassisted defendants were seldom able to make such a showing. Even where judges had an obligation to appoint counsel on request of the accused, many failed to advise defendants of that right, or interpreted statements like "could I see a lawyer?" as too "general" to constitute a request for representation.[10]

One transcript from a 1933 Georgia case typifies circumstances in which a trial proceeded despite a defendant's obvious need for assistance.

> George, have you got a lawyer?
> No, Sir.
> Have you tried to get one?
> No, Sir, I ain't . . . . I was just caught up yesterday.
> Call the first 12 jurors to the box. George, does that jury look all
>   right to you?
> Yes, Sir, I guess they will do.

At the close of the evidence:

> George, do you want to argue the case?
> If I had a lawyer I would like to argue it.

Some appellate courts were equally willing to find that defendants who failed to request assistance had waived their right even if they had not been informed of the option. A businessman who "[knew] his way around," or an accused who had prior trial experience were presumed to be aware of an opportunity for representation; the presiding judge need not draw it to their attention.[11]

By the twentieth century, social and economic forces also converged to make defendants' theoretical right to counsel only theoretical. An ad hoc appointment system relying heavily on unpaid lawyers and unrepresented litigants might have seemed tolerable in small-town America, where the number and complexity of criminal cases were modest, and the visibility of trial proceedings encouraged adequate preparation by appointed counsel. But such a system could not keep pace with the needs of a rapidly growing urban population with a large class of poor, uneducated, and immigrant defendants. Writing in 1917, Reginald Heber Smith declared that in principle the system of court-assigned lawyers might appear adequate, but "[p]ractically it has been no solution at all . . . as a whole it has proved a dismal failure. . . . The system is so thoroughly in disuse that in many quarters its very existence is denied."[12]

Even after Smith's exposé, and the growth of public defender services beginning around the turn of the twentieth century, the system for indigent defense was shockingly inadequate. A comprehensive 1951 study echoed many of Smith's conclusions. It reported that in about 40 percent of surveyed jurisdictions, felony defendants generally lacked representation. Moreover, many defendants who did receive lawyers got help too late in the process to do any good. A common practice was to appoint counsel only after arraignment, when 70 to 80 percent of defendants had already pleaded guilty, and others had made incriminating statements to police. What passed for due process concerning petty offenses was similarly problematic. One 1956 study of a city court handling vagrants and drunkards found a system utterly lacking in lawyers or any opportunity to present a legal defense; it took only fifteen minutes to find fifteen defendants guilty and to impose three-month jail terms for each.[13]

The main problem was money. As late as 1950, over half the states made no provision for paying court-appointed attorneys in noncapital cases. States that did authorize compensation set rates far below prevailing fees. In some jurisdictions, payments remained at little more than token levels, such as five or ten dollars for a felony matter. Only two states provided reimbursement for expenses such as investigation or expert witnesses. Unsurprisingly, the lawyers willing to accept court assignments under such circumstances were among the least qualified members of the bar: new entrants seeking experience or more senior attorneys who could not attract paying clients.[14]

These volunteers were often inadequate to fill the need, particularly in jurisdictions that authorized no payment or nominal fees. Courts then resorted to a variation of the English practice of dock briefs. As one appellate judge described the process:

> When advised that an indigent needs help the judge usually picks out some lawyer who happens to be in the court. . . . The lawyer then spends a few minutes with his new client at the side of the courtroom or perhaps in an anteroom. . . . In most of such assignments, after a few minutes of conference, the defendant is advised to plead guilty and he feels he has no choice but to do so. This mock assignment of counsel and the cursory hurry-up job of a busy uncompensated lawyer makes a farce of due process of law. . . .

Poor defendants whose families and friends scraped together sufficient funds to hire an attorney did not necessarily fare better. Many "jailhouse lawyers" seemed "hardly distinguishable" from those they sought to represent. They preyed on fears, extorted excessive fees, and botched the defense.[15]

Reform Efforts

This sorry situation did not pass unnoticed, and beginning in the early twentieth century, judges, bar leaders, and social activists launched a series of reform efforts. One involved establishment of government public defender systems. Such systems were in place in some European nations and were proposed for American courts at the turn of the twentieth century by Clara Shortridge Foltz, one of the nation's first female trial lawyers. As she conceived it, a network of specialized, competent advocates would "protect the poor, save the innocent, and remove an unjust burden from a generous profession." Los Angeles County launched the first office in 1914, and within a few years, other major metropolitan areas followed suit. To early advocates, including Reginald Heber Smith, this approach appeared a "complete solution" to the inequalities and injustices that plagued the criminal process. By providing experienced trial attorneys, public defender programs promised more competent representation at lower costs than systems relying on unpaid or poorly compensated appointed counsel. Bar leaders also saw such programs as a way to raise the "tone" of the criminal courts and eliminate the "shifty and shady" "shysters" who extorted unconscionable fees for unmerited defenses. Salaried government lawyers presumably would have no financial incentive to manufacture claims for the guilty and would be reluctant to jeopardize cooperative ongoing relationships with prosecutors and judges.[16]

Not all segments of the profession shared this enthusiasm. The strongest opposition to public defenders predictably came from the criminal defense attorneys who depended on paid court appointments. But they were joined by bar leaders. Some felt that the state should not "champion criminals" or that it would be unseemly for the government to be "prosecuting . . . with one hand and defending with the other." A further concern was that a state-controlled office would lead to "socialization" of the profession and threaten lawyers' independence. The title of a widely circulated article in the *American Bar Association Journal* put the matter squarely: "The Public Defender: A Step Towards a Police State?" The author, a prominent New York practitioner, left no doubt that he considered the question rhetorical. A democratic order could not long survive if a "citizen in legal conflict with the state could get no counsel except as was vouchsafed him by the state." Critics also worried that public defenders' desire to retain collegial relationships with judges and prosecutors would undermine client trust and loyalty. From opponents' perspective, a preferable alternative was adequate compensation for retained attorneys or nongovernmental defender services subsidized, or at least controlled, by private charities.[17]

As experience with government-funded criminal and civil legal aid programs increased, most of the critics' concerns appeared unfounded. Public defenders were not demonstrably more dependent on good relationships with judges and prosecutors than appointed or retained lawyers who specialized in criminal defense. Efforts to establish which system was more effective were often inconclusive. However, the limited evidence available from case dispositions and evaluations by judges and prosecutors suggested that public defenders performed somewhat better than assigned counsel. Yet on the rare occasions when anyone thought to ask clients, they were less enthusiastic. The dominant view was captured in an interview response that became the title of a celebrated study: "Did You Have a Lawyer When You Went to Court? No, I Had a Public Defender." Most surveyed clients saw defenders as part of the law enforcement process, and nearly all would have preferred private practitioners. The assumption was that a salaried government lawyer had nothing to gain from vigorously defending clients. As one defendant put it, "[h]e gets his money either way," regardless of the outcome. By contrast, private practitioners had to worry about their reputations, and therefore were perceived to be more zealous advocates.[18]

How widely this view was shared is impossible to gauge. From an objective standpoint, it clearly did not fairly characterize well-funded defender programs that became the prototype of the modern system. In any event, decision makers within and outside the profession did not appear much influenced by clients' concerns. By the early 1970s, about two-thirds of the population was served by public defenders. The growth of this system had much to do with a series of Supreme Court cases that expanded the right to counsel and increased the need for efficient structures of legal aid.[19]

Constitutional Requirements

The first of these decisions was the celebrated 1932 Scottsboro case of *Powell v. Alabama*. There, nine out-of-state black youths accused of raping two white girls on a train were perfunctorily tried in an atmosphere surrounded by potential lynch mobs. Their only aid came from a lawyer from another state who volunteered to help, but not to appear as counsel, and one local practitioner, who said he would "do what he could under the circumstances" to assist that lawyer. The "circumstances" were unpromising, to say the least, and it does not appear that much assistance was forthcoming. Neither attorney was given time to prepare or to advise the defendants. The Supreme Court found that the convictions violated the Fourteenth Amendment's guarantee of due process, which included the Sixth Amendment right to be heard by counsel. However, the Court narrowly limited its ruling to the factual circumstances presented: "in a capital case where the defendant is unable to employ counsel and is incapable of making his own defense because of ignorance, feeble-mindedness, illiteracy or the like, it is the duty of the court, whether requested or not, to assign counsel for him. . . ."[20]

The next cases to reach the Court made clear the limited scope of the *Powell* holding. In 1936, the Court held that the Sixth Amendment entitled felony defendants in federal cases to have appointed counsel unless they "competently and intelligently" waived the right. But federal cases constituted a small fraction of the nation's criminal docket, and most judges were reluctant to force states to assume the far greater burden of subsidizing legal representation in all of their proceedings. Accordingly, the Supreme Court's 1942 ruling, *Betts v. Brady,* held that a failure to grant counsel on the defendant's request in a noncapital state case was consistent with due process unless "special circumstances" made the trial lack "fundamental fairness."[21]

Over the next two decades, judicial efforts to apply this "special circumstances" standard yielded results that were neither consistent nor convincing, even to the conservative Justices who had resisted granting a broader entitlement to counsel. In the nineteen cases that reached the Supreme Court, the majority reversed convictions in over half. Taken together, these rulings identified some twenty circumstances that were relevant, such as the age, experience, and intelligence of the defendant, the complexity of the case, and the trial judge's errors or assistance to the accused. Yet at the state court level, appellate judges rarely second guessed a refusal to appoint counsel; the reversal rate was less than 10 percent. Lower courts managed to find no unfairness under circumstances hard to describe in any other terms. In one Michigan case, a seventeen-year-old boy was arraigned, tried, convicted of first degree murder, and sentenced to life imprisonment, all in a single day, without the possibility of counsel ever mentioned and "without a word . . . said in his defense." A Pennsylvania court denied relief to an unrepresented eighteen-year-old whose mental capacity was equivalent to age nine. The indeterminacy of the fairness standard created confusion at all levels of the criminal process. In arguing to the Supreme Court that the standard was unwork-able, one appellate lawyer noted: "How can a judge, when a man is ar-raigned, look at him and say there are special circumstances: Does the judge say, 'You look stupid?'"[22]

In the case that finally guaranteed counsel for all serious criminal offenses, the defendant was anything but stupid. Earl Gideon, the ap-pellant in *Gideon v. Wainwright*, wrote a handwritten petition to the Supreme Court that prompted one of the nation's landmark legal rul-ings. The case involved no "special circumstances." At issue was a rela-tively simple charge of robbery, and the defendant was not inexperi-enced in criminal trials, having been in and out of prison much of his adult life. Nor was he entirely without skills as an advocate. His Supreme Court filings, although "full of surprises" in matters of punctuation and spelling, were impressively cogent on the point that mattered. His claim was simply that "a citizen of the State of Florida cannot get a just and fair trial without the aid of counsel."[23]

Ultimately, the Supreme Court agreed. By the time *Gideon* was ar-gued, about two-thirds of states generally appointed counsel in felony cases. It was hard, therefore, to credit the claim of Florida's Attorney General that extending such a right would be a "tremendous burden on the taxpayer," open the door to countless claims for other forms of gov-ernment assistance, and thus pave the way to socialism. Writing for the Court, Justice Black largely ignored such claims. He also acknowledged that Gideon had "conducted his defense about as well as could be ex-pected from a layman." But that was not enough to ensure due process of law. He had not known of his right to examine prospective jurors dur-ing voir dire and strike those who might be prejudiced for cause. Nor was he aware of his right to object to hearsay and opinion testimony, or to make requests concerning jury instructions. And he had made no statement at the time of sentencing. On this record, Justice Black saw an "obvious truth," although one that had eluded the Court for the preced-ing two centuries: "any person hauled into court, who is too poor to hire a lawyer, cannot be assured a fair trial unless counsel is provided for him. . . . That government hires lawyers to prosecute and defendants who have the money hire lawyers to defend are the strongest indications of the widespread belief that lawyers in criminal courts are necessities not luxuries."[24]

Now, four decades after *Gideon*, that truth is widely accepted. But its logic is not easily confined and neither courts nor legislatures have de-veloped satisfactory limiting principles. Subsequent Supreme Court decisions have required counsel for misdemeanor proceedings where incarceration is possible. But as subsequent chapters note, the Court has not acknowledged the need for assistance in other civil and criminal appellate contexts where equally fundamental rights are at stake. Nor has adequate attention focused on the near poor, who do not qualify for court-appointed counsel, but who cannot realistically afford an effective defense. The burden on taxpayers has remained minimal, but at the cost of untold injustice.[25]

Civil Legal Services for the (Deserving) Poor

Until the late nineteenth century, the limited legal services available to the poor were provided by individual lawyers on an ad hoc basis. Efforts to create a more stable and systematic structure of assistance evolved in three phases. The first organizations were private charities for particular groups. Many of these organizations then expanded to provide routine assistance to all "deserving poor." In their most recent form, legal aid programs generally receive public support and focus on law reform as well as individual services. But in none of these phases has civil legal assistance been considered a basic individual right, and the aid programs have never been able to meet more than a small fraction of the needs of low-income communities.

Legal Aid as Private Charity

The nation's first legal aid organization began in 1876 as part of an effort by New York German-American merchants to assist German immigrants. As initially conceived, the mission of what became the New York Legal Aid Society was to "render legal aid and assistance, gratuitously, to those of German birth, who may appear worthy thereof, but who from poverty are unable to procure it." Fifteen years later, the Society dropped the restriction of German nationality, authorized charging its clients small fees, and broadened its base of charitable sponsors. Around the same time, two other legal aid organizations formed in Chicago. One was the Protective Agency for Women and Children. It was launched by the Chicago Women's Club to address sexual exploitation of innocent immigrants lured into sin by false promises of legitimate employment. This agency also outgrew its initial mission and soon began providing legal services of all sorts to women and children. A second organization, the Bureau of Justice, was sponsored by Chicago's Ethical Culture Society to assist needy individuals regardless of sex, race, or nationality. Shortly after the turn of the twentieth century, these organizations merged, and similar legal aid societies had formed in a half dozen major cities. By 1917, there were forty-one such societies across the nation, but with only sixty-two full-time attorneys and a combined budget of under $200,000.[26]

The founders of these organizations had mixed motives that were typical of other progressive reformers throughout this period. Early supporters of legal aid were primarily concerned about the working poor, whose inability to assert basic rights made them vulnerable to exploitation. But most of these supporters had a profoundly conservative view of the mission of legal assistance. Their objective was not to reform the law but to enhance its credibility and ensure its acceptance in the eyes of the lower classes, who might otherwise be led astray by "social agitators." In *Justice and the Poor*, Smith confidently asserted that "the substantive law, as a whole, is remarkably free from any taint of partiality. The legal disabilities of the poor in nearly every instance result from defects in the machinery of the law," not in its substance. But, Smith warned, the machinery had to be fixed: "Injustice leads directly to contempt for law, [and] disloyalty to the government, and plants the seeds of anarchy." Arthur Von Breisen, the first Director of the New York Legal Aid Society, sounded similar themes. Legal assistance "keeps the poor satisfied because it establishes and protects their rights; it produces better working men . . . and better house servants; it antagonizes the tendency toward communism. . . ." Speakers at the twenty-fifth anniversary of the Legal Aid Society delivered the same message. Legal assistance, as Theodore Roosevelt put it, was a bulwark against "violent revolution." Other proponents stressed professional as well as societal interests. Aid to the deserving poor could serve as an ideal "vehicle for public relations"; it could renew popular "faith in the integrity of the bar and relieve the profession [of] its legal and ethical burden" to provide such services free.[27]

The Role of the Bar

Yet most lawyers remained unconvinced or unconcerned. As Smith noted with frustration, "the majority of our judges and lawyers view the situation with indifference. They fail to see behind the denial of justice the suffering and tragedy which it causes."[28] The American Bar Association did make some efforts to address the situation. In 1917, it passed a resolution urging state and local bars to "foster the formation and efficient administration of Legal Aid societies . . . for the worthy poor," and appointed its own legal aid committee in 1920. But the response among the rank and file was less than enthusiastic. Smith's 1919 study found that fewer than 10 percent of the lawyers in any surveyed city contributed support, and in some metropolitan areas, the proportion was only 2 or 3 percent. A representative Chicago campaign in 1913 found only twenty firms willing to donate at least $250 for legal services; the New York Legal Aid Society's 1934 effort yielded support from only 229 of the city's some 17,000 attorneys. In other metropolitan areas, after much debate and dispute, bar associations contributed only token amounts, on the order of $100. As late as 1950, only about 9 percent of legal aid funding came from the profession. The majority was from local charities, supplemented by private contributions. The "unhappy truth," reported a comprehensive 1951 bar survey, was that "no substantial progress" in expanding services had occurred since Smith's study in 1919.[29]

Not only were most lawyers unprepared to contribute their own funds to legal aid programs, they were unwilling to support public subsidies. Summarizing widespread views, the ABA's president warned in 1950 that the "entry of the government into the field of legal services is too dangerous to be permitted to come about in our free America." Among elite lawyers, the primary concern was "socialization" of the profession and the threat to an independent bar. Among small and solo practitioners, an additional concern was loss of income from prospective clients who might be poached by government-supported legal services offices.[30]

The Scope of Assistance

To allay such concerns and retain support from conservative donors, legal aid offices throughout the first part of the twentieth century generally steered clear of public funding and took only the most unremunerative and uncontroversial cases. Clients had to be "worthy," and claims had to be meritorious, but not financially rewarding enough to attract any private practitioners. The policy of the New York Legal Aid Society was typical. According to its director, Von Breisen, "Whoever receives our attention must show that he has done some work and that he is entitled to a corresponding consideration." Yet financial eligibility standards were set so low that they often excluded not only the working poor, but even families officially below the poverty line. Some offices also charged modest retainer fees to encourage "self-respect" and a "responsible" attitude toward legal aid bureaus. Almost all offices required clients to subsidize court costs. Such policies helped to reduce caseloads and to discourage time-consuming legal proceedings, but at the cost of foreclosing assistance to many who needed it most.[31]

Legal aid agencies also operated with highly moralistic and frequently condescending policies in selecting among the "deserving" poor. Some societies excluded bankruptcies entirely or imposed restrictions, such as requirements that the claimant have a "reputation for honesty." Part of the reason was to avoid antagonizing creditors whose good will was necessary in negotiating settlements for other clients. But some bar members of legal aid boards were reluctant to sanction "technical" defenses to merchants' claims. Similar policies governed consumer debt cases, and aid was often denied in matters involving "luxury goods," such as automobiles or television sets. Divorce was also excluded unless there were special circumstances demonstrating a "social need," such as a defendant who was in a mental institution or in prison for a "heinous" crime, or who was engaging in "actual physical violence," or "continuing molestation." A client's "desire to remarry" was not enough. The class bias underlying such policies was occasionally explicit. As one attorney put it, most members of the local bar "feel that the poor don't need divorce in quite the same way middle-income people do." As late as 1966, fewer than 15 percent of legal aid offices had unrestrictive policies concerning divorce.[32]

Lack of resources also severely limited the number of clients legal aid programs could reach and the quality of assistance they could provide. In 1963, only about 400 lawyers were available to serve some 50 million eligible clients, which worked out to about one attorney for every 120,000 poor persons. Some estimates suggested that legal aid reached fewer than 1 percent of those in need. Less than two-tenths of 1 percent of the nation's total legal expenditures went to provide representation for the quarter of the population unable to afford it. Despite a high frequency of legal problems, two-thirds of low-income Americans had never consulted a lawyer. Many programs refused to take appeals, appear in court or administrative proceedings, or handle "complicated" matters. Some agencies followed policies of seeking "reasonable compromise," regardless of the client's preferences. On average, assistance consisted of one meeting with an attorney. Legal aid attorneys did not pursue class actions or law reform, and seldom undertook community education or outreach for fear of antagonizing the local bar and creating demands that they could not satisfy. Prior to 1965, no legal aid case ever reached the Supreme Court. The low pay, routine work, and crushing caseloads made it difficult to recruit and retain qualified lawyers. Persevering advocates who attempted to challenge settled doctrine or procedures often met resistance from trial judges, whose crowded dockets made any novel claims and pretrial motions unwelcome. In one telling example, a Chicago judge wadded up a motion and threw it at the offending legal aid attorney with the advice that if he wanted the matter decided, he should "take it to the Supreme Court."[33]

Legal Aid as a Public Responsibility

The social activism of the 1960s brought new resources, new priorities, and new disciples to legal aid work. The transformation began with a series of foundation grants to law reform projects as part of multiservice programs for low-income communities. Then, in the mid-1960s, in a burst of rhetorical exuberance, the nation declared war on poverty. Lawyers were among the first recruits. A newly created Office of Economic Opportunity launched a legal services program inspired by the foundation-sponsored projects. Although the American Bar Association had traditionally opposed government funding and had not been consulted about the OEO's initiative, ABA leaders saw a need to become partners, not opponents, in the venture. This change in position reflected multiple considerations. One was the long-standing inability of privately funded programs to generate anywhere near the resources necessary to provide adequate service. A more effective approach could respond to growing societal concern about access to justice and enhance the profession's image. Bar leaders also were aware of the public relations disaster that had resulted from the American Medical Association's opposition to Medicare. The prudent course was for the organized bar to help shape program design and for local lawyers to maintain control of governing boards of federally funded programs.[34]

Many of the rank and file were initially unconvinced. Some local bar groups brought legal challenges or filed ethical grievances against the new programs. Other lawyers sought OEO funding themselves, as part of Judicare programs that would reimburse private attorneys who took legal aid cases. Some board members resisted the OEO's insistence on law reform as a guiding priority. One representative case history of local bar responses to the new national program reported substantial turf battles among attorneys, including "fisticuffs" in the hallways of an open meeting.[35]

By the close of the 1960s, however, much of the opposition had been overcome, partly because it was apparent that expanded legal services programs were not reducing the client base of private lawyers. To the contrary, subsidized advocacy for the poor created new opportunities for paid work on behalf of their opponents, such as landlords, creditors, and employers. A consensus also developed among bar leaders and OEO officials that Judicare was not a desirable model. Such approaches would not create the kind of efficiency, expertise, and law reform capacity that staffed offices provided and might unleash an unseemly scramble for business among marginal practitioners. With powerful backing from the legal profession, federal funding grew at a healthy clip. Annual expenditures for legal aid increased from $4 million in 1963 to $72 million in 1971. Law schools, often with the support of private foundations, also dramatically increased their support of legal clinics serving low-income communities. This exposure to poverty law, together with the greater status and challenge associated with reform-oriented work, helped recruit a new corps of highly qualified practitioners.[36]

The heightened emphasis on law reform was also supported by national backup centers with expertise in the specific needs of low-income clients. Results were quickly apparent, as offices scored major victories on welfare, housing, education, tenant, consumer, and related issues. Between 1967 and 1972, legal aid lawyers brought over 200 cases before the Supreme Court and won most of the decisions that reached the merits. But these legal achievements also brought a political backlash. Suits against state, local, and national governmental entities provoked the greatest resistance, as many politicians began questioning whether taxpayers should be financing both sides of a lawsuit. During the early 1970s, Congress came close to passing an amendment that would have barred such suits, and the Nixon Administration succeeded in curtailing program activities and budgets.[37]

To provide greater political insulation for poverty law offices, Congress in 1974 established the Legal Services Corporation, with board members appointed by the President and confirmed by the Senate. In exchange for support from conservative critics, the authorizing legislation prohibited Corporation-funded attorneys from engaging in lobbying, political organization, and representation in controversial areas such as school desegregation, abortion, and military service. Under the new Corporation charter, the earlier OEO rhetoric of "law reform" and "social change" was also absent. Emphasis shifted to the more neutral goal of enhancing "access to justice." Although financial support initially remained strong, another round of restrictions soon followed. The Reagan Administration initially recommended dissolving the Legal Services Corporation, and subsequently secured legislation that reduced its budget by about a third and limited permissible activities. Congress imposed further restrictions in the 1990s. Recipients of government funds could not, for example, represent aliens, pursue cases involving homosexual rights, or initiate class actions.[38]

This history underscores both the capacities and constraints of American approaches to civil legal assistance. The evolution from private charity to public responsibility has brought vastly expanded resources and a new reformist ethic to poverty lawyering. Support from the organized bar has also helped to preserve some measure of independence through a separate Legal Services Corporation, decentralized priority setting by individual offices, and ethical rules safeguarding lawyer–client relationships. But restrictions on the cases and strategies that publicly funded programs can pursue have deprived attorneys of their most effective methods of law reform and have prevented legal representation of unpopular clients who need it most.

The reliance on a small group of poverty law practitioners to provide assistance to a relatively narrow band of the population has also been a mixed blessing. This approach provides the most efficient services to those at the bottom of the socio-economic scale. But it lacks the widespread political support that some countries have achieved by at least partially subsidizing private practitioners to represent a broader group of individuals. As chapter 5 notes, too few lawyers and clients have a stake in the American system to provide the political base necessary for adequate coverage. And despite impressive efforts, the contributions of privately subsidized pro bono and public interest attorneys have failed to fill the gap.

From Clients to Causes: Pro Bono and Public Interest Representation

The Pro Bono Tradition

The tradition of providing unpaid legal assistance *pro bono publico*—"for the good of the public"—has extended historical roots, although what it entails has been subject to dispute. Representation without a fee has been traced to Roman and medieval ecclesiastical practices, as well as to English common law and other European traditions. How often it occurred, either voluntarily or by judicial or bar mandate, is unclear. As noted earlier, courts have been divided on the extent of their inherent authority to compel service, but for the most part, they have been reluctant to impose substantial obligations on unwilling practitioners. Early state and national bar ethical codes recognized no obligation to provide pro bono assistance to the poor. Until the 1970s, the closest the profession came were two exhortatory provisions in the ABA's 1908 nonbinding Canons of Professional Ethics. Canon 4 advised that "[a] lawyer assigned as counsel for an indigent prisoner ought not to ask to be excused for any nontrivial reason," and Canon 12 noted that "a client's poverty" might require a reduced fee or "even none at all," and that "[t]he reasonable requests [for assistance] of brother lawyers, and of their widows and orphans without ample means, should receive special and kindly consideration." However generous the bar's response to widows and orphans of colleagues, its solicitude for poverty communities generally was noticeable for its absence.[39]

During the mid-twentieth century, the bar sought to encourage greater pro bono involvement. Part of the motivation was to prevent the government from responding to pervasive unmet needs, either by allowing more assistance from nonlawyer competitors or by "socializing" the profession through broad-scale funding for legal aid. The growth of antipoverty and public interest law movements in the 1960s and early 1970s also generated more interest in pro bono work. The demand for such legal assistance increased as the poor acquired additional legal rights. And as the profession grew more diverse and socially conscious, more lawyers and law students began pressuring employers to offer pro bono opportunities.[40]

This growing support for public service found recognition in the ABA's new Code of Professional Responsibility, adopted in the 1970s. Its Ethical Consideration 2-25 provides:

> Historically, the need for legal services of those unable to pay reasonable fees has been met in part by lawyers who donated their services or accepted court appointments on behalf of such individuals. The basic responsibility for providing legal services for those unable to pay ultimately rests upon the individual lawyer, and personal involvement in the problems of the disadvantaged can be

one of the most rewarding experiences in the life of a lawyer. Every lawyer, regardless of professional prominence or professional workload, should find time to participate in serving the disadvantaged.[41]

No disciplinary rule reinforced this "basic responsibility," and the rewards of aiding the disadvantaged proved inadequate to the occasion. No comprehensive research on bar pro bono contributions before the 1970s exists, but the limited information available confirms the assessment offered by one New York attorney in 1927:

> There is no other profession quite so smug and self-satisfied, and at the same time quite so lacking in social obligation. An occasional rare soul, a Clarence Darrow, may dedicate his energies to the defense of unpopular causes and earn the supercilious disapproval of his more orthodox brethren. . . . But these are . . . to use that most devastating epithet, the radicals.[42]

Studies from the 1960s found that the most generous firms averaged only about five hours of pro bono work a year per attorney, less than 1 percent of the firms' billable time. In the 1980s, surveyed lawyers averaged between five to fifteen hours per year, and only about 5 percent of this work went to legal aid and indigent criminal defense. Most pro bono assistance benefited friends, family members, and employees of lawyers and their clients, or bar associations and middle-class and upper middle-class organizations such as Jaycees, Little Leagues, garden clubs, and symphonies. Fewer than 15 percent of lawyers reported any involvement in law reform.[43]

The Evolution of Public Interest Law

The inadequacy of bar pro bono work, as well as government subsidized legal services, left a void that "public interest" legal organizations attempted to fill. Although that term is relatively recent, the concept has its roots in earlier social movements, particularly those involving civil liberties and civil rights. The civil liberties movement began during World War I, when a small group of pacifists founded an antimilitarism association that became the American Civil Liberties Union. Its activities quickly broadened to include free speech and eventually reproductive rights and antidiscrimination efforts. America's first major civil rights organization, the National Association for the Advancement of Colored People, also emerged early in the twentieth century. The catalyst was a brutal 1908 race riot in Springfield, Illinois, and, several decades later, the association spun off the NAACP Legal Defense Fund as a separate organization. Its efforts focused on test-case litigation challenging racial segregation and subordination. By the mid-1950s, NAACP lawyers had won thirty-four of thirty-eight Supreme Court decisions, including the landmark school desegregation decision in *Brown v. Board of Education.* Organizations such as the Lawyers' Committee for Civil Rights under Law and the National Lawyers Guild joined these early antidiscrimination efforts and served as models for other legal reform associations.[44]

During the late 1960s and early 1970s, a rise in political activism, together with a large increase in foundation founding, gave birth to new "public interest" legal groups. Judicial and legislative initiatives further encouraged this development. Courts became more responsive to law reform claims and class action litigation. Congress began authorizing fee awards to "prevailing parties" in civil rights, consumer, environmental, and analogous cases.[45]

These public interest organizations, as defined by the Council for Public Interest Law, included tax-exempt nonprofit groups that employ at least one attorney and devote at least 30 percent of their total resources to the legal representation of previously unrepresented interests on matters of public policy. By that definition, at the close of the 1960s, some 23 public interest centers employing about fifty lawyers had emerged. By the 1990s, over 200 centers with more than 1,000 lawyers spanned a broad range of issues including poverty, civil rights, civil liberties, women's rights, gay and lesbian rights, disability rights, consumer interests, and environmental quality. In addition, a substantial number of firms that did not qualify for tax-exempt status devoted a major portion of their work to public interest matters, and others provided significant pro bono assistance.[46]

Conservative legal foundations also formed to broaden the groups represented. Organizations such as the Washington Legal Foundation, the Rocky Mountain Legal Foundation, and the Pacific Legal Foundation waged often successful campaigns against affirmative action, environmental regulation, and—ironically—publicly funded legal services for the poor. Although these foundations operated with tax-exempt status, some fell outside the National Council's definition of a public interest organization because they took positions that were already well represented by their corporate funders.[47]

Despite substantial differences in size, structure, and objectives, public interest legal organizations generally have shared a common premise. They have assumed that many significant social concerns go unrepresented because individuals cannot afford legal assistance or because the benefits to any single claimant are insufficient to justify the costs. Litigation has often been the strategy of choice for several reasons; it is less expensive than other means of securing social change; it is the only way of ensuring that rights available in principle are enforced in practice; and it can be an effective catalyst for political organization and community education.

Although public interest legal organizations have played a crucial role in increasing access to justice, their efforts have been limited by chronic resource constraints. Relatively few organizations have managed to secure a stable funding base of the size necessary to fully support their work. The increasing conservatism of federal judicial appointees, and their growing reluctance to authorize statutory fee awards, have also made lawsuits a less effective strategy. All too often, law-reform litigation has become a war of attrition in which underfinanced public interests are the greatest casualties.[48]

Moreover, even under the best of circumstances, litigation has inherent limits in achieving lasting social change. As Harvard Professor Gary Bellow once noted:

> [T]he problem of unjust laws is almost invariably a problem of distribution of political and economic power. . . . [If a major goal] is to redistribute power, it is debatable whether the judicial process is a very effective means toward the end. . . . There is generally not much doctrinal judicial basis for adequately dealing with such problems, and lawyers find themselves developing cases whose outcomes are peripheral to the basic issues that these problems raise. Secondly, "rule" change, without a political base to support it, just doesn't produce any substantial result because rules are not self-executing: they require an enforcement mechanism.

Public interest lawyers often lack resources to ensure compliance with test-case decrees, and some defendants—particularly governmental institutions such as prisons, schools, or mental hospitals—have inadequate funds to implement judicial remedies. Decisions that lack political support are also vulnerable to statutory reversal or administrative agency resistance. Over the past two decades, these limitations have encouraged public interest legal organizations to focus more attention on nonlitigation strategies such as lobbying, counseling, organizing, education, and policy-related research. But funding constraints have compromised these approaches as well. The small number and highly limited budgets of public interest organizations have made other access-to-justice efforts all the more critical.[49]

Restraints on Competition: Advertising, Solicitation, Minimum Fees, and Group Legal Services

For most Americans, access to law has been limited not only by the inadequacy of subsidized assistance but also by restrictions on the delivery of routine services. Bar efforts to restrain lawyers' competitive practices have inflated the costs and reduced the accessibility of legal assistance. Although the courts have increasingly curtailed these efforts through constitutional rulings, the bar's regulatory structure has remained overly responsive to professional interests at the expense of the public.

Overbroad Restrictions

To most attorneys, mass marketing of legal services seems a recent and regrettable development. In fact, what is recent are restrictions on marketing. Practitioners in ancient Greece and Rome were not hesitant to advertise their services. Nor were some of this country's most distinguished nineteenth-century attorneys, including Abraham Lincoln. Personal solicitation of clients also has an extended lineage, but one that inspired earlier and more sustained efforts at prohibition. In medieval England, at a time when tribunals were all too easily corrupted, the profession sought to discourage misconduct that often accompanied solicitation: maintenance (assisting others to prosecute or defend a suit without just cause); champerty (helping to maintain a suit in return for a share of the recovery); and barratry (continuing to stir up quarrels and litigation). However, in America, until the twentieth century, advertising and solicitation unaccompanied by other abuses went largely unregulated.[50]

Such self-promotion was, however, often condemned by the well-established lawyers who were leaders of the bar and who had no need to engage in such indecorous conduct themselves. "Let business seek the young attorney," declared George Sharswood in his 1854 *Essay on Professional Ethics*. In his view, "[h]abits of neatness, accuracy, and . . . strict honor" would insure ample work while maintaining the dignity of the profession. By and large, that was also the position of bar ethical codes and disciplinary committees for the next century. The ABA's 1908 Canons of Ethics declared that it was "unprofessional to solicit professional employment" through advertisements or personal contact. Even indirect promotional methods, such as comments to newspapers, were deemed inappropriate. "Self-laudation" of any form was thought to "offend the traditions and lower the tone of our profession."[51]

Competition in legal fees was equally offensive. The Canons of Ethics condemned "underbidding," and, not coincidentally, bar associations during the Depression made more active attempts to suppress the practice by developing minimum fee schedules. By the early 1960s, over half the state bars and some 700 local associations had promulgated such schedules and ethics committees had ruled that the "habitual charging of fees less than those [specified]" could result in disciplinary action. An ABA Practice Manual advised lawyers to present clients with the approved fee lists in attractive folders, preferably evidencing a "degree of dignity and substance." A black leather cover with gold lettering was recommended, although a plain but neat paper version was acceptable.[52]

These prohibitions on promotional and competitive practices ill-served the public whose interest was frequently invoked but seldom seriously considered in bar decision making. Broad prohibitions on self-promotion were tolerable in small towns or commercial settings where reputation was a matter of common knowledge and virtue was not its only reward. But as the profession grew in size and shifted much of its practice to large cities, these restrictions became increasingly anachronistic. Ordinary Americans were often unaware of their rights or how to obtain assistance at a price that they could afford. Such ignorance carried a substantial cost. A representative study on industrial accidents just after the turn of the twentieth century found that a majority of injured workers received no compensation and only 5 percent secured full remedies.[53]

To reach such potential clients, some form of advertising or personal solicitation was necessary. In its most unsavory form, the conduct involved ambulance chasing. Lawyers, or "runners" hired by lawyers, would use contacts with police, doctors, and hospital workers to identify potentially profitable cases. To beat other rivals, including insurance adjusters who faced no ethical prohibitions on solicitation, the most enterprising lawyers or their agents turned up at hospital bedsides and funeral parlors with retainer agreements thoughtfully prepared for signature. In its more benign forms, solicitation occurred by mail or through recommendations of organizations such as unions or public interest groups. Lawyers in some landmark civil rights cases, including *Brown v. Board of Education*, reported that potential clients initially were "anything but eager" to initiate legal proceedings in hostile white communities.

Plaintiffs in other contexts, although not necessarily reluctant to sue, did need to be recruited; they typically lacked information about the possibility of remedies and assistance financed by lawyers through contingent fees. Attorneys willing to skirt the official rules on solicitation thus served a crucial social function. Even the most intrusive practices of personal injury lawyers were not without benefit. As one National Lawyers Guild member noted in 1938, if attorneys "didn't collar the clients" many victims would go uncompensated and those responsible for accidents would have little incentive to reduce them.[54]

Yet established lawyers who drafted and interpreted ethics rules generally found such considerations less compelling than their own interests in preserving a public image "above trade." Henry Drinker, a prominent mid-twentieth-century legal ethics expert, captured prevailing views in reminding his colleagues that "American lawyers differ radically from the milkman [or] . . . liquor dealer. They differ in being members of a profession not a business," and the distinction was "not a fanciful conceit but a cherished tradition." To preserve that tradition, constant vigilance was essential. Until the 1970s, bar ethics committees spent more time enforcing restrictions on advertising and solicitation than on any other subject. Impermissible practices included distributing calendars, embossed matchbooks, or Christmas cards with a lawyer's name and profession; displaying office signs with ostentatiously large lettering; wearing jewelry with the state bar insignia; and using boldface type in telephone books.[55]

Legal Challenges to Anticompetitive Practices

In the 1960s and 1970s, these sweeping prohibitions on advertising, solicitation, and underbidding prompted legal challenge. Various forces fueled concerns about restrictive bar policies: the increasing diversity and competitiveness of the profession, the rise of a consumer movement, the emergence of public interest organizations concerned with access to justice, and the growth of legal clinics needing a large volume of routine work in order to keep fees affordable. These developments set the stage for legal claims that eventually reached the Supreme Court.

One of the first rulings occurred in the mid-1970s in a case brought by Public Citizen, a national consumer group. It sued on behalf of a Virginia couple, Lewis and Ruth Goldfarb, who could not find an attorney willing to perform a title examination for less than the minimum charge set forth in the county bar's fee schedule. The Goldfarbs' claim was that the fee schedule constituted price-fixing in violation of federal antitrust laws. The Supreme Court agreed and held that "learned professions" involved "trade or commerce" within the scope of statutory prohibitions. This recognition that lawyers were not entirely "above trade" laid the foundations for the Court's subsequent rulings on advertising and solicitation.[56]

The initial case came in 1977. *Bates v. State Bar of Arizona* involved a somewhat colorless advertisement for a legal clinic offering "legal services at very reasonable fees." The ad also listed charges for certain routine services such as uncontested divorces, adoptions, and simple personal bankruptcies. The Supreme Court held that such claims were not misleading and fell within First Amendment protections for commercial speech. In subsequent decisions, the Court struck down restrictions on graphic illustrations, targeted mailings concerning mortgage-related services, and solicitation by public interest lawyers who had no financial stake in the proceedings. However, the Court left open the scope of permissible regulations concerning tasteless advertisements. The Justices also sustained prohibitions on personal contact with accident victims, and on mailings to victims within 30 days of an accident. In essence, the Court required that restraints on lawyers' commercial speech must be justified by a substantial state interest and must be narrowly drawn to further that interest. Yet what constitutes a sufficient interest has remained subject to dispute. And as chapter 4 notes, the profession's concern with maintaining its image still too often trumps the public's concern with access to competitive, cost-effective services.[57]

Group Legal Services

The same is true with respect to one final marketing issue—that of legal services targeted to groups rather than individuals. The first efforts to provide such services began at the turn of the twentieth century in the form of legal insurance for physicians in malpractice proceedings. Similar efforts followed from other providers: employers, who wanted to extend legal coverage to their workers; organizations such as unions and automobile clubs, which sought to offer legal services to their members; and insurance companies, which wanted to sell legal policies to their customers. From the outset, the organized bar opposed the entire concept of group services and sued, often successfully, to shut them down entirely or hamstring their development through various marketing and ownership restrictions. The most common objections were that such plans violated ethical rules prohibiting the practice of law by corporations, fee sharing between lawyers and nonlawyers, and solicitation of clients. In effect, bar ethical codes allowed lawyers to provide services to an organization but not to its members, employees, or customers. The stated rationales for this restriction were that corporations were not subject to bar ethical regulation, that nonlawyers should not exercise control over lawyers' professional judgment, and that conflicts of interest might arise between organizations and the groups targeted for services. The unstated rationales, widely acknowledged by bar members, were that group plans restricted access to clients by lawyers who were not part of the plan, and limited the fees available to attorneys who were participants.[58]

The profession's preferred alternative was a referral system run under bar auspices. Los Angeles established the first of these systems in 1937, and by the turn of this century, several hundred were in operation, handling some five to six million requests for information per year. From a consumer standpoint, however, these plans have fallen far short of what is necessary to find cost-effective assistance. Until the 1980s, the plans remained largely unregulated. Then, an increase of competitors from the private sector and the inadequacies of consumer protection prompted a few states to impose minimum requirements and the American Bar Association to adopt model standards. But only about half of all systems have complied with those standards, and even those in compliance have provided relatively little by way of price and quality control. Typically, any lawyer has been able to participate in a bar referral system if he or she accepts a few basic terms, such as maintaining malpractice insurance and limiting fees for the first half hour of consultation. No information has been available concerning the participants' prior performance, average fees, or complaint record. Moreover, many consumers have suspected that lawyers who need to place themselves on bar panels in order to obtain work have not been the cream of the profession. As a consequence, only about 6 percent of surveyed clients have relied on such referral systems.[59]

Interest in group services apart from those controlled by the bar has increased substantially since the 1960s, partly in response to the rise of consumer and public interest legal organizations. These groups, joined by unions, launched a series of challenges to restrictive bar policies that ultimately reached the Supreme Court. In 1963 the first of these challenges, *NAACP v. Button*, involved the NAACP's right to seek plaintiffs among its members and to provide them with counsel in civil rights suits. Subsequent cases concerned union practices of referring members to selected lawyers or employing attorneys to handle members' legal claims. Despite the united opposition of national and state bar associations, the Court upheld all of these activities. In essence, it ruled that "collective activity undertaken to obtain meaningful access to the courts is a fundamental right within the protection of the First Amendment." Requests by the ABA and forty state bar associations for reconsideration of that position proved unavailing.[60]

These rulings cleared the way for expanded marketing of group plans. The profession gradually relaxed its opposition to group coverage once lawyers generally discovered that it presented little economic threat to their own practices. However, the organized bar has resisted proposals to share profits and control over the delivery of group services. The result has been that far fewer individuals have coverage for basic needs in this country than in Europe, where legal assistance is commonly included in comprehensive insurance plans. One major obstacle to the growth of such plans in the United States has been the bar's continued prohibition on lawyers' sharing profits with nonlawyers. In 1987, during debates over revision of bar ethical rules, the ABA overwhelmingly rejected a reform proposal that proponents conceded would allow companies like Sears Roebuck to operate a law office. These constraints on nonlawyer financing of legal services should be reconsidered. As chapter 4 indicates, more targeted safeguards concerning conflicts of interest and preservation of lawyers' independent judgment might better serve the consumer. Achieving such reforms will, in turn, require a regulatory process less hostage to the profession's own self-interest.

Nonlawyer Services

A similar point could be made about the profession's role in preempting competition from nonlawyers. Although bar leaders have long claimed that the "fight to stop unauthorized practice is the public's fight," the public has been demonstrably unsupportive of the effort. So also were most lawyers, until competitive economic pressures during the Depression brought new appreciation of the grave public danger that unauthorized practice ostensibly posed. As noted earlier, for most of American history, lawyers held no monopoly over legal advice. During the early years of the Republic, many lay practitioners with a smattering of legal knowledge even represented parties in court proceedings. Although some states enacted statutes prohibiting unauthorized practice of law before the 1930s, these prohibitions typically applied only to nonlawyer appearances in court or to legal services by court officials such as bailiffs, clerks, and sheriffs. So too, the scattered cases against lay practitioners before the Depression generally involved such courtroom conduct or individuals who had fraudulently held themselves out as attorneys. But in a few major commercial centers, the rapid growth of business corporations in areas overlapping traditional legal work triggered bar challenges in the earlier part of the century. The Chicago Bar Association appointed the first committee on unauthorized practice in 1904 and New York followed in 1914. The efforts of these and similar committees in other states resulted in a growing series of cases against corporations, particularly title and trust companies.[61]

Unauthorized Practice Prohibitions

During the Depression, however, virtually all bar associations came to perceive a serious problem of lay competition. In 1930, the ABA appointed its first Committee on the Unauthorized Practice of Law. By 1938, over four hundred state and local bar organizations had established similar committees, and many had successfully lobbied for the passage of broader statutes on unauthorized practice. Although bar leaders have often asserted that these initiatives "arose as the result of public demand," the consensus among historians is to the contrary. Virtually all complaints about nonlawyer practice came from lawyers, not aggrieved consumers. As J. Willard Hurst diplomatically noted, "the coincidence of events ill fitted claims that [unauthorized practice] activity was moved simply by regard for protecting the public against the incompetent or unscrupulous."[62]

What constituted legal practice was, however, extremely murky around the edges. The ABA's ethical codes avoided difficult definitional issues by avoiding definition and deferring instead to the laws of the relevant jurisdiction. But these laws were often equally unilluminating. Some prohibited, without defining, unauthorized practice. Others took a circular approach: The practice of law was what lawyers did and therefore only lawyers could permissibly do it. A third strategy was to list specific tasks reserved to lawyers. This approach did little to clarify matters because the lists were extensive and included legal advice and preparation of legal documents—activities that were essential for many other occupations. Realtors, insurance agents, accountants, and financial advisors often could not provide competent assistance without preparing legal forms or counseling customers on legal issues.[63]

In response to these realities, some courts carved out exceptions to broad statutory prohibitions for nonlawyer services involving routine tasks that were within the competence of the average citizen, widespread in the community, or incidental to other established businesses. While these exceptions were steps in the right direction, they were not directly responsive to the public interests that nominally justified unauthorized practice prohibitions. In applying the "routine tasks" exception, courts typically announced that the conduct was or was not beyond an average individual's abilities without reference to any evidence about what those abilities were, whether the offending lay practitioners had above average expertise, or whether the public had been demonstrably harmed by their activities. Since advice was never considered routine, nonlawyers who prepared legal forms were expected to remain silent in the face of even the simplest questions or most obvious mistakes. The other exceptions for widespread or incidental lay services were equally problematic. As one consumer advocate noted, they seemed little more than a "rationalization for territorial truces between the warring professions."[64]

Often those truces had been negotiated by the groups themselves, without any apparant regard for the public interest. Beginning in the 1920s, national, state, and local bar associations entered into formal "Statements of Principles" with trade associations for accountants, architects, bankers, claims adjusters, collection agents, engineers, social workers, law book publishers, realtors, and insurance brokers. Not until the late 1970s, after adverse judicial rulings and pressure from the Justice Department's Antitrust Division, did bar associations rescind their formal statements of principles.[65]

Challenges to the Professional Monopoly

By that time, other forces were also at work to challenge anticompetitive bar policies, a trend that continued over the next quarter century. A rise in consumer consciousness triggered demands for greater choice in legal services. Simplification of various procedures, such as those involving uncontested divorces and uncomplicated estates, encouraged more individuals to proceed pro se, and to look for less costly alternatives to lawyers. Information available through computer programs and Internet sites enabled more individuals to represent themselves in simple matters. Greater specialization in legal work, coupled with a growing reliance on paralegals and routinized case-processing systems, undercut competence-related justifications for banning lay competitors. Yet as chapter 4 notes, the bar has resisted reforms that would increase consumers' access to qualified nonlawyer providers of legal services. Significant progress will require the public to play a greater role in policing the scope of the profession's monopoly.

The Historical Legacy

In a 1953 history of the legal profession prepared under ABA auspices, Harvard professor Roscoe Pound assured his sponsor that the organized bar was not the "same sort of thing as a retail grocer's association." If he was right, it was for the wrong reasons. Lawyers, no less than other occupational groups, form trade associations in pursuit of profits and status. The chief difference between the organizations of the bar and those of other groups is that lawyers have succeeded in maintaining a wider scope for self-regulation and self-interest in restricting commercial practices.[66]

Part of that success lies in the ability of lawyers, and former lawyers who serve as judges, to convince themselves that the profession's interest is the same as the public's. Opposition to group legal services and government-subsidized aid for civil and criminal matters has proceeded under the banner of protecting lawyers' independence in serving their clients. Restraints on advertising and solicitation have been justified as preventing overly commercial and intrusive tactics, and preserving public confidence in the profession. Bans on unauthorized practice have been defended as necessary to prevent incompetent and unethical services. But how well these restrictions protect societal interests, and at what cost, have been questions too seldom seriously considered.

This is not to suggest that lawyers have always been unconcerned with the effects of bar policies on access to justice. Especially in recent years, many efforts to increase government funding of legal aid and to challenge anticompetitive practices have been led by lawyers. But on issues where its power, status, and economic well-being are strongly implicated, the legal profession, like other occupational groups, has often had difficulty perceiving, let alone pursuing, interests at odds with its own.

In another, frequently quoted passage in his history of the bar, Pound defined professionalism as the practice of a "learned art in the spirit of public service." By that definition, too many of the bar's efforts have fallen short. True professionalism implies not some particular structure of legal practice or decorum in commercial conduct, but rather a willingness to put public interests first. Much of the progress in achieving greater access to justice over the last quarter century has occurred when bar leaders became willing to do just that. It is in this spirit that the following chapters are offered.

⩵ 4 ⩵

ACCESS TO WHAT?

Law without Lawyers and New

Models of Legal Assistance

A quarter of a century ago, in a widely publicized speech before the Los Angeles County Bar Association, then President Jimmy Carter took his audience to task for the nation's inequitable delivery of legal services. The United States, he noted, had "the heaviest concentration of lawyers on earth . . . but no resource of talent and training . . . is more wastefully or unfairly distributed than legal skills. Ninety percent of our lawyers serve ten percent of our people. We are overlawyered and under-represented." The situation has not improved. And then as now, the problem has been in large part of the bar's own making. The profession's policies on legal services and legal processes bear much of the responsibility for pricing most Americans out of the justice system.[1]

The scope of unmet legal needs is difficult to quantify with any precision. Chapter 5 addresses the estimated four-fifths of legal needs of the poor that remain unmet. With respect to middle-income Americans, the best estimates come from a large national survey by the ABA's Consortium on Legal Services. It found that about two-thirds of the civil legal needs of moderate-income consumers were not taken to lawyers or the justice system. State surveys have reached similar results. In one representative study, almost three-quarters of Maryland's "middle class citizens . . . no longer contact a lawyer when faced with a legal problem." Such studies underestimate the full range of unrepresented interests, since their findings rely heavily on subjective perceptions and do not register many collective concerns, such as environmental risks, or other problems of which individuals are unaware. Part of the reason that Americans do not turn to the legal profession or the legal system to address problems that they do recognize is that the matters do not appear sufficiently significant or beyond their own ability to handle. But two other consistently cited explanations are cost and the lack of conviction that lawyers or lawsuits would help. Two-thirds of surveyed Americans agree that it is "not affordable to bring a case to court." Neither does it appear cost-effective to bring many routine needs to lawyers. Simple wills, uncontested divorces, minor accidents, consumer disputes, landlord–tenant problems, employee grievances, and government benefit claims are the kinds of matters for which legal representation often seems an unaffordable luxury.[2]

Yet it is also clear that many individuals are unhappy with the results that they are able to achieve on their own. In the ABA's study, only about half of middle income Americans reported satisfaction with their own resolution of legal problems. Of those who took no action, only about a third were satisfied. By contrast, of those who turned to lawyers or the legal system, about two-thirds were satisfied. Yet even many of these individuals did not give high ratings to the performance of lawyers or courts. About a third were not completely satisfied with many dimensions of their attorney's representation, such as promptness, providing information, giving attention to their matters, and expressing interest or concern. A majority of Americans also were not completely satisfied with any aspect of their experience with courts or other hearings, including treatment by staff and judges, help in filing their cases, and the fairness and timeliness of the proceedings. Other more objective studies also demonstrate that individuals who try to resolve matters without legal assistance often fare poorly in processes that are designed by and for lawyers. The experience of one lawyerless litigant seeking to alter a child custody arrangement was all too typical. An impatient trial judge, after briefly listening to ill-prepared arguments by each pro se parent, offered platitudes to the estranged couple, such as "it takes two to fight." He then informed the father that he lacked crucial third party evidence to justify altering the arrangement or a draft order that would authorize a referral to counseling. When the father began asking questions about how to prepare the order, the judge snapped back "I'm not your secretary." He then shooed the couple out of the courtroom with the observation, "There's only so much I can do." If, as other evidence suggests, that is the dominant view among overburdened trial judges, then other reforms are clearly necessary.[3]

Strategies for better addressing the needs of moderate-income individuals fall into three basic categories, which parallel and partly overlap those necessary for low-income individuals. One set of initiatives involves reducing the necessity for legal intervention and assistance. A second cluster of strategies aims at reducing the cost and increasing the effectiveness of legal procedures and services. A third group of efforts involves increasing individuals' capacity to identify and afford appropriate legal assistance and dispute resolution processes.

Law without Lawyers

The bar's debates about access to justice have traditionally assumed that the main problem is inadequate access to lawyers and that the solution is to make their services more broadly available. From the profession's standpoint, this approach has obvious advantages. But from the public's vantage, such frameworks mischaracterize both the problem and the prescription. What Americans want is more justice, not necessarily more lawyering. They want a way of handling legal needs that is timely, fair, and affordable. In many contexts, the most cost-effective strategies are those that individuals can pursue themselves. Yet when it comes to facilitating those strategies, the bar often has been part of the problem instead of the solution. Most lawyers have resisted reform efforts that would help individuals help themselves, and most courts have failed to adopt sufficient strategies to make self-representation feasible and effective.[4]

The Growth of Self-Representation

The need for law without lawyers is by no means a new phenomenon. What is, however, new is the extent to which Americans are attempting to address their legal needs without professional assistance, and the increase in information and services available to help them. Eighteenth-century litigants had to make do with a few manuals like *Every Man His Own Lawyer*. Today's consumer has thousands of options. Over the last several decades, the market for do-it-yourself legal materials has grown dramatically in response to broader social trends. Beginning in the 1960s, a rise in political activism launched greater demands for legal remedies. The simplification of procedures involving issues such as divorce and probate has both reflected and reinforced those demands. Increased consumer consciousness, coupled with cutbacks in government-subsidized legal aid, has fueled more interest in self-help strategies. Technological innovations have also expanded the services that individuals can obtain quickly and cheaply through the Internet or computer software.[5]

The result has been a vast array of information, advice, document preparation assistance, and dispute resolution processes for individuals who want to take law into their own hands. For example, most state and federal statutes and agency regulations are available on-line, and websites like Findlaw make court opinions and other legal materials readily available. Websites run by courts, nonprofit organizations, and commercial providers offer blank forms for free; other sites like LegalDocs sell form templates for prices beginning as low as $6. Some courthouse kiosks and self-help centers, as well as commercial websites and off-line CD-ROMs, provide interactive form preparation services. Consumers answer a series of questions and then receive completed forms. Individuals can also purchase on-line legal advice, post their legal questions, and participate in chatroom discussions of legal issues. Internet alternative dispute resolution services are available as well. For example, SquareTrade provides a forum for resolving real estate disputes or complaints resulting from on-line auction transactions. Another service, Cybersettle, offers a patented bidding process designed to reach parties' optimal settlement point.[6]

All of these developments have contributed to a dramatic increase in pro se litigation. Pro se filings now account for about a quarter of all new civil cases, and surveyed jurisdictions report that between 65 to 90 percent of uncontested divorce cases have at least one party appearing without a lawyer, up from 25 percent in 1980. High rates of self-representation also occur in courts handling landlord–tenant disputes, bankruptcies, simple estates, domestic violence, and misdemeanor criminal charges. Small claims courts are specifically designed for pro se parties, and some states ban lawyers entirely or permit them only when both sides are represented. The income and educational level of these litigants varies. In some state courts, the poor are overrepresented; in others, the typical pro se party is at the upper level of the middle-class income and educational range. One of the few surveys of unrepresented litigants found that about half thought the matter was simple enough to handle themselves; another third indicated that they could not afford a lawyer.[7]

Resistance from the Legal Profession

For obvious reasons, the organized bar has not welcomed these trends. In a purportedly selfless effort to "protect the public" from unauthorized practice of law, the profession has attempted to ban do-it-yourself kits, document preparation services, computer software, and interactive on-line information. The stated concern is that ignorant consumers will suffer from assistance offered by individuals who do not meet the competence and ethical standards established for licensed attorneys. The unstated concern is that the bar will suffer from unrestricted competition. As subsequent discussion notes, bar opposition has had diminishing success, but it continues to play an important role in restricting nonlawyer practitioners. It has also discouraged courts and legislatures from developing streamlined procedures and adequate pro se services. Elected judges are often reluctant to antagonize the organized bar, whose support is critical for their retention and advancement. And most state politicians have been equally wary of opposing the bar's powerful lobby on issues where consumers have not mobilized countervailing pressures.[8]

The result is that a majority of surveyed courts lack formal services to assist pro se litigants. Others have services that are grossly inadequate, particularly for individuals with limited education, computer skills, or English language facility. Many jurisdictions rely on court clerks to provide assistance, yet fail to provide adequate staff or resources. Neither clerks nor pro se advisors are usually allowed to provide legal advice because that would violate state unauthorized practice prohibitions. Only general information is permissible; court staff may not counsel parties on which forms they should file or correct obvious errors. Some courthouses even have signs stating that clerks "can't answer questions of a legal nature." Yet as one California judge noted, those are the only questions that clerks generally encounter, other than "where is the restroom?"[9]

State court surveys also find that many clerks are particularly unresponsive to domestic violence claimants, whom they believe demand too much assistance and too frequently end up dropping charges. Some staff fail to inform battered women about the availability of civil protection orders or refuse to provide the assistance necessary to obtain them. Other clerks tell abuse victims (incorrectly) that they can only apply for protection once, so they "had better be sure this [is] the time they really need it." The absence of help for these women is particularly disturbing in light of the serious risks of injury if court orders are not available. Counties that fail to provide legal assistance along with other services for battered women have been found to have a higher incidence of domestic violence than counties that offer such aid.[10]

Small Claims Courts

Although virtually all states have small claims courts that are designed to enable individuals to represent themselves, most of these courts are seriously inadequate to the task. The same concerns that have led the profession to resist consumer access to nonlawyer competitors have restricted access to small claims tribunals. Their major limitation involves jurisdiction. Typically they can only handle claims involving extremely low dollar amounts; ceilings of $3,000 to $5,000 are common, and some are set below $2,000. So too, in most states, small claims courts can only grant money damages; they may not order parties to refrain from violating the law and may not enforce their own judgments. If losing opponents refuse to pay, successful parties usually must bring another suit in a court of general jurisdiction to collect their awards. Small claims courts generally are not user-friendly in other ways. Hours are too limited, forms are too complicated, and personal assistance is too often unavailable. Some jurisdictions permit appearances by attorneys even if the other side is unrepresented, which creates a playing field that is anything but level.[11]

Courts for Lawyers Not Litigants

The problems are compounded in other civil proceedings. Even courts with large numbers of pro se litigants are rarely designed with their needs in view. Hours and locations are inconvenient, forms are unintelligible, and processes are intimidating. Extended delays and fragmented jurisdictional structures force many pro se parties to spend an entire day waiting for their case to be called or to lose even more time shuttling between various courts to address related needs. For example, domestic violence victims may have to navigate one process to obtain a protective order against further abuse and file claims in another location to obtain temporary child support. Unrepresented parties are also at severe disadvantage when negotiating a settlement with an opponent who has counsel, and many are misled into giving up crucial rights and remedies.[12]

Judges often lack the time, expertise, or inclination to assist these pro se litigants. Over 90 percent of surveyed courts have no established policies concerning individuals who represent themselves. Although some judges attempt to prevent exploitation of the ignorance of a pro se party, others decline to do so out of concern that such efforts will compromise their impartiality or encourage more individuals to proceed without attorneys. Trial courts are sometimes openly hostile to unrepresented litigants, whom they view as tying up the system or attempting to gain tactical advantages. Tenants attempting to demonstrate housing code violations, divorced spouses seeking to modify support awards, or consumers trying to file valid bankruptcy petitions are frequently unprepared both for the technical requirements necessary to establish their claims and resistance from judges and courthouse staff. Domestic violence plaintiffs are particularly likely to be victimized twice: once by the abuse and once by the process of proving it. Many trial courts blame battered women for provoking assaults or burdening court dockets with avoidable squabbles. Almost half of surveyed service providers for domestic violence victims report that judges refuse to consider awarding remedies that are clearly authorized by statute, such as custody, child support, and other temporary financial relief. Some battered women have even been sanctioned or threatened with sanctions for repeated claims; one North Dakota judge informed a petitioner, "if you go back [to the abuser] one more time, I'll hit you myself."[13]

In many legal contexts, Americans experience a frustrating mismatch between what they need and what the justice system is prepared to supply. Cases in lower courts, particularly those involving pro se litigants, are often symptomatic of broader social and personal problems: mental health disabilities, substance abuse, and inadequate employment or financial management skills, coupled with local shortages in jobs, housing, and health services. Yet overburdened trial judges typically lack the time, resources, or training to engage in problem solving. "The court is not in the social work business" is a common refrain. But as John Feinblatt, founder of New York City's Center for Court Innovation notes, for better or worse, many courts are inevitably "the social services of last resort." Too often, it is for the worse.[14]

Court Reform

In short, while law without lawyers is an increasing possibility for many Americans, it is frequently law without justice. Part of the solution, as subsequent discussion suggests, is to expand Americans' access to legal services from both lawyers and qualified nonlawyers. But dispute resolution processes also need to be more effective for the public that they ostensibly serve. We do not lack for appropriate models. Many jurisdictions have begun to redesign courts in ways that improve their responsiveness to individual litigants, especially those who proceed pro se. One cluster of reforms involves creating more user-friendly legal procedures. Eliminating archaic jargon, extended delays, and fragmented court structures are crucial steps in that direction. Other key strategies include extended hours and adequate pro se services in community and courthouse settings. Some courts permit handwritten petitions and electronic filings; others offer hotlines, on site childcare, and form preparation assistance through websites and computer kiosks. A growing number provide at least some personal assistance in multiple languages for pro se litigants through centers in courthouses, community organizations, or even traveling outreach units. A few jurisdictions have substantially raised the dollar limits of small claims courts, offered assistance to their users, and banned appearances by lawyers in all cases or in proceedings where the opponent is unrepresented. Such reforms should be more widely adopted and courts should develop policies, training, and monitoring structures to promote fair treatment of unrepresented parties.[15]

More jurisdictions should also follow the example of states that have effectively implemented specialized "holistic," "therapeutic,"or "community" courts and alternative dispute resolution procedures to deal with problems like domestic violence, homelessness, and misdemeanors such as prostitution, drug possession, and juvenile offenses. Judges in these proceedings receive special training and resources. Their goal is to partner with other social service providers offering treatment approaches that can address root causes not just legal symptoms. Well-designed mediation and other dispute resolution approaches can also engage parties in productive, collaborative problem solving. What limited data are available suggest that these innovative approaches are moving in the right direction. Many have been successful in reducing repeat offenses.[16]

None of these approaches are, of course, panaceas. Many confront long-standing challenges in new forms. How can informal tribunals provide adequate procedural protections and prevent the exploitation or coercion of weaker, unrepresented parties? How can courts ensure that pro se programs are effective for lower income individuals who need them most and that litigants who represent themselves are not systematically disadvantaged as a consequence? These are not insignificant challenges, and far more research and evaluation is necessary to identify effective responses.[17]

It is not enough, however, to focus only on courts. A wide array of studies find that individuals prefer to resolve disputes in informal settings. To make that possible, we could follow the lead of countries like Australia that require certain large organizations to establish internal complaint procedures or to participate in industry-wide grievance systems that meet prescribed standards of procedural fairness. Many American organizations now lack such processes or have arbitration and mediation systems that are skewed against complainants. Considerable evidence suggests that well-designed employee and consumer grievance procedures benefit both institutional and individual participants. Giving organizations greater responsibility for "doing justice" internally is likely to prove more cost-effective than relying on lawyers and judges to resolve minor disputes.[18]

Policing the Professional Monopoly

Formal Rules and Daily Realities

Giving qualified nonlawyers a greater role in providing routine legal assistance is likely to have a similar positive effect, but the organized bar is pushing hard in the opposite direction. And its campaign has the advantage of criminal statutes and judicial rulings that prohibit the "unauthorized practice of law." Every state has such prohibitions and millions of Americans violate them on a daily basis. Many occupations cannot provide competent services without engaging in activities that fall within prevailing definitions of legal practice. Those definitions vary somewhat by jurisdiction, but the dominant approach is to permit nonlawyers to provide general information but not personalized legal advice. Nonlawyers may type legal documents but may neither correct errors in their selection and preparation nor offer other substantive assistance. Yet accountants, real estate brokers, insurance agents, financial advisors, and even newspaper advice columnists routinely engage in such prohibited activities. Ann Landers was a notorious habitual offender. In one typical column, Landers told a worried "El Paso Wings" what would happen to her eight-year-old son if she and her husband died in a plane crash. If, as the mother indicated, her closest relatives "hate[d] kids," Landers suggested that the couple make a will naming other guardians. The advice was sound; it was also a criminal misdemeanor.[19]

Recent technological advances, coupled with Americans' escalating interest in legal self- help, have expanded opportunities for such nonlawyer practice. A celebrated recent case involved a fifteen-year-old, Marcus Arnold, who presented himself as a "legal expert" on a website that allows anyone to volunteer answers to posted questions. By his own account, Arnold had never read a law book; his answers were based on information from Court TV and the Internet or common sense. Users of the site rated the advisors and ranked Arnold number three, ahead of many lawyers. After Arnold revealed that he was only a high school student without legal training, his popularity initially dipped, but he eventually gained the number one spot and was inundated with requests to represent parties in legal matters.[20]

Bar Opposition

From the profession's standpoint, such examples are cautionary tales of what can happen without stringent enforcement of unauthorized practice prohibitions. State bar leaders repeatedly sound alarms along the lines issued by one Arizona committee that nonlawyer services are causing "a crisis of faith" in the legal system. Over four-fifths of surveyed attorneys have supported prosecution of lay practitioners, and the profession has repeatedly blocked licensing proposals that would enable independent paralegals to offer routine services. Many local, state, and national bar associations have recently launched initiatives to broaden the definition, raise the penalties, and increase the enforcement of unauthorized practice prohibitions. In 2001, the ABA voted to strengthen enforcement efforts, and in 2003 it considered a task force proposal for a stringent model definition of unauthorized practice. When the Justice Department, Federal Trade Commission, and the ABA's own antitrust division protested that the proposal would inappropriately restrict client choices and increase prices, the Association's president flatly denied any such effects. The ABA's sole objective, he assured his critics, was to provide a clearer definition of permissible and impermissible activities, thus "enhancing consumer access and protection, not limiting competition."[21]

Occasionally, however, a bar leader will go off message. One former president of the New Jersey Bar expressed common views with uncommon candor when he acknowledged "no difficulty saying my position is protecting the interests of lawyers." Why should the ABA pretend that it is willing to "find work for nonlawyers[?] . . . This is the American Bar Association, not the American Paralegal Association." That fact is not lost on consumer advocates. In testimony before a recent ABA Public Hearing on Access to Justice, David Vladeck of Public Citizen put the point bluntly: "While the ABA has done good works in many areas, this is not one of them. . . . Rather than promoting reform, the ABA has instead doggedly insisted on maintaining archaic unauthorized practice of law rules that do little more than preserve the lawyer monopoly [over] the provision of legal services."[22]

The Public Interest

That view is widely shared. On the rare occasions when the public is consulted, it seems unsupportive of the protections efforts ostensibly imposed on its behalf. In one ABA survey, over four-fifths of Americans agreed that many matters lawyers handled could be "done as well and less expensively by non-lawyers." In the only reported bar survey of consumer satisfaction, nonlawyer specialists got higher ratings than lawyers. Some efforts to broaden prohibitions on unauthorized practice have resulted in political reversals. In one state constitutional referendum, Arizona voters reversed a decision giving lawyers a monopoly over routine real estate closings. And the Texas legislature hastily amended its unauthorized practice statutes to exempt computer software that the bar had succeeded in suppressing as impermissible legal advice.[23]

The public's support for greater access to lay legal services is well founded. Other nations generally permit nonlawyers to provide legal advice and assist with routine documents, and no evidence suggests that their performance has been inadequate. In this country, the American Law Institute's Restatement of the Law Governing Lawyers notes that "experience in several states with extensive nonlawyer provision of traditional legal services indicates no significant risk of harm to consumers. . . ." So too, studies of lay specialists who provide legal representation in bankruptcy and administrative agency hearings find that they generally perform as well or better than attorneys. In the most systematic survey to date, a majority of states did not report unauthorized practice complaints from consumers; the vast majority came from lawyers and involved no claims of specific injury. Such findings should come as no surprise. Three years in law school and passage of a bar exam are neither necessary nor sufficient to ensure expertise in the areas where nonlawyer services flourish; lay specialists may be better able to provide cost-effective services than lawyers who practice in multiple fields.[24]

This is not to discount the problems that can result from unqualified or unethical nonlawyer assistance. Some unlicensed practitioners, including disbarred attorneys, misrepresent their status and exploit vulnerable consumers. Immigrants are particularly common targets, both because they are generally unfamiliar with the American legal system and because they are unlikely to risk contact with law enforcement agencies in reporting abuses. However, the appropriate response to these problems is regulation, not prohibition. Consumers need an approach that balances their need for protection with their interests in competition and affordable services.[25]

Unauthorized practice restrictions are ill-suited to that task because they focus only on whether nonlawyers are providing legal assistance, not whether they are doing so effectively. The bar has repeatedly shut down lay practitioners who have helped thousands of consumers without generating a single complaint. In one all too typical recent example, the Delaware Supreme Court held that Marilyn Arons, the founder of a nonprofit Parent Information Center, had engaged in unauthorized practice of law by providing free representation of children with disabilities. Their families had sought such assistance in hearings concerning local school boards' compliance with special education requirements. The record established both that Arons was a highly qualified expert with twenty years experience in disabled children's education and that most families would be unable to find or afford lawyers with the required expertise. Yet according to the Delaware bar disciplinary counsel, Aron's qualifications were not "relevant." Nor were her clients' unmet needs. But from the public's, rather than the profession's, perspective, these should be the key concerns. The current unauthorized practice structure is both over-inclusive and under-enforced. Bar prohibitions encompass a sweeping array of competent, low-cost services. Yet strong consumer demand for such assistance makes these prohibitions difficult to enforce. As a result, most lay practice goes unsupervised, and when abuses occur, the public has inadequate remedies.[26]

A Framework for Reform

A preferable regulatory structure would provide both less and more protection—less for attorneys and more for consumers. Nonlawyers like accountants or real estate brokers who are already licensed should be allowed to provide legal assistance related to their specialties. For currently unlicensed service providers, states should develop regulatory frameworks responsive to public needs, which may vary across different practice areas. Where the risk of injury is substantial, in contexts such as immigration, consumers may benefit from licensing systems that impose minimum qualifications and offer proactive enforcement. In other fields, it could be sufficient to register practitioners and permit voluntary certification of those who meet specified standards. States also could require all lay practitioners to carry malpractice insurance and to observe basic ethical obligations governing confidentiality, competence, and conflicts of interest. Similar protections could extend to Internet services. Enforcement, of course, poses substantial challenges, but the problems are not unique to lay legal assistance. As discussion below indicates, the bar's current state-based framework for lawyer regulation is highly inadequate for services that observe no geographic borders. Devising an appropriate oversight strategy for all forms of legal practice demands national efforts.[27]

In general, however, an approach that seeks to regulate, rather than preempt, lay competition would offer a number of advantages. Experience here and abroad suggests that increased competition between lawyers and nonlawyers is likely to result in lower prices, greater efficiency, and more consumer satisfaction. Regulating the activities of lay practitioners should help curb abuses that currently go unremedied, while encouraging innovative partnerships between lawyer and nonlawyer specialists. Such partnerships could increase access to cost-effective assistance by enabling organizations to provide multidisciplinary legal services.

One-Stop Shopping: Multidisciplinary Practice

In an era of increasing specialization of law-related services, it has become increasingly unlikely that any single lawyer, or often any single law firm, can effectively meet all their clients' needs. As chapter 5 notes, opportunities for "one-stop shopping" are of particular benefit to certain low- and middle-income groups, such as elderly, juvenile, domestic violence, or immigrant clients whose problems call for diverse professional skills. Such multidisciplinary partnerships (MDPs) would also serve a wide range of other individual, corporate, and nonprofit consumers whose financial concerns cut across different legal specialties.[28]

The Profession's Interest: Competing Views

Previous collaborative efforts have bumped up against the bar's prohibitions on fee splitting and on partnerships between lawyers and nonlawyers. In effect, the ABA's Model Rules of Professional Conduct allow attorneys to work for organizations controlled by nonattorneys as long as these in-house counsel represent the organization, not its outside clients. Efforts to liberalize such rules have met with little success. After heated controversy, the ABA recently rejected reforms that would permit lawyers to form partnerships with nonlawyers to offer consolidated assistance. Bar leaders' stated concern is that such arrangements would compromise the "core values" of the profession: independent judgment, confidentiality, loyalty, and competence. In particular, opponents of MDPs maintain that they would blur the boundaries between law and business, and undermine ethical standards governing conflicts of interests and confidential communications. Underlying these concerns are more parochial anxieties about ceding turf to nonlawyer competitors.[29]

Yet a growing constituency both within and outside the bar believes that in the long run lawyers' best response to these competitors will often be to join, not fight them. From this vantage, the goal should be to craft regulation that addresses legitimate ethical concerns without unduly restricting cross-professional collaboration. Part of the impetus for reform comes from the increasing threat posed by accounting firms. Other industrialized nations generally permit nonlawyers including accountants to own organizations providing law-related services and to employ or form partnerships with lawyers. As a consequence, the largest five accounting firms have dominated the global legal market. They have a presence in 138 countries and some have over 60,000 employees. These accounting firms are also making greater inroads in the American market. Federal law provides that tax advice and representation in tax court do not constitute the practice of law. This exception to traditional unauthorized practice prohibitions enables lawyers to provide services for clients of accounting firms as long as the work can be defined as tax, not legal, assistance. Over the past decade, the large accounting firms have taken increasing liberties with this definition. Their in- house lawyers now provide many of the same services as law firms on matters including tax, financial and estate planning, and even litigation support. Although many accounting firms are undoubtedly also engaged in the unauthorized practice of law, the bar has lacked the resources and public credibility necessary to respond. As a consequence, the legal profession faces growing difficulties competing with accounting organizations, which generally offer a wider range of services, greater economies of scale, and more effective marketing, informational technology, and managerial capacities. Ironically, the world's largest providers of legal services are no longer law firms. Or, as law professor Geoffrey Hazard indelicately puts it, accountants are "eating our lunch."[30]

This realization has triggered growing controversy within the profession. Most state bar associations are reconsidering their rules on multidisciplinary partnerships, and a number have proposed a more liberal approach. Many lawyers believe that current restrictions impair their ability to compete with accounting firms and to collaborate with other service providers. From the vantage of MDP supporters, opponents' "professionalism" concerns look like window-dressing for protectionism; attorneys unable or unwilling to compete are attempting to miscast their own self-interest as a societal value.[31]

By contrast, opponents of MDPs believe that opening the door to nonlawyer partnerships would compromise independent professional judgment and bar control over the terms of legal practice. From critics' perspective, Enron et al. offer cautionary tales of what can happen if lawyers cede ethical decisions to accountants and corporate managers. Their insensitivity to conflicts of interest, particularly in the simultaneous provision of consulting and audit services, makes clear the risks of cross-professional alliances.[32]

Some opponents of MDPs are also concerned that permitting nonlawyer involvement in the financial structure of legal services would do for law what managed care has done for medicine. Before the 1970s, doctors had ethical rules on collaboration similar to those now prevailing for lawyers. Licensed physicians could not work for organizations in which profits were shared by nonphysicians. The main justification for these rules was the same as to the bar's justification for banning multidisciplinary practice: that sharing control with lay employers or investors would pose threats to independent professional judgment. The result was to restrict competition and to enable doctors unilaterally to determine what treatment was necessary and to bill patients or their insurance carriers accordingly. Such a structure offered little incentive for efficiency or cost containment. Spiraling expenses eventually convinced federal and state legislatures, as well as antitrust regulatory agencies, to take actions eliminating physicians' anticompetitive ownership restrictions. As a consequence, lay control of managed health care has become the norm and has significantly constrained physician's income and autonomy. Although this structure has led to more efficient delivery of medical services, it has also generated concerns about the quality of care and interference with professional judgment. Many managed care plans have treatment directives and reward structures that discourage expensive medical services, even though they might have some benefit for an individual patient. MDP opponents worry that lawyers working in similar lay-controlled organizations might face analogous pressures to sacrifice client interests in the service of employers' bottom line. Attorneys are also concerned that greater competition and reduced control would have the same adverse impact on income as doctors experienced in response to similar forces.[33]

The Public Interest: Competing Concerns

Multidisciplinary practice does pose significant concerns, but their formulation is problematic in several respects. All too often, the focus has been on the interests of lawyers, and only secondarily or ritualistically on the needs of clients. Seldom are clients themselves consulted, and those who testified before the ABA's Multidisciplinary Practice Commission uniformly favored access to collaborative professional services. Even less attention has centered on what law professor David Luban notes is the most crucial question: not what is good for lawyers or clients, but what is good for the rest of us. Self-interested behavior by lawyers and clients can carry substantial social costs, as is clear not just from the recent spate of corporate scandals, but also from prior debacles like the collapse of savings and loan associations. Bar rules need to take into account the concerns of the public as well as the profession.[34]

One relevant concern is conflicts of interest. But the problem is not limited to multidisciplinary contexts, and it can be addressed by regulation rather than prohibition. American attorneys already face many pressures that compromise professional independence. In-house lawyers need to please nonlawyer management. Outside lawyers need to please important clients, third parties who refer clients or pay their fees, and supervisors preoccupied with billable hours. Court-appointed counsel need to balance competing demands on their time and resources. No evidence suggests that the threats to independent judgment in multidisciplinary practice are qualitatively or quantitatively different from those in other settings. Nor is there any basis for believing that lawyers' responses to conflicts of interest are, on the whole, more "ethical" than those of other professionals. While the spotlight in recent scandals was on accountants and corporate managers, the conduct of many attorneys was scarcely above reproach, and their moral myopia in other contexts has been amply documented. As a recent Special Committee on Multidisciplinary Practice for the District of Columbia noted, there is no foundation for the "economic protectionism" implicit in mandating lawyer control. The suggestion that only lawyers can be trusted to act ethically "smacks of professional arrogance."[35]

The lessons available from doctors' experience with managed care are also more favorable than MDP opponents suggest. From the public's standpoint, the elimination of anticompetitive restrictions on lay ownership have had significant positive effects. Costs have been contained and unnecessary procedures have been curtailed. Despite some highly publicized and often tragic accounts of denial of appropriate medical services, the most comprehensive research to date finds no systematic link between the quality of care and physician incentives, and no quality differences between managed care and fee-for-service systems. The threat of malpractice liability and more intrusive government regulation appears to be reasonably effective in maintaining professional standards, and that same threat would operate if lay ownership and lay partners were permitted for lawyers. Experts who have studied the comparative financing structures of law and medicine generally believe that regulating, rather than prohibiting, lay ownership and multidisciplinary partnerships would have a positive impact on legal services; the introduction of additional capital, expertise, economies of scale, and competitive incentives is likely to make such services more affordable and cost-effective.[36]

These experts, like the ABA Multidisciplinary Practice Commission and several state task forces, identify strategies short of prohibition that could address the pressures likely to arise in multidisciplinary practice. The ABA Commission recommended holding nonlawyers to the same ethical standards governing conflicts and confidentiality as those applicable to the bar generally and imposing special audit provisions to prevent nonlawyers from interfering with lawyers' professional judgments. The attorney–client privilege could be extended to cover these settings or clients could be warned about its unavailability. The District of Columbia bar has recommended requiring lawyers to assume responsibility for nonlawyers working with them on legal matters and to make full disclosure to clients of their financial incentives and potential conflicts of interest. Such regulatory alternatives deserve a chance to work. Lay ownership and partnerships have been effective in other countries and other professions, and there is good reason to believe that the public would benefit from their availability here. At the very least, even without changes in bar ethical rules, lawyers should seek alternative ways to build cooperative relationships and "strategic alliances" with other service providers. Under these arrangements, firms agree to share clients and sometimes capital and marketing capacities. Whether these arrangements can address client needs as effectively as multidisciplinary partnerships remains to be seen. But whatever their form, multidisciplinary collaborations of some sort are and should be here to stay. Lawyers do not have a monopoly on law-related expertise. There is a strong market demand and legitimate societal need for integrated legal and nonlegal advice. The organized bar should not stand in the way.[37]

Making Lawyers' Services More Accessible

A final set of strategies for increasing middle-income consumers' access to justice involves making lawyers' services more accessible and affordable. Such approaches include reducing constraints on competitive marketing and financing strategies, and enhancing lawyers' ability to provide cost-effective assistance.

Advertising and Solicitation

As the preceding chapter noted, the legal profession has traditionally resisted competition through advertising, solicitation, and group legal services. Despite recent Supreme Court decisions forcing liberalization of bar rules, most states maintain overly broad prohibitions. For example, many jurisdictions ban advertising that bar leaders find undignified or potentially misleading, such as dramatizations, lyrics, jingles, animations, testimonials, and claims regarding past performance. The lawyers who dominate regulatory decision making often share the view of then Chief Justice Warren Burger that selling law like laxatives constitutes "'sheer shysterism,' and an outrageous breach of professional conduct." By contrast, most research indicates that consumers generally find advertising acceptable and that it is not a major factor in shaping adverse public impressions of the legal profession. Such research also indicates that advertising generally increases competition and reduces prices without diluting quality. Lower prices tend to heighten demand, expand volume, and encourage economies of scale. Entertaining television commercials of the kind that some states still prohibit have a positive effect on viewers' perceptions of lawyers' professionalism, knowledge, helpfulness, and effectiveness. Yet such evidence often has been insufficient to trump bar concerns about status and self-image.[38]

These self-interested concerns also underpin bans on solicitation, which are broader than necessary to serve the public interest. The privacy of accident victims and their families certainly deserves protection, but that interest could be served by time, place, and manner limitations, rather than categorical bans on all contact. Prohibiting solicitation by plaintiffs' lawyers while insurance agents go unregulated increases the vulnerability of unsophisticated victims. Individuals who negotiate directly with insurance companies generally receive much lower compensation than individuals who retain counsel. Yet concerns about unrepresented parties receive inadequate attention in a regulatory process controlled by the profession.[39]

Of course, restrictions on advertising and solicitation are only part of what impedes access to legal services. Cost, and uncertainty about cost, are the major reasons that consumers give for not seeking aid from a lawyer when they believe such assistance would be helpful. Constraints on competition among lawyers are by no means the only obstacles to reducing the price of services. Even for consumers whose major problem is inadequate information about how to find a qualified attorney, more advertising or personal solicitation has not been the preferred solution. Most individuals want more neutral sources of information or a referral structure that provides some assurance of quality. Part of what has gotten in the way is bar restrictions on group legal services and centralized data banks.[40]

Group Legal Services

As the preceding chapter noted, group legal service programs have grown dramatically over the last several decades. By the turn of the twenty-first century, an estimated 30 to 40 percent of Americans had some form of coverage. The extent and structure of group plans varies considerably, as does the cost. A minority of plans involve prepayment of insurance premiums by individuals or by third parties such as employers. Under some of these prepaid programs, members receive "comprehensive" coverage; that is, coverage for 80 to 90 percent of an average person's legal needs in a given year. Under other prepaid "access" programs, members are entitled only to unlimited telephone advice; they pay separately for other services. A more common form of group legal services involve no prepayments, but rather provides referrals to cooperating attorneys or employs lawyers to handle members' claims. "Closed" plans require clients to use attorneys selected by the group. "Open" plans allow participation by any attorney who accepts specified terms, such as ceilings on fees for covered services and minimum malpractice insurance. Some state laws give consumers the right to select an attorney who is not a preferred provider, but permit plans to limit reimbursements. Prices are often modest. A typical plan might cost $150 a year for the most limited coverage, or twice that amount for more comprehensive services. Prices can be kept low by handling most requests for assistance through brief telephone consultations.[41]

Despite recent expansions in group plans, far fewer individuals have coverage for basic needs in this country than in Europe, where legal services are included in comprehensive insurance programs and are as common as life insurance. As chapter 3 indicated, several factors have hampered growth in the United States. One is the bar's continued prohibition on sharing fees with nonlawyers. Although the profession gradually relaxed its opposition to group coverage once most lawyers discovered that it presented little economic threat, the organized bar has resisted proposals to share control over the delivery of legal services with lay owners or partners. An additional factor limiting the appeal of group approaches has been inadequate assurance of quality. Low rates have encouraged lawyer participants to minimize their assistance, and unsophisticated consumers have had difficulty evaluating the services that they receive. Some plans make efforts to ensure competence by surveying client satisfaction and by requiring lawyers to meet specified educational and experience standards. But other group plans do little to oversee attorneys' qualifications or the adequacy of their assistance. An absence of complaints is the only benchmark for acceptable performance. A further problem has involved marketing. It has been difficult to convince many Americans that basic legal coverage is worth the investment. Individuals who have never or rarely consulted a lawyer are often reluctant to purchase insurance or to pressure employers to provide it. An additional concern is that members of group plans will try to get their money's worth and overuse legal assistance for trivial issues.[42]

However, none of these problems seems insurmountable. Requiring some co-payment by consumers is likely to minimize excessive use. More liberal rules on the structure of group plans also could attract new investors with greater marketing capacities. To that end, rules prohibiting lawyers from sharing fees and control with nonlawyers could be replaced with more targeted safeguards, such as protection of attorneys' independent professional judgment, and requirements that they observe bar ethical rules concerning competence, confidentiality, and conflicts of interest. Additional quality controls could be imposed by statute or by standards adopted by employer purchasers, consumer protection agencies, or insurance commissioners.[43]

Databanks

Another strategy for improving the market and enhancing the attractiveness of individual legal services involves increasing the information readily available about their quality. Centralized databases concerning lawyers' qualifications and performance could reduce information barriers and enhance accountability. A useful model is the on-line clearinghouses for physicians required in about half the states. These clearinghouses include information such as education, practice area, professional affiliations, criminal convictions, disciplinary sanctions, malpractice actions, and liability insurance. More states are expected to provide such databanks, and a national consumer organization, Public Citizen, also maintains a publicly available directory of disciplined doctors. No comparable, readily accessible clearinghouses exist for lawyers. Legal directories and referral services do not provide information concerning disciplinary, criminal, and malpractice histories and many consumers who are "one shot" purchasers lack reliable sources of information. Four-fifths of surveyed Americans would like a resource that they could consult concerning the records of particular lawyers.[44]

Attorneys often object to providing such a clearinghouse on the grounds that potential clients may attach undue importance to partial information or to minor transgressions, and that the reputations of practitioners would be unjustly impaired. However, no evidence for that claim has been forthcoming, and minor indiscretions rarely trigger public disciplinary action or malpractice judgments. In any event, the public's interest in full disclosure surely should trump the profession's more parochial concerns. In a democratic market-based society, the preferred response to incomplete information has been more rather than less. Databases can include background materials such as national malpractice and disciplinary statistics that would help consumers put profiles of particular lawyers in appropriate context. Moreover, by identifying practitioners with good records and adequate malpractice insurance, such clearinghouses would create additional incentives for appropriate conduct. In the long run, an informed public is the best guarantee of an accountable profession.[45]

Unbundled Services

A further set of strategies for enhancing access to justice involves increasing lawyers' capacity to provide cost-effective services to individuals of modest means. One such strategy is unbundling legal services. Under this approach, a lawyer and client agree to limit representation to discrete, specified tasks. Although attorneys in some fields have long been offering such limited forms of assistance, the term came into vogue in the mid-1990s as interest in the concept grew. Proponents describe unbundling as analogous to ordering from an "a la carte" menu. Clients decide what services they want from lawyers and perform the remainder themselves. Common forms of unbundled assistance involve court appearances or trial representation; telephone, Internet, or brief in-person advice; and assistance with negotiations, pretrial discovery, or document preparation. Lawyers often provide these limited services through group plans, pro se clinics, and court referral arrangements. A growing number of attorneys are also offering this option in conventional small firm or solo practice settings, or in new sites such as legal coffeehouses. For example, at Legal Grind in Los Angeles, customers can get cappuccino, self-help information, and a lawyer's assistance in matters such as preparing a will or responding to an eviction letter. If given the opportunity, a growing number of clients are choosing unbundled representation. To these individuals, less is more; less assistance means more savings, more control, and more knowledge about how to prevent or resolve related legal problems in the future.[46]

Yet too many lawyers remain reluctant to offer limited services. Part of the resistance is financial. Less may be more for clients, but less may be simply less for attorneys. Sharing tasks is unappealing unless lawyers have greater demand for their assistance than they can handle or can use unbundling to attract a larger volume of new work. A second reason for resistance involves potential exposure to malpractice claims. Many lawyers worry that clients who do not successfully handle their legal problems may complain that limited assistance was *too* limited and amounted to professional negligence. Some practitioners are also concerned that once they enter a court appearance for a limited purpose, courts may be reluctant to allow their withdrawal from further representation. Bar ethical rules provide some protection from such claims, but not enough to allay all liability concerns. The ABA's Model Rules of Professional Conduct permit lawyers and clients to limit the scope of assistance, and recent amendments make clear that such limitations should be respected as long as they are "reasonable." For example, brief consultation is appropriate unless "the time allotted is insufficient to yield advice upon which the client could rely." Although these rules, together with carefully drafted written retainer agreements, may help to preempt malpractice liability, they cannot shield lawyers entirely. Courts can still refuse to permit withdrawal, or costly disputes can still arise about what was reasonable in particular circumstances.[47]

A final obstacle to unbundled services involves judicial resistance to "ghostwritten" legal documents that an attorney drafts or reviews but does not acknowledge or sign. Judges have two main concerns. One is that clients who purchase these services will receive the same leniency sometimes granted to pro se litigants who are proceeding without such assistance. A second concern is that attorneys will be shielded from accountability for their work, particularly if the claim turns out be frivolous or the documents include material misrepresentations.[48]

These are valid concerns, but they can be addressed in ways that will promote the availability of unbundled services. With respect to ghostwriting, courts and bar ethical rules can require disclosure that an attorney has assisted preparation of a document without imposing on the attorney the full responsibility of legal representation. Where sanctions for frivolous or dishonest claims are appropriate, courts and bar disciplinary authorities could also demand disclosure of the identity of the attorney. Reforms in ethical rules could recognize lawyers' right to enter limited court appearances. To reduce malpractice exposure, bar associations can provide model retainer agreements as well as training and educational materials concerning the selection of appropriate unbundled services. Insurance companies can offer malpractice coverage and protocols for limited representation. To make unbundling financially viable for attorneys, more courts and bar associations can sponsor referral services and public education programs designed to increase the client demand for such assistance.[49]

Lawyer Support Networks

A final strategy for increasing access to justice is to provide better training and support services for lawyers representing individuals of modest means. A promising example is the Law School Consortium Project, a collaborative effort to assist solo and small firm lawyers who serve middle- and low-income clients. Some law schools have participated by helping to develop model forms of support. The resources provided have included peer mentoring, assistance with information technology and client development, access to law libraries, training in office management and substantive law areas, community education opportunities, case referrals, discounts on malpractice insurance and computer software, and a forum to share advice. Some schools have also designed curricular initiatives to enhance their own students' ability to assist underserved groups. Foundation funding initially subsidized the consortium. A continuing challenge is how to create self-sustaining networks that will offer similar support.[50]

Almost two decades ago, in a prominent report on professionalism, the American Bar Association concluded that the middle class's lack of access to affordable legal services was "one of the most intractable problems confronting the legal profession today." That problem remains, but we at least have increased our capacity to address it.[51]

A wide variety of strategies are now available to make law more accessible to Americans of modest means. Technological innovation, collaborative initiatives, and reforms in judicial and bar regulatory processes can alter the legal landscape. We do not lack for innovative approaches. What remains necessary is the political will to realize their full potential.

≡ 5 ≡

LOCKED IN AND LOCKED OUT

The Legal Needs of Low-Income Communities

In expressing his support for the federal Legal Services Corporation, President George W. Bush described its role as "ensur[ing] equal access to our nation's legal system." Even for audiences hardened to rhetorical excess, this claim may have strained credulity. The Corporation Report that prominently featured the President's endorsement also highlighted a decade's research on unequal access. Bar studies consistently find that about four-fifths of the civil legal needs of low-income Americans remain unmet. The nation's poor, who most need legal assistance, are least likely to obtain it. "Equal access" is an aspiration, but by no means a description of our justice system at work.[1]

The problems of inadequate access are, of course, not limited to the poor. Millions of moderate-income Americans are similarly priced out of the legal process, and many of the reforms necessary to make law more accessible to them will benefit those in poverty as well. Yet the distinctive needs of low-income groups deserve particular attention. Not only do the poor experience more legal difficulties than the average American, their needs take on special urgency. Individuals at the economic margin are much less able to "lump it" when faced with a denial of rights or benefits. The poor and near poor are also less likely to have the education, skills, and self-confidence to handle problems effectively without assistance. In response to these needs, governments at all levels have created a program of government-subsidized assistance, but one with resources by no means adequate to the task. How best to expand and allocate those resources is the subject of this chapter.

Part of the difficulty in developing a more effective system of legal assistance arises from long-standing ideological and structural constraints. As chapter 3 notes, until the last few decades, legal aid was not viewed as either a public or a professional responsibility. Its scope in civil matters was highly limited, encompassing only the most "deserving" poor, and lawyers provided minimal pro bono contributions in time or money. Unlike many European nations, the United States never developed an entitlement program involving a sufficiently broad segment of the public or the profession to insure widespread political support. Although most Americans, including most lawyers, now endorse legal assistance in principle, their enthusiasm remains selective in practice. Popular opinion surveys find that over four-fifths of the public favor taxpayer-funded aid to the poor in at least certain kinds of cases; the broadest backing involves matters such as domestic violence, child abuse, veterans' benefits, and health care for senior citizens. But such qualified support has not provided the political leverage to ensure government funding for most low-income Americans. Nor has the profession stepped into the breach. The organized bar lobbies strongly for financial assistance from the government but has attracted relatively low levels of contributions from its own members; fewer than 10 percent have accepted referrals from legal aid programs, and the average financial contribution from surveyed lawyers is less than fifty cents a day.[2]

The political vulnerability of these programs has hobbled efforts to build more effective delivery systems. As one Denver poverty lawyer notes, the federal Legal Services Corporation (LSC) has been "caught between unloving critics and uncritical lovers." Political leaders of the far right have capitalized on unpopular cases to paint the Corporation as a "reckless and irresponsible agency" that subsidizes a "left wing political agenda." Defenders of embattled programs have not entirely avoided self-critical scrutiny, but have been understandably reluctant to call public attention to weaknesses that might further jeopardize political support. The result has been policy compromises that are often uninformed and unresponsive to crucial values. The current legal aid structure denies assistance to the politically unpopular groups who are least able to do without it and blocks the strategies most likely to address the root causes of economic deprivation. A more productive approach to civil legal assistance will require more balanced appraisals of its capacities and limitations. And that, in turn, will demand a clearer understanding of the dynamics that keep individuals locked into poverty and locked out of the decision-making processes capable of addressing it.[3]

The Challenges of Triage: Which Needs to Meet and Who Should Decide

The official mission of the federal Legal Services Corporation, like that of most privately funded poverty law programs, is to "promote equal access to the system of justice . . . [by providing] high-quality legal assistance to those who would be otherwise unable to afford legal counsel." Such broad mandates are of little assistance in defining priorities for a universe of highly elastic needs and highly limited resources. Efforts to establish more specific objectives have been helpful to a point, but they still leave the contested issues largely unaddressed. Alan Houseman, one of the most thoughtful experts on legal services over the last two decades, suggests "five overarching goals" for legal services programs: providing quality representation; ensuring adequate access for eligible groups; maximizing the efficient use of scarce resources; respecting local control of project priorities; and securing client satisfaction and support. But in pursuing those goals, the central issues for underfunded programs are which needs to meet, with what levels of service, and how to make those decisions.[4]

Eligibility and Resource Limitations

Congress has partly resolved one of those issues, yet in a way that raises as many questions as it answers. Legal services offices that receive federal funds generally may not use those funds, and in some instances may not use any other revenue, for a broad range of matters including school desegregation, labor boycotts, abortion, political redistricting, military service, welfare reform, undocumented aliens, prisoners, and public housing tenants facing eviction because of alleged drug activities. Nor may these offices engage in activities such as lobbying, community organizing, or representation in legislative and administrative rulemaking proceedings. Federally funded programs also may not bring class actions or seek attorneys' fees that would otherwise be authorized by statute. Since these are the very strategies most likely to address the causes of poverty and to deter future abuses, legal aid programs have faced an unpalatable choice. They can do without federal funds and help far fewer individual clients, but in a more effective fashion. Or they can handle greater numbers of cases, but only for politically acceptable claimants, and in ways less likely to promote broader social reforms.[5]

Given the difficulties of finding alternative sources of funding, most legal aid programs have opted for the latter course. However, a growing number of legal services programs have sought independence from federal limitations and have cobbled together support from states, localities, bar associations, court filing fees, private donors, and interest on trust fund accounts (IOLTA) in which lawyers temporarily hold clients' funds. A cut in federal support over the last decade has also encouraged LSC grantees to diversify their funding base. Adjusted for inflation, federal appropriations are now roughly half of their 1980 levels. In about a third of states, a majority of revenue comes from nonfederal sources. Yet many states impose subject-matter restrictions that parallel federal limitations. And despite efforts to broaden financial support, the United States spends only about $2.25 per capita on civil legal assistance, a ludicrously inadequate amount for a nation in which roughly a seventh of the population is in or near poverty and eligible for aid.[6]

As a consequence, legal services programs can handle only a small fraction of the cases that qualify for assistance. Quantifying the problems that remain unmet is impossible with any precision. Estimates that four-fifths of individual needs go unaddressed do not capture the magnitude of the problem. Even the most carefully designed studies generally measure only subjective perceptions of individual needs, and many potential clients are unaware of matters that could benefit from lawyers' assistance. For example, parties may not know that they are entitled to certain benefits or that their consumer loans fail to meet legal requirements. Individual legal needs surveys also leave out collective concerns such as community economic development, environmental risks, and discrimination in school financing.[7]

Legal Aid Priorities

Difficulties arise not only in gauging the incidence of unmet needs, but also in ranking their importance, determining how much assistance is adequate, and identifying who should provide it. For example, there is no consensus within the poverty law community about how to handle one of the most common needs reported by low-income Americans: uncontested divorces. Some programs exclude domestic relations matters entirely, on the ground that such assistance does nothing to address the structural causes of poverty and to serve community interests. Other programs handle a limited number of cases and have wait lists as long as two or three years. The assumption is that such a screening system will weed out all but those whose needs are greatest and who have no alternative means of assistance. A third approach is to refer clients to self-help materials and programs that may, but do not necessarily, enable them to proceed without representation. Another alternative is to attempt to provide at least minimal assistance for all who seek it, often relying heavily on paralegals. A final option is to offer quality "holistic" services to a smaller proportion of eligible individuals. Such services include not only the divorce but also related needs. For example, if the marriage has involved violence, a client may require a restraining order and referrals for counseling and shelter programs. Assistance may also be necessary for welfare benefits, tax credits, job training, and childcare.[8]

Not only must poverty law offices decide how much assistance to provide to any given client who requests it, they must also determine how actively to promote their services in the surrounding community. The main reason that low-income individuals do not seek lawyers for matters that they consider legal problems is the belief that "nothing can be done." Community outreach efforts are often necessary to counteract that assumption. Such efforts are also crucial for groups that are particularly likely to be unaware of their rights or the accessibility of free legal services, such as immigrants or those living in rural poverty. Yet many offices are reluctant to engage in such outreach when they are unable to assist large numbers of those who already seek their services.[9]

All of these issues of resource allocation require value judgments on which reasonable people can disagree. Who should make those judgments raises a further set of difficulties. Traditionally, legal aid attorneys have set priorities, subject to varying degrees of oversight by boards of directors. From a societal standpoint, however, that has hardly been an ideal arrangement. Attorneys have scarcely been disinterested and boards generally have had insufficient information and inclination to second guess staff judgments. As chapter 3 notes, personal preferences and class biases have often led to caseload restrictions that ill served the groups for whom the programs were established (e.g., bans on cases involving divorces, bankruptcies, and "luxury" goods). The problems with such autocratic decision making have not, however, escaped unnoticed. Critics from both the left and right have demanded greater accountability to communities that have to live with the decisions.[10]

One response to such concerns has been a requirement that federally funded programs conduct "an effective appraisal of the needs of eligible clients and their relative importance . . . in a manner reasonably calculated to obtain the attitude of all significant segments of the client population." The appraisal must also include "input from the recipient employees, governing body members, the private bar, and other interested persons." In practice, however, this requirement has proven difficult to implement and enforce. Although some programs have made serious efforts to engage the client community in establishing well-considered priorities, other programs have been far less successful. Questionnaires with extremely low response rates or public meetings with sparse attendance have yielded a laundry list of needs that do little to constrain lawyers' discretion. When asked to identify their most pressing concerns, many eligible clients cite only easily recognizable individual needs, rather than underlying structural problems that are widely shared. Given the limited usefulness of such surveys, they often serve only to set broad subject matter guidelines, which are also heavily shaped by staff preferences and funding pressures. To preserve political support, the Legal Service Corporation has encouraged grant recipients to maximize the number of clients reached, particularly in cases that hold greatest public appeal, such as those involving domestic violence and family matters. As then Corporation President John McKay has explained to local program directors, "We're trying to find programs we do well that Congress is willing to fund." And the "strong Congressional message [is that] federally funded legal services should focus on individual case representation," not on broader law reform efforts or community empowerment.[11]

That strategy has had mixed success. After two decades of caseload restrictions and budgetary cutbacks, the Corporation has managed to secure a fairly stable base of bipartisan support. But the price has been substantial and has been paid by groups least able to afford it. Many programs have ended up providing minimal assistance, often on a first-come-first-served basis, in substantive areas determined largely by staff and funder preferences. Such a structure leaves much to be desired for the communities that it is designed to serve. To build a more effective system of legal assistance will require a fundamental expansion in program services and resources. To make that possible, we need a way out of the national impasse on legal services, in which critics from the left and right speak past each other on all the key issues.

Critics from the Right; Critics from the Left

Conservative Critiques

Legal services programs have long been a favorite target of the political right. A common refrain is that such programs are a pathological example of "big government" and a "leading tool to promote . . . liberal causes."

In critics' view, lawyers have a "right to promote their own agenda but they do not have a right to do it with the taxpayers' money." As one Wall Street op-ed put it, "Let them do it on their own nickel." Legal aid programs allegedly have been "taking money away from law-abiding, hardworking taxpayers and then giving it to the likes of convicted felons, delinquent fathers, illegal aliens, and even drug dealers." Moreover, according to opponents, much of this government-funded aid worsens the plight of its intended beneficiaries. Commonly cited examples include efforts to prevent expulsions of disruptive students; challenges to health ordinances that push out the homeless; and farmworkers' lawsuits that increase labor costs and decrease employment. Critics maintain that the lawyer "liberators" who bring these cases seldom confront the costs of their advocacy; "abstract compassion" is the luxury of professionals who can afford to shield themselves and their families from the problems caused by homeless vagrants, disruptive students, or erosion of agricultural jobs. Worse still, poverty lawyers have assertedly allowed their own career interests to drive resource decisions. As then Senator Robert Dole maintained, "The impoverished individual who has run-of-the-mill, but important, legal needs is shunted aside by legal services lawyers in search of sexy issues. . . ."[12]

Such claims are problematic on many grounds that seldom surface in popular debate. Most conservative critiques are really objections not to legal assistance per se, but to the rights that it makes possible to assert. Opponents would have the same concerns about advocacy in welfare, homelessness, and school disciplinary proceedings no matter who was paying the bill. Restrictions on the activities and budgets of legal aid programs is a way of accomplishing indirectly what opponents have been unable to do directly: curtail rights and social services benefiting the ostensibly "undeserving" poor.

It is, moreover, by no means clear that the cases critics cite reflect counterproductive advocacy. The perennial parade of horrors includes many examples that have never been verified. Others rest on dubious premises. Opponents generally assume that the costs of defending such lawsuits will all be passed on to other poor people. But whether the employer will in fact cut jobs is a complicated empirical question that depends heavily on context and local market conditions. And whether such consequences would be offset by other benefits is equally complicated, particularly if, as the research available suggests, clients represented by legal aid attorneys typically have valid claims. Understaffed legal services offices have no reason to spend substantial scarce resources litigating the "marginal" or meritless cases that critics' arguments invoke. Similar points could be made about other litigation that assertedly hurts the poor more than it helps. For example, contesting expulsions does not necessarily result in more classroom disruptions; it can instead force school districts to respect appropriate procedural norms and to find more constructive solutions to disciplinary issues. This is not to suggest that society in general or the poor in particular would benefit if every potential claim were fully litigated. But neither is ability to pay an effective way of screening out meritless cases. And determining when the costs of legal assistance exceed its benefits involves far more complex and contested judgments than critics' simplistic sound bites have acknowledged.[13]

Opponents' claims of ideological bias are equally problematic. A common assertion is that legal services lawyers are always representing the "liberal" side of issues like school suspensions or evictions of drug-dealing tenants. Never do poverty law programs seek to assist embattled inner city schools trying to maintain classroom order or housing projects seeking to maintain a safe environment for other poor residents. But such cases would not meet the eligibility guidelines for legal services programs, which require that clients' incomes not exceed 125 percent of poverty levels. Other government-subsidized lawyers are available to assert the interests of schools and housing programs. And if the interests of poor people who qualify for assistance generally line up on the liberal side of the political spectrum, it is because conservatives have seldom supported such interests at more than a rhetorical level.[14]

Left Critiques

The more substantial criticisms of legal aid programs come from the left. A long-standing concern is that neither the direct personal services that government-funded programs encourage, nor the test-case litigation that many poverty lawyers have preferred, are effective means of addressing the structural sources of poverty. Routine cases deal with symptoms not causes of deprivation, and courtroom victories are seldom significant or enduring without a political base to support them. Yet many legal services lawyers lack the skills or resources to help low-income communities help themselves. Lawyers who do have that commitment are hobbled by restrictions on government-funded programs. Federal legislation excludes recipients from a sweeping range of political and organizational activity, including organizing client groups, conducting training programs for policy-related advocacy, representing client interests before legislative and rulemaking bodies (except under highly limited circumstances), and encouraging or engaging in political demonstrations, picketing, voter registration, and labor-related initiatives.[15]

These restrictions have reinforced the tendency of lawyers trained in legal analysis, not community organizing, to focus on matters where their expertise is most relevant. But that focus risks narrowing problems to fit legal frameworks that cannot provide effective solutions. Representing individual tenants in cases involving evictions or building code violations is less likely to help poor communities than assisting grassroots organizations find ways to increase the supply of safe, affordable housing. Although litigation can sometimes be a catalyst to organizing efforts, any approach that keeps lawyers in a position of dominance may perpetuate the powerlessness that they seek to address. Enabling individual clients and communities to develop their own problem-solving capacities is generally the most productive way of achieving significant long-term change. That, in turn, often requires lawyers to expand their own capabilities and to integrate strategies involving organizing, lobbying, and public communications as well as litigation.[16]

Among legal services programs, the response to such critiques has alternated between embrace and avoidance. Poverty lawyers have increasingly acknowledged the need to broaden their focus and to collaborate more effectively with clients and local organizations, and many have initiated efforts along the lines described below. Other LSC administrators and grant recipients believe that their hands are tied by congressional restrictions. As the then Corporation's vice-president for governmental relations and public affairs has explained, "LSC is not an institution created to 'address the causes' of poverty. Rather, the authorizing legislation . . . directed LSC to focus on providing legal assistance to solve the basic legal problems of the poor, not to end poverty." Yet it is difficult to imagine how lawyers could "solve" these problems without focusing on their causes. And nothing in the statute prevents recipients from representing existing grassroots organizations or developing community education and self-help support services.[17]

A related criticism is that many programs have given insufficient priority to issues of diversity and racial justice. Problems of poverty are especially acute for communities of color, and a recurrent complaint is that not all legal aid offices have focused on the role of race and ethnicity in institutionalizing inequality. Nor, historically, has enough attention centered on ensuring diversity at leadership levels, and providing training in the strategies necessary to promote racial justice. Yet recognition of these problems has increased substantially in recent years. A growing range of initiatives, including national conferences, publications, workshops, and discrimination litigation campaigns, have helped make these concerns more central to the legal services agenda.[18]

A final criticism of the current system is, however, impossible to dispute and more difficult to address: its failure to cope with the vast majority of poor Americans' legal needs or the forces that create them. A more effective approach to civil legal assistance system will, at a minimum, require changes on two levels: a significant expansion in resources and permissible activities, and a redirection of program priorities toward more cost-effective, coordinated, and multidisciplinary services.

Expanding the Scope of Legal Assistance: More Funds, Fewer Restrictions

Funding Strategies

The most crucial priorities for legal services programs are to find ways of increasing funds and reducing restrictions on subsidized activities. Over the last decade, the reduction in federal support has prompted most poverty law offices to seek more diversified sources of financial assistance, and in a growing number of instances, to relinquish LSC grants that come with disabling conditions. Annual state funding has increased to $85 million, up almost 50 percent since the late 1990s, and private funding has increased to $24 million, up over 400 percent. Yet the United States still spends far less than other Western developed nations. America's per capita government allocation for civil legal aid is $2.25, while the equivalent figure is $32 in England, and about $12 in New Zealand and Ontario. Contributions from many states are shamefully inadequate; some provide no allocations or only token amounts, on the order of $50,000. With few exceptions, bar associations have done no better. Only a fifth of state bars have attempted broad-based fund-raising campaigns, and in some, the effort has raised less than $50,000. In many jurisdictions, the largest source of nonfederal legal aid subsidies is the interest on lawyers' trust fund accounts, which now provides about $160 million annually. Although a recent U.S. Supreme Court decision has upheld the constitutionality of this revenue-raising method, recent declines in interest rates have substantially reduced funding. For example, in California, IOLTA grants have dropped over 40 percent in the last several years.[19]

Additional possibilities for financial support are urgently needed and readily available. One possibility is to increase court filing fees. Only twenty states now dedicate some of these fees to legal aid, and in many of these states, the amounts are minimal, such as one or two dollars per case. A more generous surcharge by all states could substantially increase resources. Other proposals include a tax on gross revenues of law firms, and an increase in attorney registration fees or bar association dues. Courts could also expand the circumstances in which they appoint counsel for indigents in civil cases. Poverty law advocates have long argued for a civil version of *Gideon v. Wainright*. That decision, as chapter 3 noted, guaranteed a right to counsel in criminal cases. Establishing a similar entitlement for at least some categories of civil matters should remain a priority. Where public funding is inadequate, the judiciary could require lawyers to serve pro bono or to make a financial contribution in lieu of service along the lines proposed in chapter 7.[20]

Eligibility Restrictions

Courts, legislatures, and bar ethics committees need also to reconsider the restrictions placed on legal services activities. None of these decision-making bodies have adequately acknowledged the unjust burden that such constraints place on clients' due process and First Amendment rights. Under the prevailing view, these limitations impose no unconstitutional conditions on the receipt of government funds because legal aid programs have alternative channels to pursue protected activities. The programs can create affiliated organizations to engage in restricted activities as long as they use separate funds, personnel, and facilities. Any hardship for clients simply leaves them in the same position that they would occupy if Congress had never allocated funds for legal services. Claims that the restrictions impermissibly interfere with recipients' lawyer–client relationships have also been rejected on the ground that this relationship enjoys no special constitutional protection from governmental regulation. The only limitation that has failed to survive judicial scrutiny is a provision that barred representation of welfare claims involving a challenge to existing law. This, in the Supreme Court's view, constitutes viewpoint discrimination in violation of the First Amendment.[21]

The decisions sustaining these restrictions are problematic on several grounds. It is, of course, true that legal aid clients are no worse off as a result of the restrictions than they would have been if the government had never provided funding. But that is often true in cases where the Supreme Court has found unconstitutional conditions; the point of the doctrine is to require the government to respect constitutional rights if it chooses to provide assistance. Once Congress decides to subsidize certain attorney–client relationships, it should not be permitted to undermine their effectiveness. Foreclosing strategies like class actions, requests for attorneys' fees, or legislative advocacy often has that effect. In many jurisdictions, no nonfederally funded organizations are available to pursue restricted activities.[22]

Moreover, contrary to courts' implication, the attorney–client relationship has long been recognized to serve crucial First Amendment values of expression and association. Current LSC restrictions undercut those values and compromise lawyers' ethical obligations to serve their clients' best interests. For example, it is generally advantageous for plaintiffs with similar claims to pursue them as class actions, since such collective efforts offer broader relief, higher stakes and visibility, and greater bargaining leverage. By foreclosing such strategies, LSC restrictions impair lawyers' ethical obligations to provide effective representation and to exercise independent professional judgment about what that representation requires.[23]

Prohibitions on class actions and claims allowing statutory attorneys' fees also undercut the interests of courts and the public in ensuring effective relief, avoiding redundant litigation, promoting efficient use of legal services funding, and deterring unlawful conduct. For example, when cases proceed only on behalf of individual plaintiffs, their lawyers may not be able to obtain evidence indicating that the challenged conduct reflects a systemic problem or ongoing pattern affecting a broader group. Nor will courts have authority to order remedies preventing future violations. Some defendants have found that the unavailability of class litigation allows them to engage in conduct that has been held unlawful; as long as they grant relief to any individual who complains, they can foreclose judicial review of illegal actions that affect hundreds of others. Preventing classwide relief forces legal services organizations to squander limited resources in enforcing the same laws for different claimants. And requiring federally funded offices to establish separate organizations to handle restricted cases wastes large amounts of money on duplicative administrative and overhead costs. Almost no programs have been able to afford this option.[24]

The ban on attorneys' fees also discourages enforcement efforts when actual damages are too small to justify suits, even where legislatures have explicitly authorized fee-shifting remedies. Defenders of this prohibition generally claim that it is needed to prevent recipients from giving undue priority to fee-generating cases, and to prevent defendants who are already subsidizing legal services through their tax contributions from "double paying" their opponents' expenses. But that latter objection could be made whenever any organization that receives government funding sues to recover fees. To deny awards in such cases would undermine the purposes of authorizing fees in the first instance: to ensure legal compliance in contexts where the costs of litigation would otherwise be prohibitive. And the current prohibition on fees for legal services organizations prevents them from using such recoveries to underwrite other, equally critical but nonpaying cases. The ban on class actions is similarly difficult to justify. Those who oppose such suits generally complain about the use of taxpayer funds to subsidize "law reform." But in many instances, the point of the litigation is to provide effective enforcement of what the law already requires. And in cases that do prompt reforms, lawmakers generally have ample opportunity to reverse decisions that are inconsistent with legislative intent.[25]

Restrictive interpretations of attorneys' fees legislation should also be reversed. A leading example is a 2001 Supreme Court decision, *Buckhannon Board and Care Home Inc. v. West Virginia Department of Health and Human Resources*. There, a narrow majority of Justices held that a federal statute authorizing fees to "prevailing parties" did not encompass lawyers who achieved their desired outcome through settlement. A "judicially sanctioned change in the legal relationship of the parties" was necessary. Yet forcing lawyers to forego fees whenever an opponent is prepared to settle either requires them to incur needless risk and expense by proceeding to trial or withholds the compensation necessary to underwrite similar claims in the future. Moreover, this interpretation is at odds with both the language and legislative history of federal fee-shifting statutes. They impose no requirement of a judicial resolution, and accompanying congressional reports explicitly state that "prevailing parties" are not limited to those who obtain a final judgment after trial. The Court's restrictive interpretation is also inconsistent with the purpose underlying fee-shifting statutes, which is to encourage protection of legal rights in areas where it would otherwise be unaffordable. Proposed legislation that would explicitly broaden the definition of prevailing parties should be a priority.[26]

Restrictions that exclude certain categories of clients or cases should also be reconsidered, and more attention should focus on identifying alternative sources of funding. Political debates have often proceeded with a highly distorted view of what is at stake. Contrary to conventional wisdom, removal of limitations on federal funds would not dramatically alter the legal services landscape. The cases that Congress has found objectionable never constituted a significant portion of most offices' caseload. But many of those excluded have nowhere else to go for the protection of fundamental interests. Prisoners are one such group. They are among the least sympathetic and most vulnerable victims of serious abuses such as sexual assault or inadequate medical care. Recent estimates suggest that at least a fifth of the nation's two million inmates experience forced sexual activity during incarceration. Without the prospect of legal accountability, guards and administrators often have inadequate incentives to prevent abuse. And the private bar has been notably unwilling to handle cases involving prison conditions. So too, in other contexts, such as those involving undocumented aliens, the possibility of legal representation is crucial to creating a credible deterrent to exploitation.[27]

Courts, bar associations, public interest groups, and legal services providers all must take more active roles in educating the public on these issues and in attracting additional support for restricted cases. Recent survey research finds that "legal aid as an institution is largely invisible to the public. Only thirteen percent [of Americans] can identify a legal aid organization in their community." The public in general, and policymakers in particular, need a better understanding of the plight of unrepresented Americans and the human costs of current restrictions. In effect, we need efforts comparable to the Innocence Project, which has exposed how inadequate representation has led to erroneous convictions and untold misery for impoverished criminal defendants. Examples of comparable civil cases are in ample supply: a ten-year-old denied disability benefits, a quadriplegic father of two suffering from Lou Gehrig's disease whose home health care services are terminated; a senior citizen on fixed income victimized by fraudulent debt collection services; an impoverished immigrant woman inappropriately denied prenatal care; individuals committed to a mental institution without any hearing or with only rubber stamp review. Bar leaders should take a far more active role in educating the public and the profession about the importance of legal services programs and the gross injustices of current restrictions. In the absence of expanded state or federal funding, more subsidies are necessary from the bar and from court filing fees targeted to restricted cases.

More efforts should also focus on enlisting private lawyers as co-counsel in fee-generating cases, since these attorneys are not subject to federal restrictions on fee awards.[28]

Legal service programs should also reconsider financial eligibility limitations that exclude the near poor, or experiment with copayment systems that provide partially subsidized assistance. Many other nations use sliding fee scales based on income to allow some government aid for individuals of limited means. Some of these countries also have developed alternative delivery structures that are not constrained by financial eligibility standards. For example, Britain's Citizen Advice Bureaus rely on volunteers to provide routine legal information to all who seek it. Broader systems of eligibility in this country are particularly necessary for groups like domestic violence victims, who may in theory have assets that put them over income limits, but who do not have control over sufficient financial resources for legal assistance as well as other crucial social services. An additional advantage of expanded coverage is that it could build a broader base of political support than systems that serve only the most economically and politically powerless constituencies.[29]

A related strategy would be to develop other structures for delivering services that might be politically appealing. One such proposal is to enlarge and remodel the National Legal Service Corps, which currently involves only a few hundred law school students and graduates. That program runs under the auspices of Americorps, which provides national service volunteers with a minimal stipend to help cover college expenses or repay student loans. An expanded program, with more generous loan forgiveness features, could attract greater numbers of law graduates. Such programs could assist not only low-income communities, but also other underserved groups such as mass-disaster victims and nursing home residents.[30]

Ensuring an Effective System

Collaboration and Coordination

Further reforms are also necessary to ensure the most effective use of program resources. To that end, legal aid offices must work toward greater coordination and collaboration with other service providers, as well as more innovative delivery structures. Efforts in this direction are already well underway. With support from the Legal Services Corporation and groups such as the Project for the Future of Equal Justice, states are beginning to coordinate providers into a unified system. Yet more efforts are needed to reach all low-income individuals and to provide specialized expertise for particularly underserved groups, including elderly, disabled, immigrant, rural, migrant, and homeless Americans. Centralized intake structures, mobile self-help centers for rural areas, and telephone hotlines in multiple languages are among the necessary innovations. Greater reliance on new technologies could also enable programs to provide more web-based assistance to clients, along with additional resources and training for providers. Too many jurisdictions still lack these innovations, and too many potential clients fall through the cracks. Here again, other nations with more centralized systems that reach broader constituencies can provide useful models.[31]

Legal services offices also need to develop more effective ways of empowering clients and strengthening communities. Greater attention should focus on working with grassroots organizations to provide information concerning legal rights, develop referral networks, and establish caseload priorities. Another promising strategy is for programs to require that clients perform some volunteer work in exchange for legal services or to give preference to clients willing to do so. For example, the District of Columbia's Time Dollars Institute coordinates arrangements in which legal aid recipients volunteer for tasks such as assisting food co-ops or neighborhood cleanup efforts. Other programs have clients help community members with similar legal needs, including immigration, wage enforcement, and domestic violence. Legal aid programs can also expand their reliance on other volunteers, such as retired individuals, law students, and lawyers willing to provide pro bono assistance. Effective use of such volunteers will, however, require additional training, supervision, and backup support which may, in turn, entail additional funding efforts. Federally subsidized programs are currently required to spend 12 percent of their grants to involve the private bar. However, more support is necessary to create volunteer involvement on the scale needed to broaden program services. Law schools, bar associations, local governments, and private donors all must be enlisted in that effort.[32]

Legal assistance programs also need to build more collaborative relationships with other service providers. Many clients have problems that cut across occupational boundaries and require holistic approaches.

Homeless individuals may require not just assistance with law-related housing issues but also with disability benefits, education, and substance abuse. Individuals who need legal restraining orders for protection from domestic violence may also need temporary shelters, counseling, childcare, employment assistance, and relocation resources. As one expert notes, many victims will not turn to the legal system when "basic safety and survival needs are not [also] met. . . ." Multidisciplinary assistance enables providers to address a broader range of concerns and to offer a broader array of solutions than traditional forms of legal aid. Such partnerships may also give practitioners additional problem-solving skills and create the coalitions necessary for policy reforms. Offering multiple services in the same program or at the same location can ensure that individuals get help, not simply referrals. "One-stop shopping" is particularly critical for groups like elderly or disabled clients, mothers with small children, or full-time employees who cannot readily shuttle between multiple agencies.[33]

Yet the evolution of effective collaborative relationships has been hampered by funders' policies, staff preferences, and bar ethical rules. In a world of severe resource constraints, the LSC's priority on increasing the number of individuals served gets in the way of full assistance to any single client. Restrictions on the groups that federally funded legal services can assist have also discouraged partnerships with organizations not subject to such limitations. Further barriers arise from differences in professional backgrounds and values. Not all practitioners "play well with others" and staff attorneys' reluctance to share authority has sometimes worked against collaborative initiatives. A final obstacle is the ethical prohibition on multidisciplinary partnerships between lawyers and nonlawyers discussed in the preceding chapter.[34]

None of these barriers are, however, insurmountable. Many of the objections to multidisciplinary partnerships based on the threat to professionalism from profit-oriented values are not present in the legal aid context. So too, concerns about confidentiality and conflicts of interest can be addressed either by holding nonlawyers to the same rules as lawyers or by developing protocols for handling different ethical obligations. For example, some jurisdictions require professionals other than lawyers to report or disclose confidential information under certain circumstances, such as those suggesting child abuse. Organizations that employ lawyers, social workers, and mental health professionals can ensure that all staff and clients are aware of different ethical obligations.

These organizations can also create structures to ensure that attorneys obtain confidential information in separate interviews and record it in secure filing and computer systems.[35]

Models for successful collaborations are readily available. Bread for the City and Zacchaeus Free Clinic in Washington, D.C. is a neighborhood-based service center that offers food, clothing, medical, legal, and social work assistance to low-income individuals. The Child Advocacy Clinic of the University of New Mexico involves law students, law professors, pediatricians, mental health professionals, child development specialists, and educational experts who all focus on children at risk of abuse and neglect. Many programs partially funded by the Violence Against Women Act provide holistic assistance for domestic violence clients. Where full partnership is not feasible, legal aid organizations can work more closely with other service providers. An example is the Clayton/Mile High Family Future Project, in which twenty-three community-based agencies and the Denver Legal Aid Society assist families through legal advocacy, child care, a medical clinic, job readiness training, vocational education, and literacy, GED, and college classes. So too, the San Francisco Legal Services Program relies on volunteer attorneys to partner with various community organizations such as the One Stop Women's Clinic, which offers a range of legal, medical, vocational, and parental services.[36]

Poverty law offices can also collaborate more effectively with federal, state, and local agencies to leverage greater governmental resources in support of economic development and racial justice. For example, some legal services offices have used testers to establish patterns of racial bias, and then have enlisted equal opportunity commissions and housing agencies to enforce antidiscrimination requirements. Other offices have challenged discriminatory practices by the agencies themselves in contexts such as assistance to welfare applicants and enforcement of zoning, health, and safety ordinances. Making government officials more aware of the class, racial, and ethnic biases underpinning seemingly neutral practices can be a crucial and relatively inexpensive means of securing widespread change.[37]

Research, Evaluation, and Training

Finally, and perhaps most importantly, legal service programs need more support for evaluation, research, and training. Program assessments have been hampered by the lack of clear and objective standards, and by the insufficiency of data concerning the satisfaction of clients, the quality of assistance, and its impact on the individuals and communities served. These inadequacies may partly reflect concerns about the political uses to which such information might be put in debates over legal services funding. Moreover, systematic empirical research seldom comes cheap. In a context of declining governmental funds, many programs have been unwilling to make further cuts in client service in order to collect data on performance. Yet in the long run, such information is essential to ensure the most cost-effective use of resources. For example, a recent comprehensive assessment of hotlines has made clear their inadequacies in assisting certain groups, such as non-English-speaking clients with low education levels, and individuals whose personal situation creates special barriers in following the advice they receive. A lack of transportation or childcare and fear of retaliation by a spouse or ex-partner are common examples. Other studies have found similar limitations in individuals' ability to use pro se clinics and other brief advice services. Further assessments of strategies to aid these groups should be a central priority.[38]

Unless we know more about what happens to clients who receive different forms of assistance and how low-income individuals assess the responsiveness of various service providers, we cannot make rational choices about program design. More efforts must focus on identifying additional resources for such evaluation efforts, and on enlisting law schools, foundations, and pro bono consultants in that process. If the point of subsidizing legal assistance is to give economically vulnerable groups a voice in the justice system, then that voice must register more effectively in the legal aid system designed to serve them.

≡ 6 ≡

PRESUMED GUILTY

Class Injustice in Criminal Justice

The court is most merciful when the defendant is most rich.
—HEBREW PROVERB

That proverb describes the criminal justice systems in much of the world, but Americans want to believe that their courts are an exception. "Getting what you pay for" is an accepted fact of life, but justice, we hope, is different, particularly in criminal cases. Punishment for a crime should reflect the guilt of defendants, not the quality of lawyering that they can afford.

But in fact, the unfairness in the criminal justice system mirrors that of the legal system generally. The mother of a Georgia defendant had it right: "There's no fair trial unless you can buy one." In most jurisdictions, it is safer to be rich and guilty than poor and innocent. What is, however, distinctively unjust about criminal proceedings is both the gap between formal rights and daily realities, and the price that is paid in human lives and liberty. The Sixth Amendment of the American Constitution guarantees the right to counsel in criminal proceedings. Under prevailing judicial interpretations, that right requires the government to provide "effective assistance of counsel" for any indigent defendant who faces a risk of incarceration. About three-quarters of the roughly one million individuals arrested for felonies each year are poor enough to qualify for court-appointed lawyers, as are a large number of the eight million arrested for misdemeanors. The adequacy of these lawyers is crucial to the fairness and legitimacy of the justice system. Yet in practice, what counts as "effective assistance" makes a mockery of formal guarantees. Courts have been unwilling to require that an appointed attorney have any experience or expertise in criminal defense. And they have upheld convictions where lawyers have failed to do any investigation, cross-examine any witnesses, consult any experts, present any evidence, or even remain awake and sober during the proceedings.[1]

Poor lawyering for poor defendants compounds other inequities in the legal system and ultimately undermines its legitimacy. Without effective assistance of counsel, individuals who are unjustly accused or denied their constitutional rights are also without effective remedies. Moreover, the unequal representation available to rich and poor defendants carries racial and ethnic consequences. African Americans, Hispanics, and other minorities who are disproportionately represented within low-income communities bear a disproportionate cost of inadequate legal assistance. Fewer than half of all Americans believe that the courts generally treat all racial and ethnic groups the same, and one crucial difference in treatment involves the quality of their legal representation. Our failure to address these biases in the criminal justice system cannot help but erode its credibility. What passes for justice in many American criminal courts is a disgrace to any civilized nation, let alone one that positions itself as a world leader in human rights.[2]

Institutionalized Injustice: Defense Counsel for the Poor

Overextended and Underfunded

States have somewhat different systems of providing legal representation for the poor, but they generally share one defining characteristic: they are grossly overextended and underfinanced. And the situation is growing worse, not better. Over the past half century, after controlling for inflation, public expenditures per criminal case have declined. The United States spends about a hundred billion dollars annually on criminal justice, but only about 2 to 3 percent goes to indigent defense. Over half is allocated to the police, and poor defendants receive only an eighth of the resources per case available to prosecutors. The disparity is still greater when adjusted for the amounts available to other law enforcement officials for assistance in investigation and trial preparation. Although some jurisdictions have model public defender programs, and a few can match prosecutorial resources, they are the exception; impoverished systems for impoverished defendants are the rule.[3]

Not only does criminal defense fare poorly in comparison to prosecutorial resources, it is generally at the bottom of the pecking order in relation to other government expenditures. The reasons are obvious. Poor defendants are a singularly powerless and unpopular group. Most Americans fail to see their own stake in procedural fairness. They generally cannot envision themselves or their friends and family needing court-appointed counsel. Nor can most individuals readily empathize with the impoverished defendants who qualify for assistance. As psychologists note, we want to believe in a "just world," in which people get what they deserve and deserve what they get. It is comforting to assume that, by and large, only the guilty are prosecuted.[4]

These assumptions, in turn, underpin attitudes about legal representation. About three- quarters of Americans believe that too many criminals get off on "technicalities." Less than half believe that defendants accused of murder should not be convicted if they lack a competent lawyer. Politicians reflect and reinforce such assumptions by stressing the need to get tough on criminals, not to spend more on their defense. So, for example, one recent Georgia legislature budgeted twice as much for improvements of a highway interchange as for counsel for all indigent defendants. Each Georgia taxpayer invested about 65 cents a year in protecting the constitutional rights of those who could not afford to protect themselves.[5]

At these prices, not much due process is available. Although Georgia has recently approved a new system for appointed counsel, it has failed to allocate the resources necessary to implement it. Nor is the situation better in many other states. The result is that over 90 percent of criminal defendants plead guilty, generally without any significant time expended on their case. In recent studies, between half and four-fifths of counsel entered pleas without interviewing any prosecution witnesses, and four-fifths did so without filing any defense motions. Few jurisdictions provide adequate funds for counsel to assist post-conviction review, the only point at which many defendants can challenge the adequacy of their appointed trial attorneys or the fairness of the trial and investigative process.[6]

Yet this is seldom cause for concern among those most responsible for the current system. Defendants who lack adequate legal resources are less likely to escape on "technicalities," or to put the state to the expense and inconvenience of trial. This seems as it should be to most legislators. Judges and prosecutors who face crushing caseloads of their own seldom disagree. If, as is commonly assumed, the vast majority of defendants are in fact guilty of something, a system that expedites conviction seems a reasonable concession to financial realities. Taxpayers who place trust in elected prosecutors also may see little reason to provide ample resources for their opponents. Former law professor and federal judge Richard Posner expresses a common view with uncommon candor:

> I can confirm from my own experience as a judge that criminal defendants are generally poorly represented, but if we are to be hardheaded we must recognize that this may not be an entirely bad thing. The lawyers who represent indigent criminal defendants seem to be good enough to reduce the probability of convicting an innocent person to a very low level. If they were much better, either many guilty people would be acquitted or society would have to devote much greater resources to the prosecution of criminal cases. A bare-bones system for defense of indigent criminal defendants may be optimal.

The death penalty advisor to Florida Governor Jeb Bush was blunter still: "Bring in the witnesses, put [the defendants] on a gurney, and let's rock and roll."[7]

Due Process Disasters

Such attitudes, and the system they perpetuate, are a due process disaster. Contrary to Judge Posner's assertion, recent exonerations through DNA evidence demonstrate an unacceptable frequency of wrongful convictions. Without the prospect of an effective adversary, law enforcement officials have less incentive to investigate cases thoroughly and respect constitutional rights. Defense challenges are also essential to counter the inevitable tunnel vision of law enforcement officials who are accustomed to viewing the facts through partisan lenses. Insuring competent legal representation to all defendants, including those who are guilty, provides essential protection for those who are innocent. Such representation is also necessary to ensure that those who are convicted or who accept plea bargains receive appropriate sentences. Our "bare bones" system of indigent representation is a large part of what prevents the current system from imposing punishment in any rational or consistent fashion. All too often, the worst sentences go to those with the worst lawyers, not the worst crimes.[8]

The problems are most obvious in jurisdictions that rely on competitive bidding systems for indigent defense. In these systems, lawyers bid to provide representation for a specified percentage of the courts' total criminal caseload based on a fixed fee, regardless of the number or complexity of cases. How many jurisdictions rely on such a process is unclear, but it appears to be on the rise. In some of the less populous states, a third of all counties have block contracts. An estimated one-fifth of the nation's largest counties also cover at least part of their caseloads through competitive bidding. Where, as is often the case, the jurisdiction has no meaningful system of quality control, this process encourages a race to the bottom. The winners are attorneys who can turn over high volumes of cases, generally without benefit of any factual investigation, or God forbid, an actual trial.[9]

An *Atlanta Journal-Constitution* profile of the Georgia contract system aptly captures the process in its series title: "When Justice is a Crime." A follow-up study by the state's supreme court commission came to similar conclusions. Some of Georgia's contract lawyers have handled over 700 felony matters a year, more than four times the average recommended by the National Legal Aid and Defender Association. On a "good" day, one attorney disposes of two dozen misdemeanor cases at a flat rate of $50 each, generally after only the briefest hallway conversations with his clients. Another attorney has entered pleas for over 300 defendants without ever taking a case to trial. A third is perpetually unreachable. Clients who try to contact him by phone receive a message that invariably informs them that the lawyer is unavailable and that they should call back later. Non-English-speaking defendants may lack access to anyone who can speak their language. Some of those facing felony charges have difficulty even learning why they were arrested, let alone what their lawyer is doing (or failing to do) on their behalf.[10]

The problems are not unique to Georgia, and the price for this cut-rate representation is paid in individual liberty. Some defendants languish in jail for months before even meeting their court-appointed lawyers and providing information that might speed their release or that might be compromised by delay. A Mississippi woman accused of shoplifting $72 worth of merchandise recently spent a year in jail without any opportunity to communicate with her attorney. Another woman spoke briefly with her lawyer for the first time on the day she pleaded guilty to several serious felonies. The lawyer told her, "You are guilty, lady," and gave her five minutes to decide whether to accept a plea involving a ten-year jail sentence. Since he offered no options for a defense, she took the plea. In defending his approach, the lawyer explained to reporters that he simply could not afford to put "too much time or money into these cases." But he insisted that his clients got "adequate representation," and added: "If they want Clarence Darrow, they should hire Clarence Darrow."[11]

Yet by definition, indigent defendants cannot afford to hire counsel. Nor can many of their lawyers afford to spend the time necessary to discover evidence that might prevent their convictions or reduce their sentences. In one particularly telling Georgia case, a single mother facing charges of petty theft received an offer of several months incarceration in a detention center. Her overworked and underprepared defense counsel did not inform the prosecutor that she was the sole provider for three daughters, one of whom was disabled, and that detention might well mean the loss of her job, her home, and custody of her children. When told by a journalist of what he had not been told, the prosecutor indicated that he was "shocked" and that the information would have made a difference in plea negotiations. In another recent case, an attorney who had never tried any of the 300 matters he had handled, declined to investigate circumstances that might have exonerated a teenager charged with drunk driving. As the lawyer later explained, if he "looked into every nook and cranny there was to this case he would never get anything done." At the defendant's sentencing hearing, the lawyer not only failed to present evidence, he informed the judge that "there's no good spin that I can put on [the defendant's conduct]. He consumed a great deal of alcohol . . . and caused a terrible tragedy." With a defense like that, a prosecutor was scarcely necessary. The judge imposed the maximum sentence: fifteen years' imprisonment.[12]

Inadequate representation is also common in jurisdictions that appoint private practitioners to represent indigent defendants on an individual basis. To be eligible for appointment, attorneys generally need only put their name on a list. No experience, qualification, or training is necessary, competence is not reviewed, and a prior record of disciplinary sanctions is not disqualifying. Where insufficient numbers of lawyers volunteer, others may be conscripted even if they lack any trial experience or any familiarity with criminal law. Appointed attorneys typically receive minimal flat fees or hourly rates capped at ludicrous levels. As chapter 1 noted, limits of $1,000 frequently apply to complicated felony cases, and some states allow even less. Hourly rates can drop as low as

$4. For most court-appointed lawyers, unmanageable caseloads are an economic necessity, and trials are usually an unaffordable luxury. A *New York Times* profile of the city's appointed counsel found some with caseloads as high as 1,600 felonies per year. Unsurprisingly, these attorneys frequently missed deadlines and court appearances, and many would have been unable to pick their own clients out of a lineup. A court-commissioned study of the Texas system revealed similar problems. As one interviewed defense lawyer noted, taking a case to trial was "not financially viable." Under many jurisdictions' fee scales, a matter of any complexity will not even cover overhead or expenses, let alone provide a living wage. The situation for appellate work is seldom better. In New York, the average fee for appointed counsel is less than a quarter of what public defenders spend per case, and less than a tenth of what private practitioners routinely charge. Lawyers willing to accept court appointments at these rates often lack the experience and ability to obtain clients in other ways.[13]

Even where fees are adequate, a politicized appointment process can work against effective representation. Some judges view the selection of counsel as an opportunity for patronage. The beneficiaries are friends and election campaign supporters or contributors, who may lack the skills or incentives for competent advocacy. Only a third of the attorneys responding to the Texas study believed that the qualifications of defense counsel were a ground for appointment. By contrast, four-fifths of the attorneys reported that campaign contributions affected the selection process. In other jurisdictions, a more common factor is the lawyer's reputation for "moving" cases. Many judges decline to appoint counsel who clutter up their calendars with pretrial motions or full-fledged trials. Ironically enough, one of the surest ways to prevent being assigned to represent an indigent client is to provide a vigorous defense for one. Stephen Bright, Director of the Southern Center for Human Rights, put the point directly in testimony before the Senate Judiciary Committee: "This is a system riddled with conflicts. A judge's desire for efficiency conflicts with the duty to appoint indigent defense counsel who can provide adequate representation; a lawyer's need for business . . . [discourages effective] advocacy. And later, if there is claim of [in]effective assistance, the judge who appointed the lawyer is the one to decide the claim."[14]

Analogous problems can arise in jurisdictions that rely on public defender offices. To be sure, where funding is adequate, these offices generally can provide a high quality of representation; they specialize in indigent defense and appointment of their lawyers is not subject to patronage. But many programs operate with grossly inadequate budgets, which translate into crushing caseloads and insufficient resources for investigation and trial. The injustices that result are well illustrated by a recent Indianapolis case in which a defendant remained in jail for four months after charges were dropped. A harried public defender had neglected to inform the client or the relevant authorities that he was entitled to release. Extended backlogs in some offices mean that almost half of the clients will finish serving their sentences before their appeals are filed and resolved. Unmanageable caseloads also encourage high levels of burnout and turnover, which further compromise effective advocacy.[15]

A further problem, both for public defenders and for other appointed counsel, involves the inadequacy of budgets for investigators and experts, and the inability to provide other essential social services. Although judges generally have authority to authorize such expenses, many feel constrained to keep costs down and avoid a reputation as a "spendthrift." In Texas, courts deny about a third of requests, and half of surveyed judges report pressure to control budgets. In many jurisdictions, appointed counsel seldom go to the trouble even to seek reimbursement for investigation or experts. In a recent challenge to Mississippi's indigent defense system, one contract lawyer testified that in ten years of defense work, he had never hired an investigator. Most attorneys also lack the resources for "problem solving" approaches that focus not just on the charges at issue, but also on services that may help keep their clients out of the criminal justice system in the future. Only by addressing needs involving employment, education, housing, substance abuse, and mental health will defense counsel often be able to obtain the best disposition or reduce the chances of recidivism. Yet such assistance is an unattainable luxury for most appointed lawyers. Rather, a combination of excessive caseloads and inadequate resources perpetuates a double standard of justice. Three-quarters of surveyed judges and prosecutors agree that counsel for indigents are less prepared than privately retained lawyers.[16]

That is not to imply that defendants who hire their own counsel necessarily receive effective representation. Most of these individuals are just above the poverty line and cannot afford the cost of trial. Their lawyers typically charge a flat fee, payable in advance, which creates obvious incentives to plea bargain. Only defendants with significant resources, usually in white-collar or organized crime cases, have ready access to full-fledged advocacy. Where defendants lack such resources, unless the case is highly publicized, counsel face considerable temptations to curtail their efforts. A quick plea bargain spares lawyers not only the expense and strain of trial, but also the risk of a humiliating defeat. Such bargains also preserve good working relationships with judges and prosecutors, who face their own, often overwhelming caseloads. For all but the wealthy, zealous advocacy is the exception not the rule.[17]

Unpopular Causes: Unpopular Counsel

The disincentives for adequate representation are particularly great where the crime is heinous or the accused is a member of an especially unpopular group. Racial and homophobic bias among court-appointed counsel is all too common and seldom results in any significant responses. Indigent black defendants have been assigned attorneys who were former members of the Ku Klux Klan, and clients who object to their assignments are reminded that the Constitution gives "you a right to a lawyer, not the lawyer of your choice." When attorneys attempt to provide anything approximating effective advocacy in a death penalty or terrorist-related case, they are often treated as social pariahs, who are making "martyrs out of murderers." Individuals designated "enemy combatants" have been denied access to lawyers or have had representation conditioned on crippling restrictions that impair confidentiality and information gathering. Counsel for these and other accused terrorists also have been singled out for particular harassment. Death threats, bomb scares, and ostracism by other potential clients are part of the job description. Even defending lawyers who defend such cases can provoke outrage; my own *New York Times* op-ed on the subject unleashed a flood of hate mail from individuals who took time out of their busy day to let me know that counsel for terrorists were "vermin" and so was I. Unsurprisingly, such cases generally do not attract scores of eager volunteers, and lawyers drafted to provide representation are not always eager to do their utmost. At a press conference following his assignment to defend Timothy McVeigh in the Oklahoma City bombing case, McVeigh's lawyer stated, "I did not seek or request this appointment, or even encourage it in any way. I have been drafted [and] will do my duty." Such attitudes are unlikely to inspire the trust and candor essential for effective working relationships.[18]

This is not to imply that most court-appointed lawyers willingly compromise their clients' interests. Rather, they are caught within a legal system that does not offer the necessary resources or incentives to ensure effective representation. Nor does it provide sufficient remedies for the injustices that predictably result.

Inadequate Responses to Inadequate Representation

Given the current structure of indigent defense, it should come as no surprise that ineffective representation is a leading cause of wrongful convictions. What is, however, more striking is the lack of serious concern that this arouses among legislative and judicial decision makers. Most have remained passive spectators to injustice, despite obvious opportunities to respond. And the system that they have developed for postconviction remedies contributes as much to the problem as the solution.

Performance Standards

One of the clearest failures involves the lack of performance standards. Many bar associations have established guidelines for effective representation in individual cases and effective administration of indigent defense systems. These guidelines could be adopted by states as a condition of funding, or by courts in establishing qualifications and monitoring conduct of appointed counsel. Such guidelines typically include limits on caseloads, support for litigation-related expenses, and requirements concerning factual investigation and communication with clients, all of which could significantly improve the quality of legal representation. Yet most jurisdictions have not adopted such performance standards, and those that have do not necessarily enforce them. For example, the Executive Director of Georgia's Indigent Defense Council has reported that efforts to make the guidelines "real" have prompted legislative threats to eliminate them altogether. The chair of one of the state's local oversight Committees for Indigent Defense has acknowledged that the Committee has never met. He has also conceded that he does not know what kind of criminal defense system the locality is operating and that, when asked to serve on the Committee, he was informed that its only function was "paperwork." A nominal supervisory structure was necessary to obtain state subsidies for defense counsel, but it did not have to do anything to ensure that the money was appropriately spent or that counsel were providing effective representation.[19]

Resources

A related failure involves the judiciary's unwillingness to ensure minimally adequate resources for indigent defense. Although some legal challenges to underfunding for private attorneys and excessive caseloads for public defenders have been successful, most have not. Particularly where judges need to worry about reelection or advancement, a strong stand on indigent defense carries obvious risks. And any rewards may seem double-edged; more effective advocacy is likely to result in more time-consuming trials and pretrial motions, which adds to courts' already unmanageable dockets. Yet in the long run, the legitimacy of the criminal justice system depends on constitutional safeguards that are enforceable only through competent representation. Moreover, providing effective counsel at the trial level is the best way to avoid the reversals on appeal that have often resulted in substantial expense and extended delay. Federal judges, who have the protection of life tenure, have a special responsibility to respond to structural failures and to ensure that the right to effective representation has meaning in practice as well as in principle. Enforcing concrete funding and performance standards is an obvious first step. If, as experts have generally agreed, most politicians are disinclined to provide adequate budgets for indigent defense, then judicial intervention is the only plausible solution.[20]

Yet not only have courts failed to prevent ineffective representation, they have also failed to provide adequate remedies when incompetence occurs. Victims face two central hurdles: a lack of lawyers willing and able to demonstrate defective performance and burdens of proof that are almost impossible to meet.

Ineffective Remedies

In theory, criminal defendants who receive inadequate representation have three forms of recourse: disciplinary complaints, civil malpractice claims, and reversals of their convictions. In fact, the first two remedies are almost never available. Convicted criminals are unsympathetic claimants, and they can rarely find lawyers to help with disciplinary complaints or to file malpractice actions. Disciplinary agencies generally will not consider claims of "mere negligence," and even egregious neglect or incompetence rarely brings any response. Moreover, the sanctions typically available, such as private reprovals, public censures, or suspensions, would do nothing to assist the defendants who filed the complaints. Malpractice remedies are equally elusive, because prevailing doctrine denies recovery unless defendants can show that "but for" their counsel's incompetence, they would have been acquitted. In effect, they must prove their innocence or have their conviction set aside. The fact that inadequate investigation materially affected a plea offer or sentencing decision is not sufficient to establish malpractice. Nor is even an egregious oversight, such as failure to meet deadlines for appeal, an adequate basis for liability. Given these difficulties of proving malpractice in criminal cases, lawyers are rarely willing to bring such claims on a contingent fee basis, and victims can rarely afford to subsidize the litigation themselves.[21]

From the standpoint of individual defendants, the most desirable remedy for ineffective representation is reversal of a conviction or invalidation of a guilty plea. However, here again, the obstacles to such challenges are usually insurmountable. Even defendants who manage to prove that their counsel's performance was constitutionally deficient will not necessarily go free; they must face retrial on the original charges and run the risk that the outcome or plea agreement will be worse the second time. Obtaining an attorney to help establish the claim is a further roadblock. As a constitutional matter, indigent defendants have a right to a court-appointed lawyer only for their initial appeal. If, as is often the case, that lawyer provides inadequate assistance or if exculpatory evidence later emerges, defendants are not entitled to counsel in subsequent appeals. Nor do they have a constitutional right to assistance in state post-conviction proceedings designed to correct errors of constitutional significance that could not be raised on direct appeal. Because these post-conviction proceedings are technically "collateral" to the criminal case, they are not within the scope of Sixth Amendment guarantees. The same is true of federal habeas corpus proceedings, which serve to address constitutional violations that were raised but not remedied in state proceedings.[22]

Although statutory or judicial authority provides for appointed counsel in at least some post-conviction contexts, the scope of coverage is by no means adequate. Nor have pro bono volunteers come close to filling the gap. To obtain counsel in many state post-conviction proceedings and in noncapital federal habeas corpus cases, prisoners must first draft their own pro se petitions and present a plausible claim to relief. That, in turn, requires an understanding of procedural and substantive law beyond the capacity of most indigent petitioners. In some surveys, fewer than 1 percent of pro se prisoner petitions were granted.[23]

When post-conviction hearings are convened in the absence of counsel, the result often resembles the "farce and mockery" that prompted the extension of Sixth Amendment guarantees of counsel decades ago. For example, in one Georgia capital case, a prisoner with a subnormal IQ was forced to represent himself at a state habeas proceeding. When the court asked him if he had any evidence, the following interchange took place:

> MR. GIBSON: I don't know what to plead.
> THE COURT: I am not asking you to plead to anything. I am just asking you if you have anything . . . you want to introduce to this Court.
> MR. GIBSON: But I don't have an attorney.

When an observer pointed out that Gibson did not even have anything to write with, he was given a legal pad and a pen. The hearing then proceeded with the state attorney's examination of Dennis Mullis, the trial lawyer whose effectiveness Gibson was challenging. As the state's attorney sought to introduce various documents during the examination, the judge repeatedly asked if Gibson had any objections. Gibson repeatedly responded that he did not know what to say without an attorney. At the close of the direct testimony, a reprise of the earlier exchange occurred:

> THE COURT: Mr. Gibson, would you like to ask Mr. Mullis any questions?
> MR. GIBSON: I don't have any counsel.
> The Court: I understand that, but I am just asking, can you tell me yes or no whether you want to ask him any questions or not?
> MR. GIBSON: I'm not my own counsel . . . .
> THE COURT: I understand that, but do you want to you, yourself, individually, want to ask him anything?
> MR. GIBSON: I don't know.
> THE COURT: Okay, sir. Okay, thank you, Mr. Mullis, you can go down.[24]

Judicial Oversight

Yet even when counsel is appointed in post-conviction proceedings, the result is not necessarily better. Fee scales are generally too low to encourage adequate preparation, and judicial oversight ranges from minimal to nonexistent. Both statutory language and court rulings make clear that lawyers' representation in "collateral" proceedings need not meet constitutional standards of effectiveness, and that incompetence will not itself constitute grounds for relief. As one Tennessee court noted, the lawyer "is not required to investigate, address, and define the allegations of the pro se petition or call witnesses or present other proof" at the post-conviction hearing. Even if the attorney's error is egregious, such as missing a filing deadline in a capital case, the Supreme Court has held that the defendant must pay the price. Under that standard, negligent lawyers have forfeited appeals that might have saved their clients' lives.[25]

The obvious inadequacies in this system have prompted at least some legislative initiatives. For example, the federal Antiterrorism and Effective Death Penalty Act attempts to encourage states to ensure competent counsel in post-conviction capital proceedings. In effect, the Act narrows the scope of federal court review for states that demonstrate an effective system for appointing and compensating lawyers in such proceedings. However, this legislation has been subject to extensive criticism from all points on the political spectrum. Critics from the left believe that it may exempt too many constitutional errors from judicial oversight. Critics from the right believe that it provides too little incentive for states to incur the costs of compliance. And in fact, experience to date confirms this concern. Reforms that have been implemented generally have fallen well short of the legislation's prescribed standards. This record speaks volumes about political leaders' indifference to injustice, even when life and death are at stake.[26]

Ineffective Assistance: Problems of Proof

Similar indifference is apparent in what passes for "effective" representation under prevailing constitutional interpretations. To establish a violation of Sixth Amendment standards justifying reversal of a conviction, defendants must meet two requirements. They must demonstrate both that their lawyers' performance "fell outside the wide range of professionally competent assistance" in the community and that "there is a reasonable probability that but for counsel's unprofessional error, the result would have been different." Those requirements are rarely met. Systematic surveys of ineffective assistance claims have found that only between 1 and 4 percent are successful. Part of the problem is that the community standard of representation is often abysmally low. A further difficulty is that the vast majority of cases involve plea bargains, which lack a record of what the attorney did, or more often, did not do.[27]

Moreover, even when attorneys' performance is inarguably inadequate, it may be difficult to prove that the outcome was affected. Judges have been extremely reluctant to second guess assertedly "tactical" decisions or to speculate on how jurors might have interpreted exculpating or mitigating facts. Convictions have been upheld even where attorneys were drunk, on drugs, or suffering from severe mental health impairment. Representation has been found adequate even when attorneys were arrested for driving while intoxicated on the way to the courthouse or sent to jail midtrial to "sober up." And defendants have been executed despite their lawyers' lack of any prior trial experience, inability to cite a single death penalty precedent, ignorance of how to present a battered woman defense, or failure to offer any witnesses, closing arguments, or mitigating evidence. As one Texas judge has noted, "Competent counsel ought to require more than a human being with a law license and a pulse." But the standard as currently applied does not demand it.[28]

The appallingly ineffective implementation of the Constitution's "effective" representation requirement has recently prompted at least some Supreme Court intervention. In a 2003 decision, *Wiggins v. Smith*, a majority of Justices voted to overturn the conviction of a death-row defendant whose attorneys failed to conduct a reasonable investigation of mitigating circumstances. Even the most cursory review would have revealed facts about the defendant's history of abuse that could well have affected the jury's sentencing deliberations. However, the Court was also at pains to limit its ruling. The majority opinion made clear that defense counsel would not always be required to present mitigating evidence or even to do a full investigation. As long as "reasonable professional judgments" supported an attorney's limited inquiry or failure to raise mitigation claims, the constitutional standard would be met. This ruling is clearly a step in the right direction, but its limited scope leaves much to be desired. According to a recent study by the Capital Jury Project, most juries that hear mitigating evidence decline to impose the death penalty. Virtually all experts and bar guidelines on capital cases underscore the critical importance of such evidence. Given this consensus, it is by no means clear how counsel could ever reasonably conclude that investigation of potentially mitigating circumstances was unnecessary.[29]

How much impact *Wiggins* will have on the conduct of defense lawyers or courts that review their performance remains unclear. In a subsequent decision, the Supreme Court emphasized the limits of judicial oversight by reversing a federal appellate panel's finding of ineffective assistance. In the Court's view, the defense lawyer's failure to discuss exculpatory evidence in closing argument might have been tactical, and federal courts should be "doubly deferential" to a state's finding of competence. But such deference is part of what accounts for decades of judicial indifference to ineffective representation. The extent of judicial tolerance is well illustrated by the jurisprudence that has developed to determine how much courtroom napping is constitutionally permissible. Defense counsel have fallen asleep with sufficient frequency that courts have developed a three-step analysis to determine when their dozing violates Sixth Amendment guarantees. Did the lawyer sleep for repeated and prolonged periods? Was the lawyer actually unconscious? Were crucial defense interests at stake while the lawyer was dozing? The absurdity of that framework is compounded by the difficulties of applying it to a record made—or not made—by counsel who was dozing. Yet according to some prosecutors and judges, it would set a dangerous precedent if defendants were entitled to a second trial merely because their lawyers slept through substantial parts of the first. So, for example, in one Texas death penalty case, courts sustained a conviction although defense counsel had fallen asleep several times during witnesses' testimony that he found "boring" and had spent only about five hours in preparing for trial. In rejecting claims of inadequate representation, a Texas appellate court reasoned that the decision to sleep might have been a "strategic" ploy to gain sympathy from the jury. And a judge reviewing that decision maintained that "[t]he Constitution says that everyone is entitled to an attorney of their choice. But the Constitution does not say that the lawyer has to be awake."[30]

When the Difference Is Death

Death cases are different, a point that would be too obvious to belabor were it not so routinely overlooked. When the state seeks to impose its ultimate and irrevocable punishment, an individual whose life hangs in the balance deserves the fairest procedures and most effective representation that our system can devise. Yet as virtually all death penalty experts agree, the "competence of defense counsel is often lowest at precisely the point at which it should be highest. . . ." In capital cases, procedures are more complex and the quality of lawyering is more crucial than in any other criminal context. Yet our system of appointing counsel fails to ensure even minimally adequate performance. Justice Ruth Bader Ginsburg has put the point bluntly. In her years on the Supreme Court, she has "yet to see a death case . . . in which the defendant was well represented at trial. People who are well-represented do not get the death penalty." People who are not well represented sometimes do get it even when they are innocent. Over the last decade, more than a hundred death-row defendants have been exonerated. We have no idea how many more might have been found innocent, or undeserving of the death penalty, if competent representation had been available at trial or on appeal.[31]

Ironically enough, some politicians view overturned convictions as a vindication of the current process. President Bush, while serving as Governor of Texas, jokingly dismissed the significance of a federal court decision reversing the conviction of a death-row defendant whose lawyer had slept during trial. According to Bush, this decision proved that "the system works." But when demonstrably innocent defendants are incarcerated for decades before release, and thousands of other prisoners' potentially valid post-conviction claims lack any representation, in what sense is the system working? Moreover, the circumstances that typically lead to exoneration are not attributable to procedural safeguards designed for that end. Rather, the evidence establishing innocence is typically the result of journalistic efforts or chance events that give no grounds for confidence in the justice of our justice process. As researchers have often noted, "vindication comes not because of but in spite of the system."[32]

The Competence Needed: The Competence Missing

What makes death penalty cases so uniquely problematic is not simply the nature of the penalty. It is also the appalling gap between the lawyering that is necessary and the lawyering that most states provide. Studies of death penalty cases have consistently found that their defense requires vastly more time, effort, and expertise than noncapital matters. One survey of California Public Defenders revealed that attorneys spent, on average, four times as much time on capital representation as on cases involving any other penalty, including those that could result in life imprisonment without parole. Other studies find that several thousand hours are typically required to provide appropriate representation. Not only must counsel investigate every aspect of the crime, they also need to compile an extensive life history of the defendant in order to identify facts that might be relevant in mitigating the punishment. Because the stakes are particularly high for law enforcement officials as well as defendants in death penalty cases, the risks of police or prosecutorial misconduct are correspondingly greater. That, in turn, poses special obligations and obstacles for defense attorneys in unearthing relevant evidence. So too, a cottage industry of studies has identified substantial racial and ethnic bias in the imposition of the death penalty. And that places further responsibilities on defense attorneys to investigate all possible sources of discrimination. Where, as is often the case, trial counsel provides inadequate representation, lawyers handling post-conviction remedies must not only review the record, but also must conduct their own investigation to identify evidence that should have been presented and strategies that should have been pursued. In addition, defense counsel need to master the highly complicated and frequently changing body of law specifically governing death penalty cases. Special training, experience, and preparation are essential.[33]

They are often missing. Here again the main reason is money. Few states provide anything close to adequate compensation for death penalty cases; few lawyers are willing to take cases at rates that will not even cover their out-of-pocket expenses. As noted earlier, funding that is shockingly inadequate at the trial level is even worse or nonexistent for post-conviction representation. The situation has been exacerbated by Congress's determination in the mid-1990s to eliminate federal support for the Death Penalty Resource Centers that had provided capital representation in about twenty states. Even before that decision, these centers' resources were never close to adequate; some two hundred lawyers were available for 3,000 defendants. But these specialized counsel were extraordinarily effective not only in preparing cases, but also in recruiting pro bono volunteers and in persuading courts to establish constitutional safeguards. Indeed, it was their very effectiveness that led to their extinction. According to the leader of congressional opposition, these lawyers were "frustrating the implementation of . . . death sentences." The withdrawal of federal support left many states without a corps of attorneys willing or able to handle capital cases. To help fill the gaps, the American Bar Association formed the Death Penalty Representation Project. Yet despite enormous efforts, the Project has managed in its first five years to find only about seventy-five lawyers willing to provide pro bono assistance.[34]

The result is that many capital defendants receive assistance from counsel whose competence or motivation is inadequate to the task. The attorneys who accept court appointments in capital cases often are those who lack other work, and with reason. Surveys in Illinois, Kentucky, Tennessee, and Texas have found that a third of the defendants who received the death penalty had lawyers who were subsequently suspended, disbarred, or convicted of criminal offenses. In Texas, defendants who had court-appointed counsel were forty-four times more likely to be sentenced to death than those who were able to retain their own attorneys. In national surveys, all other things being equal, the few defendants lucky enough to receive representation by well-funded private attorneys from urban law firms were 70 percent more likely to obtain reversals on appeal than defendants from poorly staffed offices.[35]

The inadequacy of defense counsel is also reflected in the high rates of constitutional error. A painstaking review of some 6,000 capital cases found that two-thirds were reversed in appeals or habeas corpus proceedings. The records in these cases routinely reveal counsel who treat them as a spectator sport: who conduct no investigation, make no objections, and waive cross-examination or closing argument. Such ostensibly "tactical" choices are troubling in any context, but in a capital case, they may be fatal. As one leading death penalty study concluded: "Experts . . . have generally agreed that the most important variable in determining whether a capital defendant will be sentenced to death is not the details of the crime, the locale in which the case will be tried or the race of the defendant but rather the competence of the defendant's attorney in trying death cases."[36]

Courts' acquiescence in this system makes a mockery of constitutional entitlements. In the search for warm bodies to satisfy Sixth Amendment requirements, judges routinely have appointed counsel who are known to have a history of substance abuse, disciplinary violations, and mental health difficulties, or who lack any trial or criminal law experience. Attorneys who specialize in mortgage foreclosures have been assigned complex death penalty cases without any preparation. Even in the relatively rare cases in which adequate financial resources are available, adequate representation is not always forthcoming. Lawyers handling post-conviction appeals have been permitted to collect the maximum fee, sometimes over $65,000, without even bothering to meet their clients, let alone conduct an adequate investigation. The judiciary has allowed capital proceedings to continue in which lawyers are drunk, dozing, or demonstrably clueless about basic law, facts, and procedural requirements. One of the most egregious recent examples involved a Texas lawyer who had been suspended three times for neglect and mental unfitness, who was under treatment for bipolar disorder, and who had no prior experience in a capital habeas proceeding. The lawyer conducted no investigation and missed a filing deadline for federal habeas review. The Texas courts' indifference to incompetence, both at the time of counsel's appointment, and again on appeal, ultimately cost the defendant his life. That case was all too typical. A recent review of capital records by the Texas Defender Service, aptly titled Lethal Indifference, found that those sentenced to death in Texas faced a "one in three chance of being executed without having the case properly investigated by a competent attorney or without having any claims of innocence or unfairness heard."[37]

The absence of adequate representation carries an enormous price not only for those accused of capital offenses, but also for the public and the justice system. The average capital case now takes over eleven years and costs on the order of $2.5 to $4 million dollars, depending on the state. Review of these death penalty proceedings also imposes heavy burdens on an already overextended judiciary and contributes to all the problems associated with excessive caseloads throughout the legal system. A substantial part of the delay and expense of death penalty litigation is attributable to errors by counsel who lack the qualifications or incentives to provide effective representation. And when the wrong individual is convicted, the guilty criminal remains free and poses a continuing threat to the community.[38]

Rethinking the Penalty

The gross injustices of the current system have gained increasing attention. In recent polls, 94 percent of Americans agree that innocent people are wrongfully convicted of murder. A growing number of prominent national leaders, as well as political, religious, and bar organizations, have called either for abolition of the death penalty or a moratorium on its enforcement. Public support for capital punishment has also declined, and a majority of those surveyed would now prefer life imprisonment without parole. Ending the state's use of violence as a response to violence would align the United States with the international human rights community. Almost all other nations have abolished the death penalty. The few countries that retain capital punishment, such as Iran, Pakistan, and China, are not known for their commitment to due process and individual rights. In any event, unless and until America joins the consensus of civilized nations in eliminating the death penalty, addressing the inhumanity in its imposition is a moral imperative.[39]

Making Rights a Reality

The inadequacy of defense counsel is, of course, only one of the problems plaguing the criminal justice system. Other commonly cited concerns include racial and ethnic bias, sloppy or suggestive investigative techniques, unreliable informants, police and prosecutorial misconduct, limitations on judicial review, excessive sentences, politicized judicial elections, unmanageable court caseloads, and inadequate alternatives to incarceration. But the lack of effective representation is a problem that compounds all others because it forecloses the possibility of challenge. Denying an adequate defense to those who cannot afford it compromises our most fundamental constitutional commitments.[40]

Funding

Reform is necessary on several levels. The most obvious involves money.

Virtually all experts agree that defense attorneys for indigents should have pay scales and resources comparable to those available to prosecutors. Caseloads should not exceed official bar standards. Compensation for appointed lawyers should enable them to cover their overheads and to earn a reasonable hourly rate. These reforms will, in turn, require a substantial increase in funding, particularly at the state level. Fewer than half the states now subsidize at least 90 percent of the defense costs for their indigent residents. About three-fifths rely on often financially strapped counties to foot most of the bill. Such systems have proven incapable of assuring a consistent level of independent, adequately financed representation.[41]

Accordingly, the consensus among experts is that the only way to ensure a more adequate indigent defense system is to shift primary funding responsibility to the states and to give an independent body control over lawyers' appointment, performance standards, and support services. Such allocations of authority have been the best available means of reducing resource disparities, promoting quality, and insulating lawyers from pressures by individual judges and local political bodies. If, however, states choose to retain a system of local control, they can condition subsidies on county compliance with key requirements. For example, Indiana provides reimbursement of 40 percent of defense costs for counties that establish public defender boards with responsibility for ensuring caseload limitations and minimum qualifications for appointed counsel. Additional funding could come from some of the same sources that might support increased civil legal assistance such as court filing fees, bar contributions, or a tax on legal services revenue.[42]

Effective Representation

Whatever its structure, every indigent defense system should enforce qualification requirements and performance standards for indigent defense counsel. The ABA and the National Legal Aid and Defender Association have developed appropriate guidelines, and many public defender programs have instituted more specific evaluation strategies. Experience, training, participation in continuing legal education, and reviews by peers, clients, and judges can help ensure minimum competence. Procedures should also be in place for removing attorneys from the list of counsel eligible for court appointment when they have consistently neglected basic responsibilities. Here again, bar organizations have promulgated appropriate standards for removal and reinstatement. Courts and defender oversight agencies now need to adopt them. Bar disciplinary authorities should also impose significant sanctions on attorneys who seek cases for which they lack the necessary time or skills. In addition, obstacles to proving malpractice and ineffective assistance of counsel should be reduced. Victims of incompetence need more realistic remedies and lawyers need more incentives to provide adequate representation. Given the expense and difficulties of proving ineffective assistance of counsel after the fact, decision makers should do more to prevent it.[43]

By the same token, courts should also assume an affirmative obligation to ensure that the indigent defense system is structured to promote effective representation. Jurisdictions that fail to provide adequate funding and performance standards should be held accountable for the constitutional violations that inevitably result. Cases in which courts have found such violations have prompted substantial legislative improvement. To assess the adequacy of indigent defense systems, jurisdictions also should be required to keep data concerning case expenses, preparation, and outcomes. Records should be available to compare the performance of appointed counsel, public defenders, and privately retained attorneys. Information should be broken down by race and ethnicity to identify potential sources of bias and law enforcement abuses. Only through more systematic monitoring will it be possible to determine whether counsel meet constitutional requirements of effective representation.[44]

Finally, the legal profession needs to do a better job of educating the public about the importance of criminal defense and all the ways that the current system falls short. Courts and bar associations should publicize the problems and build coalitions for realistic reforms. More Americans need to understand their own stake in ensuring effective representation for those who seemingly deserve it least. The prospect of vigorous challenge by defense counsel creates incentives for law enforcement officials to do their jobs effectively and to respect individual rights. Cases involving the most brutal offenses are the ones that these officials most want to win. Not surprisingly, these also are the cases where abuses are most likely and the need for scrutiny by defense counsel is most intense. Providing effective representation for defendants who appear guilty is the best way to protect those who are not.

≡ 7 ≡

PRO BONO IN PRINCIPLE

AND IN PRACTICE

When confronted with the gap between the public's legal needs and society's response, bar leaders have generally presented lawyers' unpaid service as a critical part of the solution. The provision of assistance "pro bono publico" often expresses what is most admirable in the legal profession. But not often enough. Over the course of their careers, many lawyers contribute hundreds of unpaid hours to causes that would otherwise be priced out of the justice system. Some lawyers also give significant financial support to legal services programs. Yet the majority do not. Most lawyers make no contributions, and the average for the bar as a whole is less than half an hour a week and fifty cents a day. Moreover, much of what passes for "pro bono" is not aid to the indigent or public interest causes, but either favors for friends, family, or clients, or cases where fees turn out to be uncollectible. The bar's pro bono commitments are, in short, a reflection of both the profession's highest ideals and its most grating hypocrisies.[1]

At many bar association meetings, both pro bono traditions are on display. A case in point occurred at a recent southern bar convention. Its program included a presentation of pro bono awards for exceptional service that truly was exceptional. The attorneys who were honored had made great personal sacrifices to assist impoverished clients and communities. But the ceremony also featured lavish praise for lawyers who had volunteered during the meeting for a community service project. Their efforts were presented as emblematic of the selfless public spirit that defines the legal profession. In fact, the service project involved less than a sixth of the lawyers present, who sacrificed a few hours of golf or shopping in order to pick up trash in a local riverside park. The project reflected no ongoing commitment to environmental causes; the cleanup occurred only every other year when the bar met at that location. In alternate years, when the convention took place at an ocean resort, the community service project involved a sandcastle contest, with entrance fees donated to legal aid organizations. The previous summer, the contest reportedly had raised several hundred dollars. If these efforts reflected all that is best in our profession, the public might draw a quite different conclusion from the one that program organizers intended.

How best to reduce the gap between professional ideals and professional practice has been the subject of long-standing debate but little data. To help fill the void, the discussion that follows reviews findings from my own recent study: the first comprehensive national survey of the factors that influence lawyers' pro bono work. This study includes both an overview of the literature on altruism in general and bar contributions in particular, as well as questionnaires and interview responses from a sample of some 3,000 attorneys. These responses, together with other research on charitable participation, suggest changes in workplace and law school cultures that can more effectively translate public service principles into professional practices.

The Rationale for Pro Bono Responsibilities

Justifications

The rationale for pro bono work rests on two central claims. One involves the value to society of addressing unmet legal needs. A second justification involves the value to lawyers, individually and collectively, of such charitable contributions. The first argument begins from the premise that access to legal services is a fundamental interest. That claim, developed at length in preceding chapters, is that inadequate legal assistance jeopardizes individual rights, compounds other social inequalities, and undermines a commitment to justice.

A second rationale for pro bono service rests on the benefits to those who provide it. A wide array of research, both on charitable involvement in general and lawyers' public service in particular, finds that participants benefit personally and professionally. Regular volunteering is correlated with physical as well as mental health. Compared with the population generally, people who regularly assist others apart from family and friends have longer lives, less pain, stress, and depression, and greater self-esteem. Volunteers also report a sense of physical well-being, both immediately after helping and when the service is remembered, and are more likely to be happy with their lives. Although the correlation between volunteer activities and well-being does not establish a causal relationship, other evidence suggests that such a relationship exists, and that selfless action is good for the self. Such evidence includes the high frequency of individuals' subjective experience of benefits, the consistent association of volunteering with objective measures of health, and the biological indications of a "helper's high." The neurological basis for such heightened well-being is not well understood, but some research suggests that assisting others reduces stress, which improves the functioning of the immune system, and triggers the release of endorphins, which produces pleasurable physical sensations.[2]

Studies of the legal profession, including findings from my own survey, similarly confirm the benefits of charitable involvement. Particularly for young attorneys, pro bono work can provide valuable training, contacts, trial experience, and leadership opportunities. Through volunteer projects, lawyers can develop new areas of expertise and demonstrate marketable skills. Involvement in community groups, charitable organizations, high visibility litigation, and other public interest activities is a way for attorneys to expand their perspectives, enhance their reputations, and attract paying clients. Pro bono work also enables individuals to express the commitments to social justice that often motivated them to choose legal careers in the first instance. ABA surveys consistently find that lawyers' greatest dissatisfaction with their practice is a lack of "contribution to the social good." Volunteer work can provide that contribution.[3]

So, too, pro bono activity serves the interests of legal employers and the legal profession generally. Strong public service programs can produce tangible, although hard to quantify, organizational benefits in terms of retention, recruitment, reputation, morale, and job performance. Pro bono contributions also can enhance the reputation of lawyers as a group. In one representative survey, which asked what could improve the image of lawyers, the response most often chosen was their provision of free legal services to the needy; two-thirds of those surveyed indicated that it would improve their opinion of the profession.[4]

Mandatory Service

For all these reasons, the vast majority of lawyers believe that the bar should provide pro bono service. However, the vast majority also oppose requiring such service. The most common objection is that it is unfair to make the profession assume a public obligation. If access to law is a societal value, then society as a whole should bear its cost. The poor have fundamental unmet needs for food and medical care, but we do not require grocers or physicians to donate their help in meeting those needs. Why should the responsibilities of lawyers be greater?[5]

One answer is that the legal profession has a monopoly on the provision of essential services. Lawyers have special privileges that should entail special obligations. In the United States, attorneys have a much more extensive and exclusive right to provide legal assistance than attorneys in other countries. As chapter 4 noted, the American legal profession is responsible for creating and protecting that right, and its success in restricting lay competition has helped to price services beyond the reach of millions of consumers. Some pro bono contribution is not unreasonable to expect from lawyers in return for their privileged status. Nor would it be unfair to expect a comparable contribution from other professionals who have similar monopolies over provision of critical services.

An alternative rationale for imposing special obligations on lawyers stems from their historic role as officers of the court and their special role in our governance structure. As a prominent New York bar report explained, much of what lawyers do "is about providing *justice*, [which is] . . . nearer to the heart of our way of life . . . than services provided by other professionals. The legal profession serves as indispensable guardians of our lives, liberties and governing principles. . . ." Because lawyers occupy such a central role in our justice system, there is also particular value in exposing them to how that system functions, or fails to function, for the have-nots. Giving broad segments of the bar some experience with poverty-related problems and public interest causes can lay crucial foundations for change.[6]

A second cluster of objections to pro bono responsibilities rests on moral grounds. To many lawyers, requiring pro bono service seems an infringement of their own rights, and a form of "involuntary servitude" or "latent fascism." Other commentators view "compulsory charity" as a contradiction in terms. From their perspective, requiring assistance undermines its moral significance and compromises altruistic commitments. Drawing on studies of helping behavior, some critics argue that individuals are more likely to provide sustained and quality service if they are doing so voluntarily than if they are fulfilling a requirement.[7]

There are problems with each of these claims, beginning with the assumption that pro bono service is "charity." Rather, as the preceding discussion suggested, pro bono work is not simply a philanthropic exercise; it is also a professional responsibility. The effect that some minimum service requirement would have on overall pro bono participation is difficult to gauge. Critics have produced no evidence that voluntary assistance has declined in the small number of jurisdictions where courts now appoint lawyers to provide uncompensated representation. Nor is it self-evident that most lawyers who already make public service contributions would cease to do so simply because others were required to join them. As to the large numbers of lawyers who do not voluntarily contribute pro bono assistance but claim that required service would lack moral significance, law professor David Luban has it right: "One hesitates to state the obvious, but here it is: You can't appeal to the moral significance of a gift you have no intention of giving." Asking lawyers to make a modest contribution of service, along the lines that bar ethics codes suggest, generally between half an hour to an hour a week, hardly constitutes "servitude." And those who find it unduly burdensome could substitute a financial contribution.[8]

The stronger arguments against pro bono obligations involve pragmatic rather than moral concerns. Many opponents who support such obligations in principle worry that they would not prove efficient in practice. A threshold problem involves defining the services that would satisfy a pro bono requirement. If the definition is broad, and encompasses any unpaid legal work, then experience suggests that poor people will not be the major beneficiaries; most work will help friends, relatives, middle-class nonprofit organizations, and deadbeat clients. By contrast, if a pro bono requirement is limited to the low-income individuals given preferred status in some bar association's aspirational standards, then that definition would exclude many crucial public interest contributions, such as work for civil rights, civil liberties, or environmental organizations. Any compromise effort to permit some but not all charitable groups to qualify for pro bono credit would bump up against charges of political bias.[9]

A further objection to mandatory pro bono requirements is that lawyers who lack expertise or motivation to serve underrepresented groups will not offer cost-effective assistance. In opponents' view, corporate lawyers who dabble in poverty cases will often provide unduly expensive or incompetent services. The performance of some attorneys required to accept uncompensated appointments in criminal cases does not inspire confidence that unwillingly conscripted practitioners would provide adequate representation. Critics also worry that some lawyers' inexperience and insensitivity in dealing with low-income clients will compromise the objectives that pro bono requirements seek to advance. The basis for such concerns is often apparent in surveys of pro bono programs. Some attorneys object to spending time on "piddling matters" or representing clients who have "messed up their lives" and then, even after assistance, "do something to botch it up even more." Opponents also worry about the "Burgeoning Bureaucratic Boondoggle" that they assume would be necessary to monitor compliance. Even with a substantial expenditure of resources, it would be extremely difficult to verify the amount of time that practitioners reported for pro bono work or the quality of assistance that they provided.[10]

From critics' perspective, requiring attorneys to contribute minimal services of largely unverifiable quality cannot solve the problem of unequal access to justice. Worse still, such mandates may divert attention from more productive ways of addressing unmet needs. Preferable strategies would include those proposed in earlier chapters, such as simplification of legal procedures, expanded subsidies for poverty law programs, greater assistance for pro se litigants, and fewer restrictions on provision of routine legal services by nonlawyers.

These are significant concerns, but they are not nearly as conclusive as critics suggest. It is certainly true that some practitioners lack many of the skills necessary to serve those most in need of assistance. But, as law professor Michael Millemann notes, the current alternative is scarcely preferable: "Assume that after four years in college, three years of law school, and varying periods of law practice some lawyers are 'incompetent' to help the poor. . . . All this despairing assumption tells us is that the poor are far less competent to represent themselves, and do not have the readily available access to attaining competency that lawyers have." To be sure, subsidizing additional poverty law specialists or enlisting more willing volunteers would be a more efficient way of expanding services than relying on reluctant dilettantes. But neither strategy seems likely to be sufficient in this political climate. Nor is it clear that pro bono programs are diverting significant attention from better ways to address current needs. Whose attention? Most policymakers who have opposed adequate legal aid funding do not appear much interested in expanding access to justice through other methods.[11]

In any event, multiple strategies are available to reduce the likelihood of incompetent assistance and undue enforcement burdens. One is to allow lawyers to buy out their required service by making an equivalent financial contribution to a legal aid program. Another option is to permit lawyers in organizations to satisfy their obligations collectively by designating certain individuals responsible for fulfilling the hourly responsibilities of all their colleagues. A further possibility is to give continuing legal education (CLE) credit for time spent in training for pro bono work, and to rely on the same kind of honor system used in enforcing CLE requirements for pro bono obligations as well. Many voluntary public interest projects have effectively equipped participants through relatively brief educational workshops, coupled with well-designed manuals and accessible backup assistance. Bar associations could also provide free malpractice insurance for pro bono cases, supported by membership dues, that would cover practitioners who satisfied certain quality-related conditions.

In the absence of experience with such strategies, the effectiveness of pro bono requirements is difficult to predict. But even without such experience, a threshold question is worth considering. Suppose critics are correct that attempts to assure competent performance would be inadequate or prohibitively expensive. Would a mandatory program still make sense, despite the risks of some noncompliance? At the very least, such requirements would support lawyers who want to participate in public interest projects but work in organizations that have failed to provide adequate resources or credit for these efforts. Many of the nation's most profitable law firms and leading corporate employers fall into that category. They could readily afford a greater pro bono commitment, and a formal requirement could nudge them in that direction. For lawyers who have no interest in public interest work, buyout provisions could reduce resistance and the risks of unacceptable performance. A fallback position would be to require attorneys to report their contributions. Some evidence suggests that such requirements can result in modest increases in participation. Only through experience with mandatory pro bono initiatives will it be possible to gauge their relative costs and benefits. Yet rather than encouraging such requirements, the organized bar has remained firmly wedded to an aspirational approach. And that approach has left a wide gap between the rhetoric and reality of bar pro bono commitments.[12]

The Extent of Pro Bono Responsibilities: Rules and Realities

As chapter 3 noted, for most of this nation's history, the bar's commitment to pro bono service was noticeable for its absence. The limited data available indicate that most lawyers have never provided significant charitable assistance and that, until recently, little of their unpaid work has gone to the poor or to underrepresented public interests. Over the last two decades, the inadequacy of voluntary pro bono programs has prompted a series of proposals for bar ethics codes to require service or at least reports of contribution levels.

Bar Ethical Rules

One landmark battle over such a proposal took place in 1983 as the ABA was preparing to adopt its new Model Rules of Professional Conduct. The Commission charged with drafting the Model Rules initially proposed a pro bono requirement of forty hours a year, and then, in the face of outraged opposition, a reporting obligation. However, bar surveys found that about four-fifths of lawyers opposed any pro bono requirement. Accordingly, the Model Rules as originally adopted included only an aspirational mandate calling for an unspecified amount of "public interest legal services."[13]

Since that controversy, efforts to strengthen pro bono ethical standards have come and gone, but mainly gone. First in 1993, and then in 2001, the ABA again rejected the possibility of mandatory service. It did, however, amend its Model Rules to quantify an aspirational contribution of fifty hours per year "without expectation of fee," primarily to "persons of limited means" or to organizations assisting them. Lawyers also could satisfy their responsibility either through assistance at no fee or a reduced fee to a wide range of public interest, charitable, religious, community, and educational organizations, or through financial contributions to such groups.[14]

Reform efforts at the state level have paralleled the national experience. Over the last decade, almost half the states have amended their pro bono rules. Many jurisdictions have considered mandatory service but only three have imposed any obligations. Florida and Maryland require lawyers to report their pro bono contributions. New Jersey requires lawyers to accept court appointments in cases involving indigents, but exempts practitioners in specified categories including lawyers who have contributed twenty-five pro bono hours a year through qualifying poverty law organizations. Other states vary in their approaches, although it is by no means clear whether the differences in aspirational standards make for differences in actual practices. Some jurisdictions have no pro bono provisions in their ethical codes or include references only in code preambles. Close to half of all states have a provision similar to the 1983 version of Model Rule 6.1, which provides a highly elastic definition of pro bono work and specifies no quantifiable level of contribution. States that establish more specific standards generally suggest between twenty and fifty hours of aid per year. About a quarter of the states permit financial contributions to a legal aid organization as a full or partial alternative to service.[15]

Court Appointments

Despite the absence of mandatory pro bono rules, local courts have occasionally exercised their inherent power to appoint uncompensated counsel, generally in criminal cases where a funding appropriation runs out or where fees are set too low to attract sufficient volunteers. The scope of this appointment authority remains unsettled because it is seldom exercised and usually involves only the small number of practitioners who also seek voluntary court appointments. When courts have attempted to compel service, lawyers typically have responded with a "Pavlovian [plea]: it must be unconstitutional." Many lawsuits have challenged judges' appointment power on the grounds that compulsory representation constitutes involuntary servitude in violation of the Thirteenth Amendment, or a "taking of property" in violation of the Fifth Amendment. Most modern courts have rejected both claims. With respect to involuntary servitude, a well-settled line of precedent holds that Thirteenth Amendment prohibitions extend only to physical restraint or confinement. Because the sanctions for refusal of pro bono work have not included incarceration, courts generally have rejected involuntary servitude challenges. Most judges also have dismissed objections based on "takings" grounds on the theory that governments need not "pay for the performance of a public duty if it is already owed," and that pro bono service is such a duty. As long as the required amount of service is not unreasonable, courts generally have rejected constitutional challenges.[16]

Bar Contributions

How many lawyers meet their state's aspirational standards or are subject to court- appointed requirements is impossible to gauge with any precision. Full information on participation is lacking because only two states mandate reporting of contribution levels, because the definition of pro bono is often expansive and ambiguous, and because lawyers responding to surveys often stretch its scope to include work for which they expected to be paid but which turned out to be uncompensated or undercompensated. Many attorneys also count services for friends, family members, bar associations, and organizations that could afford to pay for assistance. For example, New York lawyers report the highest participation rates in the country. Almost half (47 percent) report engaging in pro bono work, but three-quarters include assisting a close friend or relative. An Oklahoma pro bono survey included civic, community, and charitable work, which would include coaching soccer and serving on opera boards.[17]

In most surveyed jurisdictions, participation levels in pro bono activity, variously defined, range between 15 to 18 percent, and of those who engage in pro bono work, contributions range from an average of forty-two hours per year in New York to a median of twenty hours in Texas. When adjusted for the number of lawyers who make no contributions, hourly assistance ranges from an average of twenty hours in New York to a median of five in Texas. Less than 10 percent of practitioners accept referrals from federally funded legal aid offices or bar-sponsored poverty-related programs. Only two-fifths of surveyed in-house legal departments participate in pro bono work and the average yearly commitment is less than eight hours per legal department employee. Most lawyers are no more charitable with their money than their time. Reported financial contributions range from an average of $82 per year in New York to $32 per year in Florida. In short, the best available research finds that the American bar averages less than half an hour of work per week and under half a dollar per day in support of legal services.[18]

Pro bono programs involving the profession's most affluent members reflect a particularly dispiriting distance between the bar's idealized image and actual practices. Only a third of the nation's large law firms have accepted the Pro Bono Institute Challenge, which calls on firms to contribute 3 to 5 percent of firm revenues. A substantial number of firms that accept the challenge nonetheless fail to meet its standard. Only eighteen of the nation's one hundred most financially successful firms achieve the Model Rules aspiration of fifty hours per year of pro bono service. The approximately 50,000 lawyers at these firms average less than ten minutes per day on pro bono activities. What is equally shameful is that pro bono participation in the most profitable firms declined by a third during a decade when their average revenues increased by over 50 percent. Although pro bono contributions by these firms have increased slightly since the 9/11 terrorist attack, it is not clear whether that increase will be sustained. Nor is it clear how market forces will affect volunteer activity. Neither a good economy nor a bad economy is necessarily better for pro bono. When demand for legal services is strong, many lawyers believe that they or their firms are too busy with paying work to take time for volunteer activity. Conversely, when times are hard, many view pro bono involvement as a luxury that they cannot afford.[19]

Yet a strong pro bono commitment is clearly not inconsistent with commercial success. Many of the nation's most profitable firms have high contribution levels. Indeed, surveys of large firms have found that pro bono participation is positively correlated with profitability. Such findings are consistent with the evidence noted earlier of the professional benefits of charitable service in terms of recruitment, training, client development, and so forth.[20]

The failure of so many lawyers to participate in pro bono work has prompted a broad range of initiatives. In some jurisdictions, state supreme courts have established structures to develop and monitor responses to legal needs. Many state and federal agencies have also established policies encouraging pro bono service. A growing number of organizations and websites match lawyers with potential clients, and the ABA's Pro Bono Center gives assistance to more than 1,000 volunteer programs. Major lawyers' periodicals like the *American Lawyer* and the *National Law Journal* now provide rankings and profiles of outstanding employer contributors. Yet despite such initiatives, pro bono contribution levels remain dispiritingly low, particularly when compared with lawyers' capacity to give. The limitations of current bar initiatives have prompted calls for more efforts by law schools to reach practitioners at the formative stages of their legal careers.[21]

The Evolution of Law School Pro Bono Programs

Until relatively recently, formal law school pro bono programs were rare. Most students' exposure to public interest causes and low-income clients occurred in clinical courses, externships, or summer jobs. In the late 1980s, a growing number of faculty, administrators, and students began encouraging law schools to take a more active role in promoting pro bono service, and Tulane instituted the first law school requirement. Over the next fifteen years, most schools developed formal pro bono programs, and about a fifth adopted requirements. Several initiatives encouraged that trend. In 1996 the American Bar Association amended its accreditation standards to provide that every law school "should encourage its students to participate in pro bono activities and provide opportunities for them to do so." A year later, the Association of American Law Schools appointed a Commission on Pro Bono and Public Service Opportunities in Law Schools. Recommendations in the Commission's Report led to various follow-up projects that provided additional support for public service initiatives. By 2003, 90 percent of surveyed schools had organized pro bono programs. These programs vary considerably in scope and content. Of schools that require service, obligations range from twenty to seventy hours prior to graduation. Some, but not all, institutions count non-legal work, as well as courses and internships carrying academic credit. Of schools with voluntary programs, most provide referral systems with administrative support; the remainder rely on student groups.[22]

Student and Faculty Service

Yet despite this growth of institutional support, many schools' pro bono programs leave much to be desired. Although recent data on voluntary student involvement are lacking, pro bono administrators interviewed for the AALS Commission Report estimated that only about a quarter to a third of the students at their schools participated, and that average time commitments were quite limited. Some student involvement was at token levels and seemed intended primarily as resume padding. Accordingly, the Commission concluded that the majority of students graduated without pro bono legal work as part of their educational experience. Although some schools have strengthened their pro bono programs and a few have instituted requirements since the Commission issued its report, no evidence suggests that student involvement rates have changed dramatically. The vast majority of schools remain a considerable distance from meeting the Commission recommendation that every institution "make available to all students at least once during their law school careers a well-supervised law-related pro bono opportunity and either require the students' participation or find ways to attract the great majority of students to volunteer."[23]

Quantitative information on faculty pro bono service is unavailable, but impressionistic accounts suggest room for improvement in this area as well. Few schools require contributions by faculty, and fewer still impose substantial or specific levels. In the AALS Commission survey, only half of administrators agreed that "many" faculty at their schools were providing "good role models to the students by engaging in uncompensated pro bono service themselves." And those administrators often added that many faculty were not. Yet improving pro bono programs does not appear to be a priority at most schools. About two-thirds of deans responding to the Commission survey expressed satisfaction with the level of pro bono participation by students and faculty at their law schools. So much satisfaction is itself unsatisfying, given the limited number of students involved at most institutions, the inadequate role of faculty, and the strong justifications for broad pro bono involvement.[24]

The Rationale for Service

Most of these justifications for pro bono service by law students parallel the justifications for pro bono service by lawyers. Leaders in legal education, including about 95 percent of law school deans, largely agree that such service is a professional responsibility and that their institutions should prepare future practitioners to assume it. During the formative stages of their professional identity, future lawyers need to develop the skills and values that will sustain commitments to public service. To that end, schools need to offer effective pro bono programs, and faculty need to model such service commitments themselves.[2]

This rationale for pro bono programs assumes that positive experiences in law school will encourage involvement after graduation. Evidence for this link between law school pro bono work and subsequent participation comes from research on "service learning" in general and surveys of law students in particular. Service learning refers to courses that require participants to provide unpaid assistance to selected community organizations. Students who have such experiences typically report a greater willingness to volunteer in the future than students in courses without such service opportunities. So too, between two-thirds and four-fifths of law students who have participated in a mandatory pro bono program indicate that their involvement has increased the likelihood that they will engage in comparable work as practicing attorneys. However, prior to my own study, no systematic research had attempted to corroborate such claims by comparing the amount of pro bono work by graduates who were subject to law school requirements and graduates who were not. And as noted below, my study's findings provide no such corroboration. To be sure, as research on altruism suggests, a positive experience working on public interest causes can encourage future involvement. But that experience need not be in a pro bono program; it could come from clinical courses, internships, or other legal work.[26]

Yet the rationale for public service initiatives in law school does not rest solely on their capacity to promote subsequent volunteer service. Pro bono placements have independent educational value. Like other forms of experiential learning, participation in public service helps bridge the gap between theory and practice, and enriches understanding of how law relates to life. For law students, as well as lawyers, pro bono work can provide valuable training in interviewing, negotiating, drafting, problem solving, and working with individuals from diverse racial, ethnic, and socio-economic backgrounds. Such work may also offer practical benefits such as career information, contacts, and job references. Aid to clients of limited means exposes both students and faculty to the urgency of unmet needs and to the capacities and constraints of law in addressing social problems. Such exposure also can increase awareness of ethical issues and the human costs of professional inattention or incompetence. Positive experiences may, in turn, encourage more individuals to press potential employers for information about their policies toward such work. Too many students who report interest in public service now lack this information.[27]

For law schools, pro bono programs can prove beneficial in several respects apart from their educational value for students. As over two-thirds of surveyed deans note, such programs offer valuable opportunities for cooperation with local community groups, bar organizations, and alumni. Successful projects also can contribute to law school efforts in recruitment, public relations, and development. Individual faculty can profit as well from community contacts and from opportunities to enrich their research and teaching through public service. Given this range of benefits, it is hard to find anyone who opposes law school pro bono programs, at least in principle. But in practice, considerable disagreement centers on the form that these programs should take and the priority that they should assume in a world of scarce educational resources. Many students, faculty, and administrators oppose mandatory service and are unwilling to provide the support necessary for effective voluntary programs.[28]

Opposition to Pro Bono Initiatives

The opposition to pro bono initiatives for faculty and students parallels the opposition to pro bono initiatives for lawyers. Again, the most serious objections are practical rather than moral. Critics raise concerns about the effectiveness of both mandatory and voluntary programs in enhancing professional skills and responsibilities. One objection is that a service obligation or aspiration for which no compensation or credit is available devalues the importance of public interest work and imposes disproportionate hardships on students with significant family or part-time work responsibilities. The burdens are likely to be greatest for students from economically disadvantaged backgrounds, the very group that pro bono responsibilities are intended to assist. To address this concern by minimizing the amount of work expected creates other problems. Law professor Lucie White argues that current pro bono programs too often offer only a brief experience of providing routine services to low-income clients. Such services do not address the root causes of poverty and can encourage a kind of noblesse-oblige paternalism that often leaves both providers and recipients unsatisfied. Differences in racial, ethnic, socio-economic, and educational backgrounds exacerbate the problem, particularly if students lack "cross-cultural competence" and are not in classroom or workplace settings that foster it. Clients may resent the seeming arrogance and insensitivity of students; students may resent the seeming ingratitude and unworthiness of clients.[29]

A related concern, particularly with mandatory programs, is that participants will lack the time or motivation to provide quality assistance. Some law graduates, including a significant number in my own study, have been quite critical of required service. They have felt bored and unchallenged by routine tasks. For these reluctant students, contact with clients who appear ungrateful or undeserving can confirm adverse stereotypes of poverty communities. Experience with disaffected students can, in turn, discourage overburdened field supervisors from spending the time necessary to generate adequate placements or to make them more effective.[30]

These are valid concerns. But as is true with criticism of pro bono programs for lawyers, the response is always: "Compared to what?" Not all students will have the desire or opportunities for more sustained involvement with poverty or public interest causes. And not all schools are willing or able to invest the resources necessary to provide such opportunities through clinical courses for the entire student body throughout their law school education. Pro bono placements are not a substitute for faculty-supervised coursework, but they can be a less costly supplement. Well-designed programs can offer an array of non-routine service opportunities along with training that sensitizes students to the dynamics of poverty and effective client relationships. Mandatory programs can also send a message that public service is a professional responsibility, and reach students who would not take advantage of voluntary pro bono programs, externships, or clinical courses. By their own accounts, some of these individuals become converts to public interest causes, and most participants have a sufficiently positive experience that they report an increased interest in future pro bono service.

Yet whether these benefits of required service are sufficient to offset the costs is an open question, and one on which little research has been available. One major objective of the empirical study summarized below was to help identify what law school as well as workplace strategies are most likely to promote valuable pro bono experiences.

Workplace Influences on Pro Bono Service: An Empirical Analysis

The Survey

The objective of the empirical study summarized here was to provide the first broad-scale data about the personal characteristics, educational experiences, and workplace policies that influence pro bono participation. To that end, some 3,000 detailed questionnaires went to three groups:

lawyers who were graduates of six schools that had different approaches to student pro bono work; recent individual and law firm winners of the American Bar Association's annual Pro Bono Publico Award; and firms for which annual pro bono data are available.

The first group included law school graduates of Yale, the University of Pennsylvania, Fordham, Tulane, Northwestern, and the University of Chicago. All of the schools have had strong clinical programs, but have varied in their approaches to pro bono work. Tulane and the University of Pennsylvania were among the first to require student pro bono service and have consistently invested substantial resources in their programs. Fordham and Yale have strongly encouraged pro bono work, have designated administrators to coordinate such work, and have had high levels of student involvement in public interest organizations. The University of Chicago and Northwestern were identified by the Association of American Law School's Pro Bono Project as schools with resources and student bodies roughly comparable to the others, but without a formal pro bono program or coordinator at the time of the survey. Two schools were selected in each category to minimize idiosyncrasies that might be unique to either institution. A detailed questionnaire went to all the graduates from these schools in the classes of 1993 and 1997. These classes were selected to provide a pool of lawyers who were at different seniority levels, who had been at their workplace long enough to have a good sense of its policies, priorities, and culture, and who included graduates of two law schools that required pro bono service while they were students.

A second group of survey participants included individuals or law firms that received the five annual ABA awards between 1993 and 2000 for outstanding pro bono service. The time period was selected to correspond to the one used for the law school graduates. Individual award winners received the same questionnaire that was sent to these graduates. Firms received a similar questionnaire. Individual recipients were also interviewed by telephone to obtain the fullest possible information from lawyers who had demonstrated exceptional commitment to pro bono work.

A third group of survey participants included firms consistently listed by the *American Lawyer* during the period 1993–2000 as among the nation's one hundred top law firms in terms of gross revenue. These were the only firms for which data on pro bono service were publicly available. Firms that were in the top one hundred for at least four years, ninety-four firms in all, were included in the sample. The same law firm questionnaires used for firm ABA award winners went to the pro bono coordinator or managing partner at those firms.

The survey obviously was not designed to provide a random sample of lawyers or law firms. Rather, the point was to identify groups that could yield useful information about factors most likely to influence pro bono contributions. Although the respondents are not representative of the legal profession, they are either award winners or firm members who are particularly knowledgeable about factors affecting pro bono involvement, or they are part of a law school sample whose experience could be relevant in affecting such involvement. And while any survey relying on self-reports has limitations, the cumulative responses give a more comprehensive picture of pro bono contributions than is currently available.

Some 3,000 individuals and firms received surveys and those who did not respond received two follow-up mailings. Ultimately, 844 returned them, yielding an overall response rate of about 28 percent. This rate is not unusual for large mailed surveys. As with any study yielding this level of response, the margin of error was greater than 3 percent, which means that the data may not be characteristic of the entire population surveyed. Some questions also had a high number of "not applicable" responses, which further increased the margin of error for those inquiries. Survey findings need to be interpreted in light of the non-random nature of the responses. In general, however, biases in this survey's responses are likely to run in a direction that does not unduly limit the overall findings. The lawyers who took time to complete and return the questionnaire are, as noted below, individuals who are exceptionally likely to care about the issues it raised. Since the primary objective of the study was to identify factors that contribute to pro bono service, the most helpful perspectives will be from those who have strong views about such service.[31]

In terms of demographic characteristics, the individual lawyers who responded were roughly similar to other lawyers of the same age, except that women were overrepresented in the sample. Compared to the general American legal profession, the sample had a substantially higher percentage of women, racial and ethnic minorities, associates in law firms, and lawyers not engaged in legal practice. The surveyed lawyers also earned more income, billed more hours, and made substantially greater pro bono contributions than is typical of the profession generally. The average number of pro bono hours per year for responding lawyers was 70. The range was between 255 hours for individual award winners and 37 hours for University of Chicago graduates. Based on the limited data available for the profession generally, the sampled lawyers contributed well over three times as many hours as the national average; the award winners contributed over ten times as many hours. It is less clear whether responding lawyers were also more generous than the bar as a whole in making financial contributions. Of the 180 lawyers who reported contributions to organizations providing legal assistance for persons of limited means, a majority contributed $100 or less; a fifth contributed $101–$200; and 4 percent contributed over $200 annually. Comparable national data are unavailable, but in the few states that compile statistics, the average annual lawyer contributions for roughly the same time period ranged from $32 to $82.[32]

Questionnaire responses that were susceptible to statistical evaluation were analyzed in several ways: percentage calculations, regression analysis, a correlation test (t-test), and a significance test. In each case, the dependent variable, hours of pro bono work, was factored against independent variables such as law school programs, law firm policies, and respondents' demographic characteristics. Each of these independent variables was tested to see if it was correlated positively or negatively with pro bono contributions. The correlations that were identified do not, of course, demonstrate that the independent variable caused an increase or decrease in pro bono work. However, the overall pattern of relationships, together with other data, can cast light on the factors likely to influence pro bono contributions.[33]

Almost none of the factors that responding lawyers or prior research identified as having the greatest influence on pro bono contributions were statistically significant by themselves in predicting pro bono service. That lack of correlation may partly reflect noise in the data, but it may also highlight the interrelationships among forces that affect behavior. As the following analysis suggests, individual characteristics, workplace practices, and educational experiences all play a role that is difficult to disentangle in professional settings.

Motivations for Pro Bono Work

To gauge the relative importance of factors influencing pro bono participation, the questionnaire asked lawyers to rank commonly cited factors on a scale of 1 to 5, with 5 being "very significant" and 1 being "not significant." In general, the rankings that emerged were consistent with other research on altruistic behavior. That research finds that people are motivated both by intrinsic factors, such as personal values and characteristics, and by extrinsic factors such as rewards and reinforcement. For surveyed lawyers, the most commonly emphasized forces driving pro bono participation were intrinsic: the satisfaction that comes from the work (4.2) and a sense of obligation to pursue it (3.7). Of secondary importance were extrinsic factors such as: employer policies (2.7) or encouragement (2.7); and professional benefits such as contacts, referrals, and training (2.7), trial experience (2.5), involvement with clients (2.4), and opportunities for control over the work (2.4). Of slightly less significance were personal characteristics such as political commitment (2.3) or religious commitment (2.1). Awards by employers or bar associations had least importance (1.7). A regression analysis was also performed to determine whether any of the demographic characteristics of respondents were significantly correlated with pro bono work. As is the case with altruistic behavior generally, no such correlations were identified. Race, ethnicity, gender, income, and the importance of religion did not predict involvement. The only factors that were strongly positively correlated were political commitment and employer encouragement.[34]

Some lawyers also volunteered comments about these influences on their pro bono work, as did many of the ABA award winners. The most significant motivations were a commitment to public service and the personal satisfaction that it provided. Some attorneys had gone to law school or had taken a particular job partly out of a desire to be involved in public interest work. For these lawyers, family influences, early volunteer involvement, or personal hardships often instilled a commitment to community service in general or to certain causes in particular. Other attorneys developed interests in law school or through exposure to pro bono programs at their firms. A number of lawyers, mainly Tulane graduates and ABA award winners, expressed a conviction that such work was a "professional obligation" and part of the "price for lawyers' license to practice law."

A much larger group of lawyers, spread across the entire sample, mentioned the rewards of particular kinds of work; examples included death-row criminal appeals, prison suits, sweatshop labor litigation, and political asylum claims. For many of those attorneys, pro bono matters provided their most rewarding professional experiences. As one ABA winner put it, after lawyers leave law school, the "altruistic sense of what the profession is about . . . disappears pretty quickly. Pro bono is a way to get this passion back. This makes you feel alive and like you are doing something worthwhile." Other award winners offered similar views, and some believed that they had benefited more than their clients. One attorney noted, "If I couldn't do pro bono, I wouldn't practice law. It makes me feel like I am making a difference." Lawyers often contrasted their public service with their largely commercial practices, and reported greater satisfaction from promoting social reform or from helping a disadvantaged client than from wrangling over money. Some attorneys found it especially rewarding to work on matters within their field of expertise, such as assisting a nonprofit organization protect its intellectual property. By contrast, others enjoyed the chance to work in areas "not part of daily practice," particularly where the cases involved important constitutional issues or social justice causes. Many lawyers also cited professional benefits from pro bono service. It was often a way to develop expertise in a particular area in which they wanted to practice. Others gained trial experience or community contacts, which sometimes had direct payoffs in obtaining paid work.

Obstacles to Service

Lawyers were also asked about the relative importance of factors limiting pro bono work. Here again, the findings are consistent with more general research on the factors discouraging altruistic behavior. For surveyed lawyers, the most important constraints were workload demands (4.5), family obligations (3.4), and billable hour expectations (3.0). Other factors included employer attitude (2.6), lack of opportunities in their practice area (2.6), lack of expertise (2.4), lack of information about opportunities (2.4), employer bonus policies excluding pro bono work (2.2), lack of interest (2.2), lack of resources (e.g., support staff) (2.2), inconvenient or unpleasant aspects of work (2.1), and lack of malpractice insurance (1.9).[35]

Again, many attorneys' written comments and interview responses amplified these views. Some lawyers, especially those who did not find their legal careers intrinsically satisfying, explicitly denied that pro bono work was a professional responsibility. As one Pennsylvania graduate put it, "I hate practicing law and only do it to pay the bills. I refuse to undertake additional legal work." Other lawyers simply registered their lack of interest in pro bono work or their sense that it was often "pointless," "unnecessary," or unlikely to do much good in the world. One Northwestern graduate noted: "I now realize how elusive the notion of 'social justice' is and have become more selfish—meaning less willing to sacrifice my own well-being in the interest of social justice. . . . I have grown discouraged about anything substantially changing." Even law-yers who did substantial pro bono work cited frustrations inherent in the work as a constraint on involvement. From their perspective, pro bono assistance was an "inadequate band-aid" for social problems. Such dis-illusionment, or a general lack of enthusiasm for legal practice, led these attorneys to prefer investing their volunteer efforts in other nonlegal projects. "Frankly," said one Tulane graduate, these other activities feel "less like work."

Some attorneys cited negative pro bono experiences as the major factor limiting their participation. The work was uninteresting, unim-portant, or emotionally draining, or the clients were unethical, unrea-sonable, or unappreciative. Other lawyers identified their field of prac-tice as the main problem in finding appropriate cases. Attorneys who specialized in areas such as securities law, mergers and acquisitions, or trusts and estates could not find cases matching their expertise, or felt limited to routine "unrewarding" matters like incorporation of nonprofit organizations. So too, lawyers who ventured outside their field some-times ended up with unchallenging cases, particularly where their em-ployers failed to make adequate resources available. In the experience of one Chicago graduate, "Helping people avoid paying credit card bills is what you get in a small firm that doesn't spend millions on [pro bono programs]."

Other attorneys' negative feelings about volunteer work stemmed from client relationships. Some lawyers had represented individuals who seemed to be dishonest or to be "abusing the system." One attorney who handled landlord–tenant cases found that his clients were "usually liable and often have lied in an effort to fashion a defense." Other lawyers believed that because individuals were not paying for the rep-resentation, they did not really value or appreciate the effort involved. In some cases, this attitude led to seemingly unreasonable rejections of settlement offers. Clients reportedly found "no downside to rolling the dice and going to trial."

Finally, some attorneys felt that they simply could not afford to do pro bono work. One partner in a two-person civil rights/criminal de-fense firm already represented many low-income clients on a contingent fee basis. The firm ended up with "a lot of 'de facto' pro bono work" and the partner found it impossible at this point in her career to build the practice, support its staff, and take on additional matters that she knew would be pro bono. Another lawyer, currently "a stay-at-home mother," would "love to do pro bono work" but the malpractice insurance and childcare costs were too great. Many lawyers cited family obligations, coupled with heavy workload pressures, as a primary constraint. One attorney who found it impossible to find time for optional public service when combining 2,400 billable hours a year with a family, added: "*I* need pro bono!" Or at least, as noted below, lawyers in this situation need a policy that counts pro bono work as part of their billable hour quota.

Lawyers with substantial family responsibilities not only had competing demands on their time, they also had greater financial obligations, which pushed them to focus on paying work and client development activities that would generate it. However, the extent to which money mattered in constraining pro bono involvement was a matter of dispute. Some ABA award winners emphasized the need to make financial sacrifices—"to live a pro bono lifestyle"—and acknowledged the cultural pressures pushing in the opposite direction. Others were unconvinced that colleagues' lack of commitment reflected financial constraints. As one award winner put it, "I have clients who make less than $300 [a] month and still give to charity or volunteer their time. I think [lawyers who fail to contribute] enjoy their position of power in society and they don't have an interest in altering it."

In describing their own behavior, attorneys provided a more nuanced portrait. Many cited significant educational debts and the high cost of living in cities like New York as major deterrents to public service. Some lawyers described themselves as "not driven by money," but rather as "realists" about supporting a family, especially if they had multiple educational tuitions to pay or children with special needs. A few interviewees were candid about their own lifestyle desires. As one attorney acknowledged, there are "certain comforts . . . [I don't] want to live without." Yet by the same token, some lawyers, particularly ABA award winners, saw pro bono work as a way to reconcile their economic needs with their service commitments. Although they would have preferred full-time public interest work, a well-paying private-sector job offering pro bono opportunities was the next best alternative.

Taken together, the data collected and reviewed for this study make clear that financial considerations are neither decisive nor unimportant in explaining pro bono contributions. As is true with altruistic behavior generally, economic ability does not determine charitable involvement. Rather, the most powerful influences are a sense of satisfaction and obligation, together with the professional benefits or costs associated with pro bono work. Yet some of these benefits and costs are influenced by external factors, particularly workplace policies. Even seemingly personal motivations, such as the satisfaction that lawyers experience from pro bono involvement, may be in part a function of the opportunities, training, and support that their employers provide or fail to provide. So too, the negative pro bono experiences that some lawyers reported may reflect a mismatch between their interests or expertise and the volunteer options readily available. Certain adverse reactions to clients also may indicate a lack of understanding or "cultural competence" in dealing with low-income individuals. As earlier discussion of law school programs indicated, it can be counterproductive to assign poverty-related work to lawyers who have little appreciation of the life experiences that may cause impoverished clients to distrust their attorneys or assentedly "abuse" the system.[36]

Workplace Policies

Not only could well-designed workplace programs affect satisfaction with pro bono work, they also could reduce the costs of pursuing it. Yet as the survey findings make clear, most programs leave much to be desired. Lawyers were asked a range of questions about employer practices beginning with whether their workplace had a policy concerning pro bono work, and if so, whether such work counted in full or in part toward billable hours. It is both surprising and dispiriting that almost half of employers (47 percent) have no pro bono policy, and only a third (35 percent) have a formal policy. It may not be coincidental that a higher percentage of ABA award winners, about half of both individuals and firms, reported a formal policy. Particularly in large or midsize organizations, lawyers interpreted the absence of a formal policy as an absence of support for pro bono work.

Even more disheartening is the content of formal policies. Only a quarter of the employers fully counted pro bono work toward billable hours. Less than a third counted a certain number of hours (20 percent) or a certain kind of work (10 percent). Such findings are consistent with other recent survey data and signal a priority structure that undermines public service commitments. Many lawyers volunteered comments critical of their employers' failure to credit pro bono work toward billable hour quotas. A common attitude was "do it if you want," but "don't expect to have less 'real' work" and "make sure you've got [your billables] at the end of the year." In effect, pro bono work was permissible only if it occurred "outside the normal work hours." Given what passes for "normal" in many firms, the price of public service is often prohibitive.[37]

Other limitations on pro bono participation arise from workplace practices concerning resources, rewards, and recognition. Only about half of the surveyed workplaces (7%) subsidized all the costs of pro bono matters; another 10 percent provided partial support. Again, award winners had greater access to resources than the sample as a whole; over four-fifths of the individual winners reported full subsidies. A significant number of lawyers volunteered comments clarifying their organization's policy. About half (75/147) indicated that their employer provided no support for pro bono work. A third indicated that some support was available, typically staff time, but that costs, such as fees for experts, were not covered. Some employers provided resources for approved cases, but limited their approval to "small inexpensive matters."

A more pervasive limitation of workplace policies is the effect of pro bono work on promotion and bonus decisions. Only 10 percent of surveyed lawyers indicated that their organizations valued such work as much as billable hours. About a fifth (18%) believed that pro bono contributions were not viewed as important, and almost half felt that they were negatively viewed (44%). Unsurprisingly, award winners were more likely to be in workplaces that valued, or at least did not penalize, public service. Almost three-quarters of the individual winners (73%) and half of the firm award winners (50%) reported that pro bono work was valued as much as paid work.

Again, a substantial number of lawyers wrote comments concerning their employer's treatment of pro bono service. Of these, two-thirds (100/152) indicated that nonpaying work was a negative factor in promotion and bonus decisions. Most lawyers who provided details reported attitudes ranging from active discouragement to not-so-benign neglect. Sometimes the message was explicit. One Tulane graduate was told by a partner that "I was putting myself at risk if I did too much public service work." In other firms, the negative attitude was conveyed through promotion decisions or bonuses that were linked to billable hours and that excluded charitable activities. As one Yale graduate noted, the "overwhelming emphasis" in performance evaluations is "client work [which] makes it difficult to volunteer for unpaid matters." A Chicago graduate similarly observed that "you would never rise to the top on the basis of pro bono work, and a lack of pro bono work wouldn't be counted against you." Some firms were selective in their support. Junior associates were free to work on public interest matters likely to yield generalizable skills; senior associates had no such option.

Over a third of surveyed lawyers noted that their organizations' informal reward structures were at odds with formal policies supporting pro bono work. Some attorneys volunteered comments that were highly critical: firm leaders simply paid "lip service" to pro bono work for purposes of recruiting or self-image; others "encouraged pro bono on the surface but [provided] . . . no incentive to do it." In large firms, a feudal management structure frequently permitted a "disconnect" between the organization's stated policy and the "practical realities" enforced by supervising partners and department heads. In small firms or corporate legal departments, the necessary resources often seemed unavailable. But as some lawyers noted, the key impediment was not so much the organization's size, structure, or financial capacity, as it was the choice to make profits preeminent. Moreover, the economic trends in private practice suggest that these bottom-line priorities are having an increasing impact. Almost half of responding attorneys (46%) believed that recent escalation in salaries and hourly work expectations had caused practitioners to decline pro bono work.

Dissatisfaction with Pro Bono Policies and Practices

These trends are taking a toll on workplace satisfaction. Less than a quarter of surveyed attorneys were very satisfied (22%) with the amount of time that they spent on pro bono work. About a fifth (19%) were somewhat satisfied and a quarter (25%) were neutral. A third of the sample were dissatisfied, about a quarter, somewhat dissatisfied, and about 10 percent very dissatisfied (11%). Satisfaction rates were considerably higher for the method of obtaining pro bono work, but only about a third of the sample (35%) were very satisfied with how they got pro bono work. Another quarter were somewhat satisfied, and the remainder were neutral (29%) or dissatisfied (11%). Again, the award winners were significantly happier with both the amount and method of obtaining pro bono work. Almost half of the individual winners and a third of the firm winners were very satisfied with the amount of time they spent on public service. Even greater numbers, two-thirds of the firm winners (67%), and half of the individual winners, were very satisfied with how they obtained such opportunities.

The Nature of Pro Bono Work

The most common method for obtaining pro bono work was through an employer's pro bono committee or coordinator. About a third of the overall sample (35%) relied on this method. The next most common sources of opportunities were bar association programs (17%), friends (12%), and supervising attorneys (8%). Only a small number took referrals from public interest (4%) or legal services organizations (3%). The patterns were slightly different for award winners who relied less on employer programs and more on other sources. About a hundred lawyers also wrote in responses that identified additional sources of referrals. The most common were court appointments, religious or charitable organizations, law schools, and networking activities. A surprisingly high percentage of lawyers, about half of the overall sample (54%), worked in organizations with no pro bono committee or coordinator to facilitate placements. Yet where such a structure was in place, the vast majority of attorneys believed it was either very effective (38%) or somewhat effective (49%). However, no consensus emerged in response to a follow-up question asking whether, if the respondent's organization had no facilitator, it should appoint one; slightly under half (43%) advocated such a position and slightly over half (56%) did not.

Lawyers' responses concerning the types of work available did, however, make clear the problems that can arise when no well-designed structure exists to screen pro bono opportunities and to handle concerns about what cases qualify. One question asked attorneys how their organizations dealt with matters that might prove objectionable to clients, other lawyers, or the community. Another question asked how satisfied attorneys were with the types of cases that were permitted. A relatively small number of individuals answered these questions. Of those who did, about two-fifths were in organizations that discouraged work likely to advance positions inconsistent with client interests or values. Slightly over a third were in organizations that limited support to cases approved by a committee or coordinator, and about 10 percent encouraged associates to work on cases selected by partners. Only about 10 percent allowed attorneys to take any cases that did not pose conflicts of interests under bar ethical rules. Policies among award winners were more permissive. About four-fifths (83%) of the individual winners and half of the firm winners (50%) reported that attorneys could take any cases that did not involve conflicts of interests; the remainder limited support to matters that had approval from committees or coordinators.

Close to half (43%) of respondents were dissatisfied with the types of cases permitted. None was very satisfied, only 13 percent were somewhat satisfied, and 11 percent were neutral. Almost a third responded "other" and wrote comments identifying significant concerns. One cluster of problems involved matters that lawyers classified as "not truly" pro bono, such as favors for clients or their relatives, or personal legal needs of partners or their families. A related concern involved the use of pro bono resources to subsidize the "pet organizations" of certain partners, particularly when these matters were objectionable to other members of the firm. Some attorneys also identified problems of ideological bias. One Chicago graduate had found no opportunities for "conservative/libertarian" matters. By contrast, a Yale graduate complained that his firm took many "conservative causes but refused to allow associates to take liberal causes." A lawyer working in house felt that his organization supported only projects that would benefit the corporate "image." The problem with these practices is not simply that they skew the allocation of scarce charitable resources. It is also that such preferential treatment can undermine the legitimacy of pro bono programs. That risk is particularly great when the lawyers' self-interests are implicated. As one Tulane graduate observed, "Right now this firm's idea of pro bono is to handle a partner's personal matters for free. It's a joke."

Another frustration with the kinds of pro bono opportunities available emerged from lawyers holding public sector positions. Internal codes of conduct, agency regulations, or conflict of interest legislation often significantly limited the volunteer legal activities that judicial and governmental employees could pursue. For example, the city charter governing one government lawyer required special permission for representation of non-municipal clients. The public defender office policy covering another attorney banned representation involving any outside legal matters. According to a U.S. Department of Justice employee, agency regulations prevented lawyers from litigating nongovernmental cases in their areas of expertise. A further problem for state employees was liability coverage; sovereign immunity protected government lawyers only for their official work, and no malpractice insurance coverage was available for other matters. Yet not all public sector lawyers found such restrictions problematic. For some, like one beleaguered public defender, overwhelming caseload pressures made volunteer service unthinkable; as it was, "there was barely time to breathe at the end of the day, much less . . . do pro bono work." Another public defender felt "all my work is pro bono," a view common among government employees.

As one lawyer noted, "I do feel that being a federal prosecutor is public service and involves some 'pro bono like' work—*i.e.,* I accept a much lower salary."

The Importance of Pro Bono Policies in Career Decisions

However, the number of attorneys holding such public service positions represents a small fraction of the legal profession. For lawyers in most practice settings, the treatment of pro bono activities leaves much to be desired. Yet although many lawyers identify inadequacies in workplace policies, their criticisms have not been sufficiently pervasive or intense to force the necessary changes. Policies on pro bono generally are not a critical factor in influencing surveyed lawyers to choose a particular employer. Only a third of attorneys considered such factors very important (13%) or somewhat important (20%) in their choices of employment. Almost half (44%) indicated that pro bono policies and practices were not important to their decisions, and about a quarter (23%) had no information about these norms at the time of decision. Unsurprisingly, award winners were far more likely to have cared about pro bono issues. Almost half of the individual winners (47%) and four-fifths (80%) of the firm winners considered such policies and practices to have been very or somewhat important in choosing an employer.

The priorities of most attorneys are undoubtedly a major obstacle to improving pro bono programs. Yet the evidence summarized above suggests that many lawyers are underestimating the personal and professional rewards that well-designed programs can provide. If so, the question then becomes how best to educate attorneys about those benefits, and what role law schools can play in that effort.

Law School Pro Bono Programs: An Empirical Analysis

Interest in Pro Bono and Public Interest Work

To determine what effect law school might have on later pro bono activities, the survey asked a range of questions concerning lawyers' career aspirations, educational experiences, and involvement in public interest work while a student. An initial set of inquiries focused on why attorneys had gone to law school, whether their goals had changed during law school, and whether those changes had affected their interest in pro bono or public interest work. In identifying their main career motivations, slightly over half of surveyed lawyers cited a desire for a financially rewarding and secure career (59%). The next most common responses were finding intellectual challenges (52%) and keeping options open (41%). Close to a third of the sample (31%) hoped to promote social justice, and slightly under a third (29%) wanted to prepare for public service. The aspirations of individual award winners were somewhat similar, including the desire for a financially rewarding career (55%). However, a slightly higher proportion were interested in promoting social justice (41%) and a lower proportion were concerned with intellectual challenge (32%).

Less than a third of the overall sample reported that their objectives had changed during law school. Of those who did, a significant number (172) wrote comments indicating a shift in attitudes concerning pro bono or public interest work. Only a fifth (22%) indicated that positive law school experiences had encouraged involvement in pro bono activities. About a third reported that student loans (24%) or an understanding of differential salary levels (8%) had steered them away from public interest work. Another fifth (19%) reported that negative law school experiences had dampened their desire to do pro bono work.

Some lawyers also took the opportunity to elaborate on the law school experiences that had influenced their interest in pro bono service. Of the forty-six lawyers who noted positive effects, a third mentioned law school culture; about a fifth described work or life experiences; and 15 percent cited personal beliefs and values. A smaller number mentioned their opportunities as a student to engage in pro bono or public service work (4%) or financial support for such opportunities (7%). A supportive culture was conveyed through a graduation requirement or the attitudes of faculty and students. The service ethic appeared particularly strong at Yale. A disproportionate number of its graduates cited evidence of the school's support, both "financially and philosophically," through curricular opportunities, public interest placements, and a relatively generous loan forgiveness program.

For the sample as a whole, the most positive specific comments typically focused on clinical experiences, which some graduates singled out as their "best" experience in law school. Other graduates felt similarly about pro bono experiences or did not distinguish between various forms of legal aid work. Favorable assessments emphasized both the educational value of skills training and the personal rewards of assisting clients "desperately in need of legal representation." Graduates liked getting a "taste of what being a real lawyer was . . . like" and the chance for direct client contact, trial experience, negotiation, and drafting briefs. Exposure to the "imperfections of the legal system" and the limitations of the "social safety net" was equally valuable. For some lawyers, the key factor was their own sense of "meaningfully contributing to society" and "making a difference in societal terms." As one Tulane graduate put it, "I helped some children have a better life—what could be more rewarding?"

Many attorneys, however, reported a far less positive experience, both with the law school culture in general and with their clinical or pro bono opportunities in particular. One of the most common complaints was that the majority of faculty showed no serious "interest in or commitment to . . . public service." Many survey participants also criticized their school's inadequate support for clinics; the course opportunities were too limited, the time or credit allotted was insufficient, or the offerings were not "valued or promoted" by the tenured faculty. A second cluster of criticisms involved the perceived elitism or ideological bias of professors, students, and administrators. Criticism came from graduates of all schools and from all points on the political spectrum. Some lawyers felt that their school's predominantly conservative attitudes "undermine[d] ethical values of students." Conversely, other lawyers complained that their institution's pro bono and public interest opportunities had a "liberal agenda" that they did not share, and a few resented the "self-righteous[ness]" or "excessive preachiness" of program proponents. Some graduates also felt that their institution's placement efforts were unduly biased toward private practice and that this orientation negatively influenced attitudes toward public service.

However, many lawyers also acknowledged that these attitudes were only part of a larger set of economic forces that undermined altruistic commitments. About two-thirds (65%) of survey participants agreed that market and financial constraints negatively affected their interest in pro bono and public interest work. Many individuals wrote comments elaborating on the impossibility of taking a public interest job while paying off student loans, supporting a family, or working in a city with a high cost of living. Some lawyers mentioned the effect of these economic factors on pro bono involvement as well. As one Tulane graduate noted, "I have paid back $78,000 in 8 years and still owe $33,000. Why should I do anything for free?"

A final set of negative influences on pro bono and public interest involvement arose from unrewarding clinical or pro bono experiences. The reasons were mixed. Some graduates cited inadequate supervision, support, or training. Others found their clients "unsavory" or undeserving for reasons similar to those arising from the practice experiences described earlier. As one Yale graduate noted, "I did not enjoy helping people who were basically trying to milk the system." Other lawyers, while more sympathetic toward their clients, found it depressing or "emotionally draining" to have such limited impact on systemic injustices or the overwhelming problems facing indigent clients. One graduate who found domestic violence work "unrewarding" explained, "[i]n most situations, a TRO (or maybe any other legal remedy) is a drop in the bucket compared to the woman's needs."

Pro Bono Policies and Support

The lawyers who cited these negative experiences did not, however, indicate whether they occurred in mandatory pro bono programs, voluntary service, or clinical work. In order to gain some sense of the impact of a school's pro bono approach, the survey asked lawyers to describe their institution's policy and its level of support for such programs. On the whole, graduates' characterizations of their school's policies were consistent with the three main approaches that the survey sought to assess: a pro bono requirement; a very strong voluntary program; and a less developed support structure. About four-fifths (83%) of the Tulane and Pennsylvania graduates recalled a requirement and four-fifths (83%) of the Yale and Fordham graduates recalled strong encouragement for pro bono activities. Only half (55%) of the Northwestern and Chicago graduates remembered strong encouragement and 40 percent remembered merely lip service or limited encouragement. It is, however, sobering that a significant number of graduates either did not recall their school's pro bono requirement (17% of the Tulane and Pennsylvania graduates) or believed erroneously that they had been subject to one (8% of Yale and Fordham graduates; 2% of Northwestern and Chicago graduates).

It also bears note that regression analysis revealed no significant correlation between law school policies and subsequent pro bono work. Although, as noted earlier, students in other surveys generally believe that law school pro bono experiences have increased the likelihood of continued contributions, this study fails to confirm that belief. Such a result is not entirely surprising, given the research on volunteer activity summarized above, as well as the factors that lawyers themselves report as most important in influencing pro bono work. Personal values and the costs and rewards of pro bono involvement in particular practice settings are likely to be more important than law school policies. While a positive student experience with public interest work can have a significant impact, such an experience need not come from a pro bono placement. Nor does a pro bono requirement insure a positive experience.

Although the vast majority of graduates reported that their schools required (37%) or strongly encouraged (51%) pro bono work, the responses to specific questions suggest substantial room for improvement. For example, less than a third of the graduates believed that their institution provided financial support for student pro bono activities. Only 1 percent reported that pro bono issues received coverage in orientation programs or professional responsibility courses. None of the graduates of schools with pro bono requirements recalled the subject arising in such courses. Only 3 percent of graduates observed a visible faculty commitment or felt that their schools provided adequate clinical opportunities for public interest work. And none of the graduates reported awards for outstanding pro bono contributions, externship programs with adequate public interest placements, or visible support by deans and administrators for public interest work. In the absence of such tangible forms of support, it is not clear what caused so many graduates to believe that their school strongly encouraged pro bono service.

Nor is it clear whether a pro bono requirement is the most effective way for a school to promote public service. Much may depend on the nature of the program and the institutional culture. Tulane graduates voiced almost no objection to mandatory service and many cited valuable experiences. By contrast, most Pennsylvania graduates who volunteered comments were highly critical, perhaps in part because the requirement was substantially greater (70 versus 20 hours). Typical observations included:

- A horrible experience, really embittered me about law firms and pro bono.
- It's a politically correct form of indentured servitude. The forced pro bono placement was an awful experience. Everyone seemed to hate feeling forced into it.
- Compulsory involuntary servitude . . . cheapened the experience and bred resentment.
- [T]he majority [of my classmates] found the requirement burdensome and a nuisance.

A smaller number of graduates voiced objections not to the requirement but to the way that it was implemented. According to some critics, a "broader spectrum of assignments" rather than the coordinator's "pet political causes" would help. Another graduate felt that grades were necessary: "Otherwise students will just blow it off. . . ."

How widely these perspectives were shared is impossible to assess. Such attitudes did not translate into lower rates of pro bono involvement after graduation; the average for Pennsylvania graduates was substantially higher (174 hours) than that of the sample as a whole (70 hours). Moreover, as noted earlier, most administrators of pro bono requirements do not believe that student resistance is a major problem. But neither is it clear how much hard evidence they have for that perception, how much unvoiced resentment is present, or how reluctant students ultimately respond to their experience. While this study cannot answer those questions, it does supply data on lawyers' perceptions of strategies that could improve pro bono programs in both law schools and legal workplaces.

An Agenda for Reform: Connecting Principles to Practice

The survey gave lawyers an opportunity to indicate whether there was anything their organization could do to encourage more pro bono work and what if any changes they would recommend in law school pro bono programs. Of 277 responses to the question about workplaces, about 15 percent thought that nothing much could be done. The most common reform proposal, cited by over a quarter of lawyers, involved modifying policies toward billable hours, either by reducing the amount of billable time required or by counting public service equally towards hourly requirements. About a fifth of the responding lawyers suggested other changes in organizational policies (12%) or reward structures (7%). Proposed reforms included adopting formal policies, counting pro bono work favorably in promotion decisions, or making it more prestigious. Smaller numbers of attorneys recommended a requirement or very strong encouragement of pro bono work (5%); a more active role for pro bono committees or coordinators (5%); more opportunities for corporate lawyers (4%); increased enthusiasm by partners (2%); and better use of local resources such as bar organizations or court-appointment programs (2%).

Many survey participants also volunteered comments about the role of legal education in encouraging pro bono. Of the 247 lawyers who responded, two-thirds were largely satisfied with their law school's program. The most common proposed change, cited by a quarter of responding lawyers, was greater financial support for pro bono and public interest work, including resources for additional placement opportunities, expanded summer funding, and more generous loan forgiveness policies. Another 10 percent advocated a change in attitudes, such as more recognition for pro bono work, greater enthusiasm for such service among faculty, and expanded outreach to students who were not planning full-time public interest careers. Smaller numbers of graduates proposed a pro bono requirement (6%); less ideological bias in placements (4%); increased service opportunities (2%); more support from career services offices (2%); or less emphasis on pro bono work (2%).

Taken together, the survey findings underscore several key points about the influences on pro bono commitments. Most of the critical factors—the rewards of service, a sense of professional obligation, and workplace practices—are themselves subject to influence. Well-designed programs of employers, law schools, and bar associations can increase the likelihood and quality of pro bono contributions. The challenge is how to make such programs a priority. An effective effort to institutionalize ideals of public service will require strategies along two main lines. One set of initiatives should increase the incentives for lawyers, legal employers, and legal educators to translate pro bono principles into practice. A second set of strategies should focus on making pro bono opportunities more accessible and successful for both providers and recipients of services. Both reform efforts will require greater collaboration among the judiciary, the organized bar, the law schools, and the public interest community.

Reporting Obligations

A first step in expanding pro bono participation is to increase its visibility. Better information is needed about the extent (or lack) of public service by lawyers, legal employers, law faculty, and law students. One obvious option is to require lawyers and legal employers to report their contributions of time or money to organizations assisting persons of limited means and nonprofit legal organizations. Since Florida established a pro bono reporting system, the number of volunteer hours and the amount of financial contributions have grown substantially. Efforts to increase reporting by law firms on their recruitment and retention of minority lawyers have similarly improved performance, particularly after large corporate clients began considering firms' diversity as a basis for selecting outside counsel. If more private and public sector clients considered pro bono commitments, significant progress might result. Organizations that purchase substantial amounts of legal work could also make pro bono contributions a condition of retainer agreements. For example, California recently passed legislation requiring such a condition in state contracts for legal services that exceed $50,000. Such contracts obligate contracting firms to "make a good faith effort to provide, during the duration of the contract, a minimum number of hours of pro bono legal services. . . . Failure to make a good effort may be cause for non-renewal of a state contract for legal services and may be taken into account when determining the award of future contracts. . . ." Some California municipalities impose similar requirements.[38]

Further pro bono incentives could come from law schools, bar associations, and other legal organizations. Law schools could, for example, require legal employers who use their placement facilities to disclose their pro bono policies and the average number of hours annually contributed by their members. Such information could assist law students in making pro bono opportunities part of their decision in selecting employment. National groups, such as the AALS Section on Pro Bono and Public Service Opportunities, the National Association for Law Placement, or the ABA Standing Committee on Pro Bono and Public Service could also publish directories with information concerning employers' pro bono policies and contributions.

Best Practices

Such organizations could also develop best practices for pro bono work and publicize lists of employers who certify that they are in compliance. These practices, based on the research summarized above, could include:

- adoption of a formal pro bono policy;
- visible commitment by the organization's leadership;
- credit for pro bono work toward billable hour requirements;
- consideration of pro bono service as a favorable factor in performance evaluations and in promotion and compensation decisions;
- recognition and showcasing of service;
- efforts to emphasize the personal and professional benefits of service;

- establishment of a pro bono coordinator to develop opportunities, to match participants with appropriate placements, and to insure adequate training, supervision, and performance;
- compliance with the Law Firm Pro Bono Challenge of 3 or 5 percent of billable hours or the ABA Model Rules standard of fifty hours per lawyer per year or the financial equivalent.

Analogous reporting requirements and best practice standards could also be developed for law schools. Although ABA accreditation standards require schools to provide appropriate pro bono service opportunities for students and to encourage service by faculty, many institutions neither keep nor disclose specific information concerning participation rates. Such information, or compliance with minimum standards, could be required as part of the accreditation process or as a condition for AALS membership. Schools that met best practice standards could also be given recognition in publications of the AALS, ABA, and other lawyers' organizations, as well as in rankings like those by *U.S. News and World Report*. Findings from this survey and from the AALS Pro Bono Project suggest that appropriate practices could include:

- a formal policy concerning pro bono work by students and professors;
- institutional support from faculty, administrators, and deans;
- an independent program with adequate staff and service opportunities;
- structures for insuring appropriate supervision and quality control;
- adequate funding for curricular development, summer placements, and program expenses;
- involvement of students in developing service opportunities and in recruiting fellow classmates;
- recognition of service through pro bono awards, notations on transcripts, and showcasing of student, faculty, and alumni projects in publications and special events;
- curricular integration of materials concerning access to justice and pro bono service in professional responsibility courses, orientation programs, and core courses;
- a program that makes available at least one significant well-supervised pro bono opportunity for every student and that involves the vast majority of students;

- pro bono contributions by faculty at levels established by the appliable rules of professional conduct;
- favorable consideration of pro bono work in faculty promotion and tenure decisions.

The message that public service is a professional responsibility needs to be reinforced not only in pro bono programs but also throughout the law school culture. Basic courses can include discussion of prominent pro bono cases and projects; ethics professors can offer credit to students who design service opportunities for their law school or postgraduate workplace; placement offices can showcase firms that comply with best practice standards; and deans can highlight pro bono work in their communications with students, faculty, and alumni.

So too, the bar, the judiciary, and the law schools need to work together to develop more effective, coordinated plans to expand pro bono participation. In some jurisdictions, impressive progress has occurred through law firm pledge drives spearheaded by prominent judges, and law school pledge drives organized by students. In other jurisdictions, representatives from the bench, the bar, and the legal academy have formed regional groups to identify program needs and a strategy for meeting them. One example is the Minnesota Justice Foundation, which coordinates placements for law students from several Minneapolis schools. Another approach is the pro bono program established by a consortium of New York law firms to provide holistic legal assistance related to the 9/11 terrorist attacks. Such initiatives could serve as models for other states.[39]

Pro Bono Requirements

Whether courts, bar associations, or law schools should take the further step of requiring pro bono contributions is a closer question. As earlier discussion suggested, mandating some modest contribution of services or financial support from practicing lawyers seems justifiable in principle. Without further experience and evaluation, it is impossible to know how effective such requirements would prove in practice. At the very least, they could assist lawyers who are interested in pro bono work, but are in organizations that fail to support it. In the current political climate, however, which lacks broad-based support for mandatory service, a prudent alternative would be to focus on strengthening voluntary initiatives and on obligating lawyers to report their contributions.

Similar points could be made concerning law schools. Findings from this research provide a strong educational justification for exposing students to Americans' unmet legal needs, the profession's responsibility to address them, and the personal rewards of doing so. But this survey's results do not demonstrate that pro bono requirements are necessarily more effective in accomplishing those objectives than well-designed voluntary programs, coupled with strong institutional support and ample clinical opportunities. The main advantages of a requirement are that it conveys a message about professional responsibility and that it forces schools to invest resources in developing service opportunities. Yet the success of mandatory programs can be compromised if the number of hours is too limited or too demanding, if the range of options is too narrow, if the quality of placements is inadequate, if supervision or preparation is insufficient, or if the importance of involvement is not reinforced throughout the educational experience. The ultimate objective should be to institutionalize the best practices noted above, however that can be achieved in a particular law school context.

Expanded Opportunities and Resources

Related strategies should focus on making public service opportunities more available, attractive, and effective. One possibility is to target particular groups of attorneys whose services have been underutilized. Obvious examples include transactional lawyers, in-house counsel, government lawyers, legal academics, retired lawyers, and lawyers in American firms abroad. Restrictions on pro bono work by public servants should be eased and special opportunities should be developed to avoid conflicts of interest. Greater efforts should be made to enlist law faculty as experts, consultants, or cooperating attorneys in their fields of expertise. Legal employers should offer more sabbatical and part-time pro bono programs in order to recruit and retain talented, socially committed lawyers. Such programs could also help law firms cope with short-term economic downturns. Rather than permanently laying off associates and incurring the substantial recruitment and retraining expenses of hiring replacements when the demand for work increases, a growing number of firms allow underutilized attorneys to pursue pro bono work. Further efforts should focus on marketing this approach as a profitable as well as charitable initiative.[40]

Other strategies for strengthening pro bono programs involve improving support structures. More website matching services could alert potential volunteers to specific project needs and offer comprehensive educational materials. More bar associations could offer back-up assistance for inexperienced volunteers, free malpractice insurance for lawyers who otherwise would lack coverage, and continuing legal education credit for pro bono training. Greater attention could focus on increasing attorneys' sensitivity in dealing with clients of a different class, race, or ethnicity. More courts could make special accommodations for pro bono cases, such as giving these cases priority on their dockets and permitting telephone conference calls in lieu of time-consuming personal appearances.[41]

Finally, pro bono initiatives need additional sources of funding. Even when lawyers' assistance is free, their recruitment, training, and back-up support are not. If the bar remains unwilling to require financial contributions as an alternative to personal assistance, other funding possibilities merit consideration. For example, courts could increase user fees for cases involving a substantial amount in controversy. Law firms could establish pro bono funds with expected financial contribution levels from lawyers who do not devote time to public interest legal work. Legislatures could impose a tax on legal revenues above a certain minimum. Whatever the strategy, the objective should be to insure a closer match between the profession's resources and rhetoric concerning pro bono service.[42]

This is not a modest agenda. But there can be no higher priority. Pro bono service reflects all that is best in the legal profession. In a celebrated 1886 Harvard address, Oliver Wendell Holmes submitted that those who have the souls of idealists "will make—I do not say find—[their] world ideal." Those who believe in pro bono service can make a professional culture that will sustain it.

≗8 ≗

A ROADMAP FOR REFORM

Equal justice . . . has been the dream of the philosopher, the aim of the lawgiver, the endeavor of the judge, the ultimate test of every government and every civilization.
—CHIEF JUSTICE WINSLOW, *Supreme Court of Wisconsin, 1912*

The ideal of equal justice is deeply embedded in American legal traditions and routinely violated in daily legal practices. Our nation prides itself on its commitment to the rule of law, but prices it out of reach of the vast majority of its citizens. We have the world's highest concentration of lawyers, but one of the least accessible systems of legal services. Our Constitution guarantees "effective assistance of counsel" in criminal cases, but what can satisfy that standard is a national disgrace. Court-appointed lawyers for the poor are not required to have any experience or expertise in criminal defense; they do not even have to be awake. In civil matters, the law is least available to those who need it most. And primary control over the legal process rests with the profession that has the least stake in reducing its expense.

At the most fundamental level, the problem involves a mismatch between what the public needs and what the system of justice delivers. Americans generally want legal services and dispute resolution procedures that are fair, efficient, and affordable. For most individuals, the current system falls well short. At a minimum, procedural fairness requires opportunities for meaningful participation before a neutral tribunal. That, in turn, typically requires access to some form of competent legal assistance. Those who need but cannot realistically afford lawyers should have opportunities for government-subsidized services. And all individuals should have access to affordable self-help assistance for routine matters. For problems that cannot be resolved informally, parties should have an adjudicative structure that offers timely, equitable, and cost-effective remedies.

The preceding chapters have explored all the ways that the American justice system fails to achieve these objectives and have identified the necessary policy correctives. What follows is an overview of that agenda for reform. The point is to chart the changes that are most needed in legal services and legal processes.

Government Funding and Bar Pro Bono Contributions

Money may not be the root of all evil in our justice system, but a lack of money is surely responsible for much of it. Most programs that assist the poor in civil and criminal matters are starved for resources. Americans do not believe that justice should be for sale, but neither do they want to pay for the alternative. Less than 1 percent of the nation's expenditures on legal services goes to civil legal assistance for the poor. And less than 3 percent of its law enforcement budget supports indigent legal defense. America spends only about two dollars per person on civil legal aid for the one-seventh of its population that is eligible. That funding level is one-sixth to one-fifteenth of that of other countries with comparable legal systems like Canada, Australia, and Great Britain. Criminal defense programs average only an eighth of resources available to the prosecution, and their lawyers sometimes must juggle over a thousand felony matters a year. The fees available for court-appointed counsel are capped at rates that make adequate preparation a financial impossibility.

At these funding levels, not much due process is available. In principle, America is deeply committed to individual rights. In practice, few Americans can afford to enforce them. Over 90 percent of indigent criminal defendants plead guilty without trial, typically before any significant effort is made to investigate their case. Civil legal aid programs operate with similarly crushing caseloads, and an estimated four-fifths of the individual needs of the poor remain unmet. Those estimates do not include millions of Americans of limited means who are above financial eligibility limits but who cannot afford lawyers. Nor do the estimates encompass collective problems such as discrimination in school funding systems or environmental hazards that legal challenges could help address.

The inadequacy of financial support is compounded by restrictions on the kinds of cases and clients that government-funded programs may handle. Politically vulnerable groups that are most in need of legal assistance are least likely to receive it. Excluded from coverage are matters such as those involving prisoners' rights, school desegregation, and undocumented aliens. Legal services organizations that receive federal subsidies are also barred from activities such as lobbying, community organizing, or class action litigation. Yet these are the very strategies that are most likely to help poor communities help themselves, and to address the root causes of poverty, rather than its symptoms.

Part of the problem is the lack of public understanding of how bad the problem is. As chapter 1 noted, about four-fifths of Americans believe, incorrectly, that the poor are entitled to counsel in civil cases. Only a third think that low-income individuals would have a very difficult time obtaining assistance. Most people have no sense of the long waits and limited services that result from chronic underfunding of legal services. Nor are Americans adequately informed about the assembly-line pleas and incompetent lawyering that are routine occurrences in indigent criminal defense. Public perceptions are shaped by well-publicized cases and fictional screenplays in which zealous advocacy is the norm. But a wide gap remains between law in prime time and law in real time, and few well-informed individuals would willingly trust their lives and liberty to a typical court-appointed counsel system.

Expanded Funding and Eligibility for Aid

The prescriptions follow obviously from the diagnosis. The government needs to expand its sources of funding for civil and criminal legal assistance and expand the groups that are eligible for services. Many European and British Commonwealth countries have systems that merit consideration. Typically, they allocate aid on a sliding scale so that individuals of limited means can receive at least partially subsidized services. Rather than excluding broad categories of unpopular causes and clients, other countries focus on the merits of the claim. Does the individual have a reasonable probability of success? What would be the likely benefits of providing aid and the harms of withholding it? Similar tests could be adapted for civil matters in this country. In criminal cases, all jurisdictions should aim for what bar commissions recommend: comparable resources for defense and prosecution. Statutory fees should permit a reasonable hourly rate for adequate preparation, and caseloads should not exceed bar guidelines for competent representation.

The costs of such a system would scarcely be prohibitive. Tripling the annual federal budget for civil legal services would cost less than a billion dollars. For a nation that has spent over $160 billion to safeguard the rule of law in Iraq, a modest additional investment in the rule of law at home should not be unthinkable. There are, moreover, ways to expand legal assistance budgets that would be more politically palatable than tapping general tax revenues. Examples include a surcharge on lawyers' gross revenues or on court filing fees. Many states already set aside a small percentage of those fees for legal services. Increasing the surcharge, at least for cases involving substantial sums, would be a relatively painless and progressive way to expand access to justice.[1]

Pro Bono Service

More pro bono assistance from the bar would serve similar ends. As chapter 7 noted, although some lawyers are extraordinarily generous, the average pro bono contribution for the profession as a whole is shamefully inadequate: less than half an hour a week and half a dollar a day. Moreover, much of the work that passes for pro bono does not assist the poor. Only about 10 percent of lawyers accept referrals from legal services or bar-sponsored programs for low-income groups. What attorneys define as "pro bono" often ends up benefiting relatives, friends, or clients who fail to pay their bills. The inadequacy of bar involvement in public service reflects a missed opportunity for both the profession and the public. Lawyers' pro bono work has made a major contribution not only to poverty law programs, but also to every important social justice movement of the last half century. And attorneys themselves benefit, both individually and collectively, from participation in public service. It can enhance their skills, contacts, reputation, and psychological well-being, as well as lawyers' public image.

The profession could do much more to promote pro bono work and the values that it serves. The most obvious strategy is for courts or bar ethical codes to require some modest contribution to legal aid or public interest programs. Resistance to such requirements might be reduced by providing a broad array of service opportunities, along with training and back-up assistance, and by allowing financial contributions as a substitute for direct assistance. Even if skeptics were correct that rules mandating pro bono work would be difficult to enforce, the benefits might still be substantial. At the very least, these requirements would support the many lawyers who would like more pro bono involvement, but who are in workplaces that fail to provide adequate resources or credit for such work. A less controversial alternative would be to require that lawyers report the contributions that they make to legal aid and public interest causes. Experience to date indicates that such reporting rules have led to modest increases in the resources available to poverty law organizations. Further improvements might result if contribution rates were widely publicized, and if clients and job candidates began paying more visible attention to employers' pro bono records.

Even without changes in the rules governing pro bono work, a wide range of strategies are available to encourage charitable commitment. Legal employers and legal educators can adopt formal policies, impose service requirements, and provide greater resources, rewards, and recognition for pro bono activities. Law schools could themselves be subject to reporting obligations concerning the public service contributions of their students and faculty. The ABA and AALS also could request such information as part of their accreditation and membership review processes. These organizations also could encourage specified best practices concerning law school pro bono programs or help other groups develop such standards and monitor compliance. It is a disgrace that most law students now graduate without a pro bono legal experience and that most surveyed lawyers report inadequate workplace support for pro bono involvement. The profession can and must do more to institutionalize its public service commitments.

Structural Changes in Dispute Resolution and the Delivery of Legal Services

A second cluster of strategies should focus on structural changes that would improve the functioning of dispute resolution processes and the delivery of legal services. Access to law is not an end in itself; the goal is justice, and formal proceedings or representation by lawyers is not always the most effective way of addressing legal concerns. Most individuals prefer to resolve law-related problems directly in out-of-court settings, so one objective of reform should be to promote more informal dispute resolution processes. For example, businesses and workplaces over a certain size could be required to establish grievance procedures that meet minimum standards of fairness.

Civil courts should also redesign their own processes to reduce costs and increase accessibility. In most states, small claims courts are too limited in jurisdiction, hours, location, and enforcement power, and assistance for self-represented litigants in these and other proceedings is inadequate at best. The tort system is inconsistent and inefficient; relatively few accident victims can afford it, and 50 to 60 percent of the payouts by defendant insurance companies end up compensating lawyers. In other contexts, particularly those involving families and petty offenses, overburdened trial courts lack the time, resources, and remedial options to address the underlying problems. Alternative models are readily available. A growing number of judicial systems offer more accessible and equitable processes. Necessary innovations include: on-line or automated document preparation services; personalized multilingual help for pro se litigants; simplified forms and procedures; evening hours and community sites for hearings and legal assistance; expanded jurisdiction for small claims courts; specialized no-fault compensation systems in areas like medical malpractice and automobile accidents; and collaborative problem-solving tribunals that partner with other social service providers.

Comparable innovations are necessary for the delivery of legal services. In essence, Americans need a wider range of choices in law-related assistance and better regulation of the choices that are available. Less protection should be available for the professional monopoly and more for individual consumers. Sweeping prohibitions on the unauthorized practice of law, multidisciplinary partnerships (MDPs), and lay ownership of organizations providing legal services should be more narrowly tailored to further the public's rather than the profession's interest. As chapter 4 noted, other nations generally permit nonlawyers to give legal advice, and no evidence suggests that their performance has been unacceptable. So too, research in this country finds that lay experts typically can provide at least as effective routine services as attorneys. Consumers need protection from unethical or incompetent practitioners, but states could meet this need through licensing or certification systems. The level of oversight should depend on lay specialists' ability to provide adequate assistance, the seriousness of harm if they do not, and the public's ability to assess providers' qualifications and remedy any deficiencies in their performance. Nonlawyers also could be held to the same ethical standards as lawyers concerning competence, confidentiality, and conflicts of interest, and could be required to carry malpractice insurance or contribute to client security funds.

So too, the concerns underlying bans on multidisciplinary partnerships and lay ownership should be addressed by rules protecting the independent disinterested judgment of lawyers. That is not to discount the difficulties that may arise in enforcing such rules, but the current structure of sweeping anticompetitive prohibitions is scarcely preferable. Unless and until serious abuses arise, consumers would be best served by access to professional services that cut across disciplinary boundaries and by greater competition in the financing and management of legal services. Here again, the experience of other European nations is instructive. They permit multidisciplinary partnerships, and these organizations now dominate the global legal market. Compared with traditional law firms, the MDPs owned by accountants offer a wider range of services, more economies of scale, and greater managerial and marketing expertise. Americans deserve access to similar arrangements, and the bar's own interests in restricting competition should not stand in the way.

Nor does the profession need to wait for changes in ethical rules in order to promote effective collaborative relationships and marketing structures. More lawyers and legal aid programs can develop strategic alliances with other professionals in order to share clients, capital, and expertise. Greater efforts can also focus on targeting low-cost services to consumers of limited means. Better design of group legal insurance, further development and regulation of on-line legal assistance, and increased support for networks of solo and small firm practitioners all could make justice more affordable for millions of Americans.

Accountability

A final set of strategies should focus on increasing the accountability of the legal profession and the legal process. More oversight is necessary both for individual lawyers and for the systems that structure their services. Courts and bar disciplinary agencies should impose more frequent and significant sanctions for frivolous claims, excessive fees, and incompetent representation. National data banks should provide ready access to information about such sanctions and other performance-related factors. Standards governing ineffective assistance of counsel in criminal cases also must be strengthened. It is appalling that courts allow cases to proceed when counsel are drunk, dozing, or demonstrably ignorant of the relevant law or facts. It is more appalling still that convictions are upheld under such circumstances, even in capital proceedings. Defendants should not have to prove their innocence in order to establish ineffective assistance. It should be enough to establish the likelihood that competent representation would have yielded a significantly better outcome.

Courts and legislatures must also assume greater responsibility to ensure effective systems for funding and regulating legal services for the poor. In civil cases, courts should be more willing to appoint counsel where fundamental rights and substantial due process concerns are at issue. The judiciary should also be more willing to strike down restrictions on government-subsidized services that seriously compromise the quality of assistance, such as prohibitions on class actions or statutory fee awards. In criminal cases, courts should demand a funding structure that insures adequate compensation and resources for indigent defense lawyers, and an independent oversight body to monitor their appointment and performance. That body should insure that counsel have appropriate qualifications, that their representation meets minimum quality standards, and that judges do not use their appointment power to reward campaign contributors or to punish zealous advocates. Public defender offices and civil legal-aid programs should also enforce performance standards and should work with other groups to improve delivery structures.

Government funders, bar associations, legal service providers, and academic researchers should all join forces in compiling greater information concerning access to justice. For example, we need to know more about the effectiveness of specific strategies involving indigent representation, self-help assistance, alternative dispute resolution, and pro bono programs. Better data are necessary concerning objective outcomes, client perceptions, and community impact. Only through more comprehensive evaluation can policymakers develop appropriate resource priorities and strategies for improvement.

Finally, we need more public and professional education about access to justice. On many crucial issues, most Americans are uninformed or misinformed. Few members of the general public have any sense of how civil and criminal assistance actually functions. Fewer still see enough reason to care. Even lawyers are often ill-informed about the unmet legal needs of middle and low-income Americans and the strategies necessary to address them. Part of the reason is that most law schools do little to include such topics in their core curricula. That only 1 percent of surveyed lawyers recall any coverage of pro bono issues in their courses on professional responsibility speaks for itself about the professional irresponsibility of legal educators.

Here again, we do not lack for promising alternatives. The Association of American Law Schools' "Equal Justice" Project and its Handbook on Law School Pro Bono Programs offer a wealth of information concerning curricular coverage and public service initiatives. Law school faculty also have a wide range of options for promoting access to justice through research, teaching, public education, and public service. Their involvement in such activities needs stronger encouragement in practice as well as principle. Legal education plays an important role in socializing the next generation of lawyers, judges, and public policymakers. As gatekeepers to the profession, law schools have a unique opportunity and obligation to make access to justice a more central social priority.[2]

The Politics of Progress

The reforms proposed throughout this volume constitute a more than modest agenda. They will require fundamental changes in the funding and structure of legal services. And substantial obstacles stand in the way. Public opinion surveys consistently find that the vast majority of Americans, while dissatisfied with the delays and expense of the current justice system, still believe that it is the best in the world. Although the vast majority also agree that wealth affects the quality of justice that a litigant receives, they have little idea of the strategies that could reduce that influence. Neither policymakers nor the public know much about how other countries encourage access to justice and what international practices could be profitably adapted for our own system. Those who suffer most from current policies are least able to affect them. The poor, who lack adequate law-related assistance, also lack leverage in legislative and judicial decision making. Primary control over the delivery of services and dispute resolution processes rests with the legal profession, which is anything but disinterested in the outcome, and which typically dwarfs its organized opposition. HALT, the only national consumer group that focuses on reforms of the legal profession and access to justice, has a membership of under 50,000 and an annual budget of only about $500,000. By contrast, the ABA has some 400,000 members, a budget of about $90 million, and powerful alliances with state and local bar associations. As a result, on matters affecting price and competition in the delivery of legal services, the profession has played a dominant role, and one that has often served its own interests at the expense of the public. For the organized bar, the stakes are money, status, and control. For elected judges, the concerns include moving cases, controlling costs, and maintaining lawyers' cooperation and campaign support. Many key participants in the justice system see too much to lose and too little to gain from any fundamental reform.[3]

Yet powerful forces are also pushing in progressive directions. Technological innovations are equipping an increasing number of Americans to solve their own legal problems directly, and they are impatient with the obstacles that stand in the way. Well-publicized abuses have heightened concern about frivolous litigation, excessive fees, and incompetent death penalty representation. Public dissatisfaction with lawyers and legal processes is increasingly visible, and public image ranks high among the bar's own concerns. At last count, Google recorded some 800,000 legal humor sites, and their frequently unflattering content underscores the need for reform. A growing number of responses have been forthcoming. Over the last decade, about three-quarters of the states have formed some official body concerned with access to justice. These bodies have begun to build the collaborative partnerships and public support that are necessary for effective reform. The prospects for significant change have never been more promising.[4]

These reform efforts are deeply rooted in American ideals. Our national pledge of allegiance affirms a faith in one nation, indivisible, with "liberty and justice for all." The challenge remaining is to make good on that commitment and to reconnect our fundamental principles with our legal practices.

⩵ NOTES ⩵

Chapter 1

1. For unmet needs of the poor, see LEGAL SERVICES CORPORATION, SERVING THE CIVIL LEGAL NEEDS OF LOW-INCOME AMERICANS: A SPECIAL REPORT TO CONGRESS 12 (2000); Alan W. Houseman, *Civil Legal Assistance for the Twenty-First Century: Achieving Equal Justice for All*, 17 YALE LAW & POLICY REVIEW 369, 402 (1998); Robert J. Rhudy, *Comparing Legal Services to the Poor in the United States with Other Western Countries: Some Preliminary Lessons*, 5 MARYLAND JOURNAL OF CONTEMPORARY LEGAL ISSUES 223, 224 (1994). For unmet needs of middle-income consumers, see ABA CONSORTIUM ON LEGAL SERVICES AND THE PUBLIC, AGENDA FOR ACCESS: THE AMERICAN PEOPLE AND CIVIL JUSTICE (1996); ABA CONSORTIUM ON LEGAL SERVICES AND THE PUBLIC, LEGAL NEEDS AND CIVIL JUSTICE: A SURVEY OF AMERICANS (1994); and ROY W. REESE & CAROLYN A. ALDRED, ABA, LEGAL NEEDS AMONG LOW-INCOME AND MODERATE-INCOME HOUSEHOLDS: SUMMARY OF FINDINGS FOR THE COMPREHENSIVE LEGAL NEEDS STUDY (1995). *See also* CALIFORNIA COMMISSION ON ACCESS TO JUSTICE, THE PATH TO EQUAL JUSTICE (2002) (estimating that almost three-quarters of the needs of California poor are unmet).

2. *See* the text accompanying note 25 and chapter 5 *infra*.

3. *See* the text accompanying notes 20, 21, and 24, and chapter 6 *infra*; Stephen B. Bright, *Sleeping on the Job*, NATIONAL LAW JOURNAL, December 4, 2000, at A26.

4. For perceptions concerning wealth, comparisons with other systems, and the ability of the poor to obtain counsel, see AMERICAN BAR ASSOCIATION, PERCEPTION OF THE U.S. JUSTICE SYSTEM 51, 59, 63, 65–66 (Chicago: American Bar Association, 1999). For similar perceptions concerning wealth, see Marc Galanter, *Farther Along*, 33 LAW AND SOCIETY REVIEW 1113 (1999). For assumptions about the entitlement to counsel, see ACCESS TO JUSTICE WORKING GROUP, REPORT TO THE STATE BAR OF CALIFORNIA 4–6 (1996); Earl Johnson, Jr., *Toward*

Equal Justice: Where the United States Stands Two Decades Later, 5 MARYLAND JOURNAL OF CONTEMPORARY LEGAL ISSUES 199 (1994). For the representation of the poor, see Paul R. Tremblay, *Aiding a Very Moral Type of God: Triage among Poor Clients*, 67 FORDHAM LAW REVIEW 2475, 2481–82 (1995).

5. Ron Ostroff, *Missouri Remains Unable to Pay Indigents' Counsel: Pro Bono Revolt Grows*, NATIONAL LAW JOURNAL, May 11, 1981, at 2.

6. *See* Geoffrey Hazard, Jr., *After Legal Aid is Abolished*, 2 JOURNAL OF THE INSTITUTE FOR THE STUDY OF LEGAL ETHICS 375, 386 (1999); Stephen Pepper, *Access to What?*, 2 JOURNAL OF THE INSTITUTE FOR THE STUDY OF LEGAL ETHICS 269, 272 (1999).

7. R. H. TAWNEY, EQUALITY 103 (London: Unwin Books, 1964).

8. For civil legal aid expenditures, see Alan W. Houseman, *Civil Legal Assistance for Low-Income Persons: Looking Back and Looking Forward*, 29 FORDHAM URBAN LAW JOURNAL 1213, 1233 (2002); Rhudy, *Comparing Legal Services*, 236–38. For figures used to calculate the federal legal aid budget per person in poverty, see U.S. CENSUS BUREAU INCOME IN THE UNITED STATES 2002 (Washington, D.C.: U.S. Department of Commerce, 2003). OFFICE OF MANAGEMENT AND BUDGET, ANALYTICAL PERSPECTIVES: BUDGET OF THE UNITED STATES GOVERNMENT, FISCAL YEAR 2003, 680 (Washington, D.C.: U.S. Office of Management and Budget, 2003). For disparities between prosecution and defense, see *State Should Pay for Indigent Defense*, ATLANTA JOURNAL CONSTITUTION, December 31, 2001, at A11.

9. *See* BRENNAN CENTER FOR JUSTICE, STRUGGLING TO MEET THE NEED: COMMUNITIES CONFRONT GAPS IN FEDERAL LEGAL AID 5 (New York: Brennan Center for Justice, 2003); Earl Johnson, Jr., *Equal Access to Justice: Comparing Access to Justice in the United States and Other Industrial Democracies*, 24 FORDHAM INTERNATIONAL LAW J. S183, 195 (2000).

10. THOMAS BURKE, LAWYERS, LAWSUITS, AND LEGAL RIGHTS 7, 179 (Berkeley: University of California Press, 2000); ROBERT A. KAGAN, ADVERSARIAL LEGALISM: THE AMERICAN WAY OF LAW (Cambridge, Mass.: Harvard University Press, 2001).

11. LAWRENCE M. FRIEDMAN, TOTAL JUSTICE (New York: Russell Sage, 1994).

12. Powell v. Alabama, 287 U.S. 45, 68–69 (1932). For requirements of counsel in criminal cases, see Alabama v. Shelton, 535 U.S. 654 (2002); Argersinger v. Hamlin, 407 U.S. 25 (1972); Douglas v. California, 372 U.S. 353 (1963); Gideon v. Wainwright, 372 U.S. 335 (1963); Griffin v. Illinois, 351 U.S. 12 (1956). *But see* Pennsylvania v. Finley, 481 U.S. 551 (1987) (finding no right to counsel in optional post-conviction proceedings). For civil cases, see Lassiter v. Department of Social Services, 452 U.S. 18, 27, 31 (1981).

13. Lassiter v. Department of Social Services, 452 U.S. at 20–22, 32–33. For a recent example of the unwillingness to appoint counsel, see M.L.B. v. S.L.J., 519 U.S. 102 (1996).

14. Two-thirds of domestic violence complaints are classified as simple misdemeanors, even though most involve serious injuries, and in surveyed cities, fewer than 10 percent of men arrested for domestic assault served any jail time. DEBORAH L. RHODE, SPEAKING OF SEX: THE DENIAL OF GENDER INEQUALITY 112 (Cambridge, Mass.: Harvard University Press, 1997) (citing studies). The risks to battered women escalate after seeking a protective order. One-half of all inter-

spousal homicides and most serious injuries occur after victims attempt to separate from their abusers. *Id.* at 114. Martha R. Mahoney, *Legal Images of Battered Women: Redefining the Issue of Separation,* 90 MICHIGAN LAW REVIEW 1, 64–65 (1991). For the right to sue, see Chambers v. Baltimore & Ohio R.R., 207 U.S. 142, 148 (1907).

15. Hazard, *After Legal Aid,* 380.

16. For counterproductive cases, see Jonathan R. Macey, *Mandatory Pro Bono: Comfort for the Poor or Welfare for the Rich?,* 77 CORNELL LAW REVIEW 1115, 1117 (1992) (quoting John A. Humbach); *see also* LEGAL SERVICES FOR THE POOR: TIME FOR REFORM 3–29, 329–36 (Douglas J. Besharov ed.) (Washington, D.C.: American Enterprise Institute, 1990); Kenneth F. Boehm, *The Legal Services Program: Unaccountable, Political, Anti-Poor, beyond Reform and Unnecessary,* 17 SAINT LOUIS UNIVERSITY PUBLIC LAW REVIEW 321 (1998); RICHARD POSNER, ECONOMIC ANALYSIS OF LAW 513–14 (New York: Aspen Law & Business, 5th ed. 1998); Charles Silver & Frank B. Cross, *What's Not to Like about Being a Lawyer?,* 109 YALE LAW JOURNAL 1443, 1481–84 (2000); and sources cited in chapter 3 *infra.*

17. BRENNAN CENTER FOR JUSTICE, LEGAL SERVICES CLIENTS TELL THEIR STORY 2 (1999); BRENNAN CENTER FOR JUSTICE, RESTRICTING LEGAL SERVICES: HOW CONGRESS LEFT THE POOR WITH ONLY HALF A LAWYER 2, 9–10, 13 (1999).

18. *See* the discussion in chapter 3 *infra.*

19. 351 U.S. 12 (1956).

20. Alan Berlow, *Requiem for a Public Defender,* AMERICAN PROSPECT, June 5, 2000, at 28; Chester Mersky, *Quality Legal Aid: Going, Going, Gone,* NATIONAL LAW JOURNAL, December 4, 1995, at A19; Stephen B. Bright, Keep the Hope of Equal Justice Alive (unpublished address, Yale Law School, May 24, 1999).

21. For private practitioners, see JIM DWYER, PETER NEUFELD & BARRY SCHECK, ACTUAL INNOCENCE 204 (New York: Doubleday, 2000); DAVID COLE, NO EQUAL JUSTICE 83–85 (New York: New Press, 1999); Marcia Coyle, *Hoping for $75 an Hour,* NATIONAL LAW JOURNAL, June 7, 1999, 1, at 18; Bob Herbert, *Cheap Justice in America,* NEW YORK TIMES, March 1, 1998, at 15. For public defenders, see COLE, NO EQUAL JUSTICE, 83; Stephen B. Bright, *Counsel for the Poor: The Death Sentence Not for the Worst Crime but for the Worst Lawyer,* 103 YALE LAW JOURNAL 1835, 1850–54 (1994).

22. *See* Leroy D. Clark, *All Defendants, Rich and Poor, Should Get Appointed Counsel in Criminal Cases: The Route to True Equal Justice,* 81 MARQUETTE LAW REVIEW 47, 51–56 (1997).

23. *See* Catherine Greene Burnett, Michael K. Moore & Allan K. Butcher, *In Pursuit of Independent, Qualified and Effective Counsel: The Past and Future of Indigent Criminal Defense in Texas,* 42 SOUTH TEXAS LAW REVIEW 595, 597, 622, 641 (2001); Mike McConnell & Chester Mersky, *Guilty Plea Courts: A Social Disciplinary Model of Criminal Justice,* 42 SOCIAL PROBLEMS 216 (1995); Robert E. Scott & William Stuntz, *Plea Bargaining as Contract,* 101 YALE LAW JOURNAL 1909, 1959 (1992); Sara Rimer & Raymond Bonner, *Texas Death Row Record a Concern,* NEW YORK TIMES, June 11, 2000, at A1.

24. For malpractice standards, see CHARLES W. WOLFRAM, MODERN LEGAL ETHICS § 5.6 (1986); John Leubsdorf, *Legal Malpractice and Professional Responsibility,* 48 RUTGERS LAW REVIEW 101, 111–19 (1995); RONALD E. MALLEN & JEF-

FREY M. SMITH, 3 LEGAL MALPRACTICE § 25.3 (4th ed. 1996). For ineffective assistance, see Victor E. Flango & Patricia McKenna, *Federal Habeas Corpus Review of State Court Convictions*, 31 CALIFORNIA WESTERN LAW REVIEW 237, 259–60 (1995). For capital cases, see Bright, Keep the Hope of Equal Justice Alive; COLE, NO EQUAL JUSTICE, 87; Bruce A. Green, *Lethal Fiction: The Meaning of 'Counsel' in the Sixth Amendment*, 78 IOWA LAW REVIEW 433, 499–501 (1993).

25. John Pickering, *Hearing on the Legal Services Corporation before the Subcommittee on Commercial and Administrative Law of the House Judiciary Committee*, 106th Cong. 54, 57–58 (September 9, 1999) (noting that approximately 10 percent of federally funded legal aid cases are litigated and the average expenditure is only about $300 per case). The Bronx Legal Aid Society office has a two-and-one-half-year waiting list to receive an appointment for a divorce. LEGAL SERVICES PROJECT, FUNDING CIVIL LEGAL SERVICES FOR THE POOR, REPORT TO THE CHIEF JUDGE (1998); *see also* Mitchell Zuckoff, *Uneven Justice: Limited Funds for Legal Aid Can Lead to Mismatches in Civil Cases*, BOSTON GLOBE, March 12, 2000, at A1. For eligibility restrictions, see 45 C.F.R. §§ 1610–42 (1999).

26. Russell Engler, *And Justice for All—Including the Unrepresented Poor: Revisiting the Roles of the Judges, Mediators, and Clerks*, 67 FORDHAM LAW REVIEW 1987, 2047 (1999). *See also* Jona Goldschmidt, *How Are Courts Handling Pro Se Litigants?*, 82 JUDICATURE 13, 20 (July/August 1998). Jona Goldschmidt et al., MEETING THE CHALLENGE OF PRO SE LITIGATION: A REPORT AND GUIDEBOOK FOR JUDGES AND COURT MANAGERS (1998); Robert B. Yegge, *Divorce Litigants Without Lawyers*, 28 FAMILY LAW QUARTERLY 407, 408 (1994).

27. JUDITH S. KAYE & JONATHAN LIPPMAN, BREAKING NEW GROUND 2 (New York: New York State Unified Court System Housing Court Program, 1997); Engler, *And Justice for All*, 2056, 2060, 2064; John M. Greacen, *No Legal Advice from Court Personnel: What Does That Mean?*, JUDGES' JOURNAL 10, 10–12 (Winter 1995); Joel Kurtzberg & Jamie Henikoff, *Freeing the Parties from the Law: Designing an Interest and Rights Focused Model of Landlord/Tenant Mediation*, 1997 JOURNAL DISPUTE RESOLUTION 53, 90 (1997); 80 Opinion of Maryland Attorney General No. 95–056 (December 19, 1995); LEGAL SERVICES PROJECT, FUNDING CIVIL LEGAL SERVICES 3 (noting that 90 percent of New York tenants lack counsel in eviction proceedings); Russell Engler, *Out of Sight and Out of Line: The Need for Regulation of Lawyers' Negotiations with Unrepresented Poor Persons*, 85 CALIFORNIA LAW REVIEW 79, 107–8, 154–55 (1997) (citing studies in which 90 percent of tenants are unrepresented and often relinquish legitimate defenses due to exploitation of their ignorance); *see* Karl Monsma & Richard Lempert, *The Value of Counsel: 20 Years of Representation before a Public Housing Eviction Board*, 26 LAW AND SOCIETY REVIEW 627, 645–53 (1992).

28. Engler, *And Justice for All*, 2014, 2016; STATE BAR OF CALIFORNIA, AND JUSTICE FOR ALL: FULFILLING THE PROMISE OF ACCESS TO CIVIL LEGAL SERVICE IN CALIFORNIA 47 (1999).

29. For experts' views, see the sources cited in Deborah L. Rhode, *Professionalism in Perspective: Alternative Approaches to Nonlawyer Practice*, 22 NEW YORK UNIVERSITY REVIEW OF LAW AND SOCIAL CHANGE 701 (1996); ABA COMMITTEE ON NONLAWYER PRACTICE, NONLAWYER ACTIVITY IN LAW-RELATED SITUATIONS: A REPORT WITH RECOMMENDATIONS (1995). For bar ethical rules, MODEL RULES

OF PROFESSIONAL CONDUCT R. 5.5 cmt. (1983); DEBORAH L. RHODE & DAVID LUBAN, LEGAL ETHICS (Westbury, N.Y.: Foundation Press, 4th ed. 2004). For ABA and bar associations actions, see Debra Baker, *Is This Woman a Threat to Lawyers?*, 85 ABA JOURNAL 54 (1999). ABA, Select Committee Report on the 2000 Midyear Meeting, *available at* http://www.abanet.org/leadership/2000hous.html; CALIFORNIA BUSINESS AND PROFESSIONAL CODE § 6126 (amended by Chapter 394 S.B. 1459). For other countries and other professions, see Technician's Report, 41; JUDITH CITRON, THE CITIZENS ADVICE BUREAU X: FOR THE COMMUNITY, BY THE COMMUNITY (London: Pluto Press, 1989); HERBERT KRITZER, LEGAL ADVOCACY 193–203 (Ann Arbor: University of Michigan Press, 1998); Matthew A. Melone, *Income Tax Practice and Certified Public Accountants: The Case for a Status Based Exemption from State Unauthorized Practice of Law Rules*, 11 AKRON TAX JOURNAL 47 (1995).

30. *See* Deborah L. Rhode, *Ethical Perspectives on Legal Practice*, 37 STANFORD LAW REVIEW 589, 611 (1985) (quoting MODEL RULES OF PROFESSIONAL CONDUCT R. 3.6, Discussion Draft 1983 and commentators on that draft); MODEL RULES OF PROFESSIONAL CONDUCT R. 4.3 (1983); *see, e.g.,* Engler, *Out of Sight*, 107–30, 133–37.

31. LOIS G. FORER, MONEY AND JUSTICE: WHO OWNS THE COURTS? 23, 99, 132–33 (New York: W. W. Norton, 1984).

32. MODEL RULES OF PROFESSIONAL CONDUCT R. 6.1 (2002); MODEL CODE OF PROFESSIONAL RESPONSIBILITY EC 2–25, 8–3 (1981); Robert L. Haig, *Lawyer-Bashing: Have We Earned It?*, NEW YORK LAW JOURNAL, November 19, 1993, at 2. *See also* James C. Moore, Legal Services for the Poor: The Unfulfilled Responsibility of an Affluent Society, Remarks at the National Press Club (October 14, 1998) ("I can think of no other profession that acts as responsibly towards those who need its help as does the legal profession.").

33. In Sparks v. Parker, 368 So. 2d 528 (Ala. 1979), the Alabama Supreme Court upheld an assignment system for indigent criminal defense, which the U.S. Supreme Court summarily dismissed on appeal. Sparks v. Parker, 444 U.S. 803 (1979). And, in earlier cases, the Court concluded that attorneys, as "officers of the court," are "bound to render service when required." Powell v. Alabama, 287 U.S. 45, 73 (1932). The Court cited with approval United States v. Dillon, 346 F.2d 633, 636 (9th Cir. 1965), which upheld required service. For state codes, see Deborah L. Rhode, *Pro Bono in Principle and in Practice*, 53 J. LEGAL EDUC. 413 (2003). For the ABA's most recent refusal to recommend mandatory pro bono, see *Mandatory Pro Bono Idea Loses Steam at Ethics 2000 Commission's Final Hearing*, 16 ABA/BNA MANUAL ON PROFESSIONAL CONDUCT 370 (2000).

34. For lawyers' definition, see CARROLL SERON, THE BUSINESS OF PRACTICING LAW 129–33 (Philadelphia: Temple University Press, 1996); Deborah L. Rhode, *Cultures of Commitment: Pro Bono for Lawyers and Law Students*, 67 FORDHAM LAW REVIEW 2415, 2423 (1999). For current pro bono contribution levels, see Rhode, *Pro Bono*; Judith L. Maute, *Pro Bono in Oklahoma: Time for Change*, 53 OKLAHOMA LAW REVIEW 527 (2001); LSC Statistics: Private Attorney Involvement, All Programs, *available at* http://www.lsc.gov/pressr/pr_pai.htm. For large firms, see Rhode, *Pro Bono*; Aric Press, *Eight Minutes*, AMERICAN LAWYER 13 (July 2000); Press Release, Judicial Council of California, Chief Justice Urges More Lawyers

to Donate Time to Pro Bono Efforts (September 16, 2000), *available at* http://www
.courtinfo.ca.gov/newsreleases/NR52-00.htm.

35. *See generally* sources cited in Rhode, *Pro Bono*; Esther F. Lardent, *Mandatory Pro Bono in Civil Cases: The Wrong Answer to the Right Question*, 49 MARYLAND LAW REVIEW 78, 97–99 (1990); Debra Baker, *Mandating Good Works: Colorado Proposal Requiring Pro Bono Draws Fire from Most Lawyers*, 85 ABA JOURNAL 22 (1999).

36. For other nations, see DEBORAH L. RHODE, IN THE INTERESTS OF JUSTICE: REFORMING THE LEGAL PROFESSION 136–37 (New York: Oxford University Press, 2001) Andrew Boon & Jennifer Levin, THE ETHICS AND CONDUCT OF LAWYERS IN ENGLAND AND WALES 55–59, 402 (Oxford: Hart Publishing, 1999); CITRON, CITIZENS ADVICE BUREAU; Christine Parker, JUST LAWYERS: REGULA-TION AND ACCESS TO JUSTICE 1–9 (Oxford: Oxford University Press, 1999). For lawyers' characterizations, see Tigran W. Eldred & Thomas Schoenherr, *The Lawyer's Duty of Public Service: More Than Charity?*, 96 WEST VIRGINIA LAW RE-VIEW 367, 391 n. 97 (1993–94); and Michael J. Mazzone, *Mandatory Pro Bono: Slavery in Disguise*, TEXAS LAWYER, October 22, 1990, at 22.

37. For opponents' claims, see Macey, *Mandatory Pro Bono*; George M. Kraw, *Pro Malo Publico*, SAN FRANCISCO RECORDER, August 25, 1999, at 4; and Gary G. Sackett, *Dear Access to Justice Task Force*, 11 UTAH BAR JOURNAL 22 (1998). For a response, see Rhode, *Pro Bono*.

38. Steven Lubet & Cathryn Steward, *A "Public Assets" Theory of Lawyers' Pro Bono Obligations*, 145 UNIVERSITY OF PENNSYLVANIA LAW REVIEW 1245, 1299 (1997); Rhode, *Pro Bono*; and Rhode, *Cultures of Commitment*, 2415, 2420.

39. ASSOCIATION OF AMERICAN LAW SCHOOLS, LEARNING TO SERVE: THE FIND-INGS AND PROPOSALS OF THE AALS COMMISSION ON PRO BONO AND PUBLIC SER-VICE OPPORTUNITIES vii (Washington, D.C.: AALS, 1999); Rhode, *Pro Bono*; Rhode, *Cultures of Commitment*, 2436, 2433–43. In 1996 the ABA amended its accredita-tion standards to call on schools to "encourage . . . students to participate in pro bono activities and provide opportunities for them to do so." RECODIFICATION OF ACCREDITATION STANDARDS 302 (1996). However, schools are not required to provide specific information about how they comply with that standard or how many students participate. In the absence of such accountability, many schools' performances leave much to be desired. About one-third either have no legal pro bono programs or have programs in which less than fifty students partici-pate. ASSOCIATION OF AMERICAN LAW SCHOOLS, LEARNING TO SERVE, 8.

40. ABA COMMISSION ON NONLAWYER PRACTICE, 137; RHODE, INTERESTS OF JUSTICE, 136–37; Rhode, *Professionalism*, 714–15.

41. *See* Christine Parker, JUST LAWYERS 184–89 (New York: Oxford University Press, 1990). For preferences regarding dispute resolution, see MICHAEL ZANDER, THE STATE OF JUSTICE 29–32 (London: Sweet & Maxwell, 2000); and HAZEL G. GENN, PATHS TO JUSTICE: WHAT PEOPLE DO AND THINK ABOUT GOING TO LAW 217–18 (Oxford: Hart Publishing, 1999).

42. For other countries, see Mark Richardson & Steven Reynolds, *The Shrinking Public Purse: Civil Legal Aid in New South Wales, Australia*, 5 MARYLAND JOURNAL OF CONTEMPORARY LEGAL ISSUES 349, 360 (1994); Jeremy Cooper, *English Legal Services: A Tale of Diminishing Returns*, 5 MARYLAND JOURNAL OF CONTEMPORARY LEGAL ISSUES 247, 253 (1994); Quail v. Municipal Court, 171 Cal. App. 3d 572,

590 n.13 (1985) (citing the German test: whether the matter would be pursued by a reasonable person able to pay the cost). For American legal aid guidelines, see 45 C.F.R. § 1611.3 (1999). For support for broader eligibility, see Houseman, *Civil Legal Assistance*, 431.

43. Johnson, *Toward Equal Justice*, at 215; Erik Cummins, *Novel Proposal Would Privatize Legal Services for Poor*, SAN FRANCISCO DAILY JOURNAL, August 22, 2001, at 1, 16; William Carlson, *San Francisco Lawyers Propose Tax on Lawyers*, SAN FRANCISCO CHRONICLE, February 7, 1989, at A7.

Chapter 2

1. An adaptation of this chapter is forthcoming *in the Duke Law Journal*. For the megasuits, as well as other issues in this chapter, see DEBORAH L. RHODE, IN THE INTERESTS OF JUSTICE: REFORMING THE LEGAL PROFESSION 83–84, 117–31 (New York: Oxford University Press, 2000). For the trivial cases, see THOMAS BURKE, LAWYERS, LAWSUITS, AND LEGAL RIGHTS 2 (Berkeley: University of California Press, 2000) (peanut butter); PHILIP K. HOWARD, THE LOST ART OF DRAWING THE LINE 14–15 (New York: Random House, 2001) (cracker jack box and playground spat); David McKibben, *Coaches Face Parents' Full Court Press*, LOS ANGELES TIMES, May 5, 2003, at A1, A11 (athletic teams); Pat Wingert, *Learn the Hard Way*, NEWSWEEK, December 5, 2003, at 51 (cheerleader).

2. Wycoff v. Emporium Video (Wyoming Supreme Court) (suit dismissed); Nevens v. Maharishi International University (D.C. D.C.) (jury award of $137,890); Lambech v. Salimes (dismissal of claim and $16,000 in sanctions against plaintiff and his attorney for frivolous claim); Baily v. McDonald's Corporation (suit dismissed but claim for attorneys' fees denied). These cases are discussed in JAMES L. PERCELAY, WHIPLASH!: AMERICA'S MOST FRIVOLOUS LAWSUITS 12, 14, 57, 54 (Kansas City: Andrews McMeel, 2000). For the prom date, see Quotes, 75 ABA JOURNAL 30 (1989). For the poodle, see Roger Cramton, *What Do Lawyer Jokes Tell Us about Lawyers and Lawyering*, CORNELL LAW FORUM 7 (July 1996).

3. For juror views, see Jeffrey Abramson, *The Jury and Popular Culture*, 50 DE PAUL LAW REVIEW 497, 515 (2000). For the public's views, see Greg Pierce, *Nation: Inside Politics*, WASHINGTON TIMES, February 28, 2003, at A5; Gary A. Hengstler, *Vox Populi: The Public Perception of Lawyers: ABA Poll*, ABA JOURNAL 60, 63 (September 1993). For the Texas study, see ROBERT A. KAGAN, ADVERSARIAL LEGALISM: THE AMERICAN WAY OF LAW 127 (Cambridge, Mass.: Harvard University Press, 2001). For the judicial study, see SAUL M. KASSIN, AN EMPIRICAL STUDY OF RULE 11 SANCTIONS (Washington, D.C.: Federal Judicial Center, 1985).

4. For complaints about litigiousness, see LAWRENCE M. FRIEDMAN, A HISTORY OF AMERICAN LAW 96 (New York: Simon & Schuster, 2d. ed. 1985) (caterpillars); Jerold R. Auerbach, *A Plague of Lawyers*, HARPERS 37 (October 1976); Terry Carter, *A Lesson Learned*, ABA JOURNAL (May 1998) (quoting Thomas Donahue, President of the American Chamber of Commerce, concerning vitality of business enterprise). *See also* Archie Dunham, Chairman of National Association for Manufacturers, speech before the National Press Club, Washington, D.C., October 28, 2002, *reprinted in* SPEECHES OF THE DAY 101 (December 2002). For

fuzz and wuzz, see LANCE BENNETT, NEWS: THE POLITICS OF ILLUSION 1, 39 (New York: Longman, 3d ed. 1996, quoting Dan Rather).

5. *Ridiculous Unjustified Suits Are Bringing Down State's Economy*, SAN JOSE AND SILICON VALLEY BUSINESS JOURNAL, May 12–18, 1997, at 43 (quoting Pete Wilson); George Bush, Presidential Debate Transcript 2–6, October 11, 1992, quoted in BURKE, LAWYERS, 171; George Bush, State of the Union Address, January 20, 2004, http://www.whitehouse.gov/news/releases/2004/01/print/20040120–7.html. George Bush, Remarks on Medical Liability Reform, University of Scranton, Scranton, Penn., January 16, 2003, *available at* http://www.whitehouse.gov/newsreleases/2003/01/print20030116-.html; David Heckler, *At ATLA, "We are at War,"* NATIONAL LAW JOURNAL, February 10, 2003, at A1, A9 (quoting George W. Bush). For ads, see Deborah L. Rhode, *A Bad Press on Bad Lawyers: The Media Sees Research, Research Sees the Media, in* SOCIAL SCIENCE, SOCIAL POLICY, AND THE LAW 141, 150–51 (Austin Sarat ed.) (New York: Russell Sage, 1999); Stephen Daniels & Joanne Martin, *"The Impact That It Has Had Is Between Peoples' Ears": Tort Reform, Mass Culture, and Plaintiffs' Lawyers*, 50 DEPAUL LAW REVIEW 453, 469–70 (2002); AAHP Launches New Television Campaign, Public Relations Newswire, January 25, 1999. For trade presses, see CATHERINE CRIER, THE CASE AGAINST LAWYERS (New York: Broadway Books, 2002); WALTER K. OLSON, THE RULE OF LAWYERS: HOW THE NEW LITIGATION ELITE THREATENS AMERICA'S RULE OF LAW (New York: St. Martin's Press, 2002).

6. Rhode, *A Bad Press*, 151–52; *On the Air*, CALIFORNIA LAWYER 12 (June 2003). *See also* OLSON, THE RULE OF LAWYERS, 284–85.

7. David A. Hyman, *Medical Malpractice and the Tort System: What Do We Know and What (If Anything) Should We Do about It?*, 80 TEXAS LAW REVIEW 1639, 1640 (2002).

8. Marc Galanter, *Reading the Landscape of Disputes: What We Know and Don't Know (and Think We Know) about our Allegedly Contentious and Litigious Society*, 31 UCLA LAW REVIEW 4, 56 n. 238 (1983); Lawrence M. Friedman, *Access to Justice: Social and Historical Context, in* 2 ACCESS TO JUSTICE 3 (Mauro Cappelletti & John Weisner eds.) (Milan: Giuffee, 1978).

9. DEBORAH L. RHODE, SPEAKING OF SEX 97–98 (Cambridge, Mass.: Harvard University Press, 1997). For costs, see *id.* & KERRY SEGRAVE, THE SEXUAL HARASSMENT OF WOMEN IN THE WORKPLACE, 1600–1993, 203 (Jefferson, N.C.: McFarland, 1994).

10. RALPH NADER & WESLEY J. SMITH, NO CONTEST: CORPORATE LAWYERS AND THE PERVERSION OF JUSTICE IN AMERICA 267 (New York: Random House, 1996).

11. Cindy Webb, *Boiling Mad*, BUSINESS WEEK, August 21, 1995, at 32. "Ridiculous" is the Chamber of Commerce's characterization. *See* NADER & SMITH, NO CONTEST, 267–73; Andrea Gerlin, *A Matter of Degree: How a Jury Decided That a Coffee Spill Is Worth $2.9 Million*, WALL STREET JOURNAL, September 1, 1994, at A1; S. Reed Morgan, *Verdict against McDonald's Is Fully Justified* (Letter to the Editor), NATIONAL LAW JOURNAL, October 24, 1994, at A20.

12. DAVID L. PALETZ & ROBERT M. ENTMAN, MEDIA POWER POLITICS 16 (New York: Free Press, 1981). For the campaign against lawsuit abuse, see KAGAN, ADVERSARIAL LEGALISM, 135. For examples, see Lynn A. Baker & Charles Silver, *Introduction: Civil Justice Fact and Fiction*, 80 TEXAS LAW REVIEW 1537 (2002); Richard

Lacayo, *Anecdotes Not Antidotes*, TIME, April 10, 1995, at 40; Michael J. Saks, *Do We Really Know Anything about the Behavior of the Tort Litigation System—and Why Not?*, 140 UNIVERSITY OF PENNSYLVANIA LAW REVIEW 1147, 1161 (1992).

13. For claims, see LAWRENCE M. FRIEDMAN, TOTAL JUSTICE 17–19, 150 (New York: Russell Sage, 1994); John Leo, *The World's Most Litigious Nation*, U.S. NEWS AND WORLD REPORT, May 22, 1995, at 24; Stephen Budiansky, with Ted Gest & David Fischer, *How Lawyers Abuse the Law*, U.S. NEWS AND WORLD REPORT, January 30, 1995, at 50, 56. For data, see BURKE, LAWYERS, 3; MICHAEL H. TROTTER, PROFIT AND THE PRACTICE OF LAW 167 (Athens, Ga.: University of Georgia Press, 1997). For rates, see FRIEDMAN, TOTAL JUSTICE, 17–19; Herbert Kritzer, *Lawyer Fees and Lawyer Behavior in Litigation: What Does the Empirical Literature Really Say?*, 80 TEXAS LAW REVIEW 1943, 1981 (2002); Marc Galanter, *The Turn against Law: The Recoil against Expanding Accountability*, 51 TEXAS LAW REVIEW 246 (2002); Marc Galanter, *Real World Torts: An Antidote to Anecdote*, 55 MARYLAND LAW REVIEW 1093, 1104–6 (1996); Marc Galanter, *News from Nowhere: The Debased Debate on Civil Justice*, 71 DENVER UNIVERSITY LAW REVIEW 77, 79–80 (1993). For uncontested divorces, see RHODE, INTERESTS OF JUSTICE, 123; FRIEDMAN, TOTAL JUSTICE, 19.

14. Greg Winter, *Jury Awards Soar as Lawsuits Decline on Defective Goods*, NEW YORK TIMES, January 30, 2001, at A1, C4; Ted Rohrlich, *We Aren't Seeing You in Court*, LOS ANGELES TIMES, February 1, 2001, at A1, A8; Theodore Eisenberg and Geoffrey P. Miller, *Attorney Fees in Class Action Settlements: An Empirical Study*, 1 JOURNAL OF EMPIRICAL LEGAL STUDIES 27 (2004). Galanter, *News from Nowhere*, 92–96.

15. For the increase in awards, see Winter, *Jury Awards*, at A1. For the increase in premiums, see Peter Eisler, Julie Appleby & Martin Kasindorf, *Hype Outraces Facts in Malpractice Debate*, USA TODAY, March 5, 2003, at A1–A3; Bush, Remarks on Medical Liability Reform. *Litigation by the Numbers*, LITIGATION, Fall, 2003, 14; Kenneth Thorpe, *The Medical Malpractice "Crisis": Recent Trends and the Impact of State Tort Reforms*, HEALTH TRACKING, January 21, 2004, at W4–20. For punitive damages, see William Glaberson, *A Study's Verdict: Jury Awards Are Not Out of Control*, NEW YORK TIMES, August 6, 2001, at A9; Theodore Eisenberg, Neil LaFountain, Brian Ostrom & David Rottman, *Juries, Judges, and Punitive Damages: An Empirical Study*, 87 CORNELL L. REV. 743 (2002).

16. Joseph B. Treaster, *Malpractice Insurance: No Clear or Easy Answers*, NEW YORK TIMES, March 5, 2003, at C1, C3; Laura Bradford, *Out of Medicine*, TIME, September 20, 2002, at 13–14. For the reasons for the increase in awards, see Richard Perez Pena, *Few New York Doctors at Insurance Protests*, NEW YORK TIMES, May 21, 2003, at A28; Eisler, Appleby & Kasindorf, *Hype*, at A1, A3. For the lack of correlation between caps and premiums, see *id.* and Treaster, *Malpractice Insurance*, at C3. For the reasons for premium increases, see Treaster, *Malpractice Insurance*, at C3; Jyoti Thottam, *He Sets Your Doctor Bills*, TIME, June 9, 2003, 50, 51; Richard A. Oppel, Jr., *With a New Push, Bush Enters Fray over Malpractice*, NEW YORK TIMES, January 17, 2003, at A1, A20. For the effect of damage caps see Thorpe, *Medical Malpractice*, W4–26 (finding caps have led to 17 percent lower premiums).

17. KAGAN, ADVERSARIAL LEGALISM, 140; DEBORAH R. HENSLER ET AL., COMPENSATION FOR ACCIDENTAL INJURIES IN THE UNITED STATES 110, 121–28 (Santa

Monica, Calif.: Rand Corporation Institute for Civil Justice, 1991); PETER A. BELL & JEFFREY O'CONNELL, ACCIDENTAL JUSTICE: THE DILEMMAS OF TORT LAW 58 (New Haven, Conn.: Yale University Press, 1997); HARVARD MEDICAL PRACTICE STUDY, PATIENTS, DOCTORS AND LAWYERS: MEDICAL INJURY, MALPRACTICE LITIGATION AND PATIENT COMPENSATION IN NEW YORK: THE REPORT OF THE HARVARD MEDICAL PRACTICE STUDY TO THE STATE OF NEW YORK 6–9 (Cambridge, Mass., 1990); Saks, *Do We Really Know Anything*, 1183–87; Marc Galanter, *The Conniving Claimant: Changing Images of Misuse of Legal Remedies*, 50 DE PAUL LAW REVIEW 647, 663 (2000); Frank A. Sloan & Stephen S. van Wert, *Cost and Compensation of Injuries in Medical Malpractice*, 54 LAW AND CONTEMPORARY PROBLEMS 131, 155 (1991).

18. For other countries, see BURKE, LAWYERS, 3; KAGAN, ADVERSARIAL LEGALISM, 136. For litigation expenses and tort reform, see Jamie Court, *Damage Cap Adds Insult to Injuries*, LOS ANGELES TIMES, February 10, 2003, at A13.

19. For concerns, see KAGAN, ADVERSARIAL LEGALISM, 142–43; Karen O'Connor, *Civil Justice Reform and Prospects for Change*, 59 BROOKLYN LAW REVIEW 917, 922 (1993); Samborn, Anti-Lawyer Attitude, 1. For evidence, see KAGAN, ADVERSARIAL LEGALISM, 142–43; Galanter, *The Regulatory Function of the Civil Jury, in* VERDICT: ASSESSING THE CIVIL JURY SYSTEM 43 (Robert E. Litan ed.) (Madison: University of Wisconsin, Law School, 1993); Robert E. Litan, *The Liability Explosion and American Trade Performance: Myths and Realities, in* TORT LAW AND THE PUBLIC INTEREST: COMPETITION, INNOVATION AND CONSUMER WELFARE 127, 128 (Peter H. Schuck ed.) (New York: Norton, 1991); NADER & SMITH, NO CONTEST, 279; NATHAN WEBER, THE CONFERENCE BOARD, PRODUCT LIABILITY: THE CORPORATE RESPONSE (Report No. 893, 1987).

20. For the fear of law, see Mortimer B. Zuckerman, *Welcome to Sue City, U.S.A.*, U.S. NEWS AND WORLD REPORT, June 16, 2003. For concerns about shifts in practice, see Eisler, Appleby & Kasindorf, *Hype*, at A3; Daniel Eisenberg & Maggie Sieger, *The Doctor Won't See You Now*, TIME, June 9, 2003, at 46; Bush, Remarks on Medical Liability Reform; *Ten-Gallon Tort Reform*, WALL STREET JOURNAL, June 6, 2003, at A10. For concerns about defensive medicine, see PHILIP HOWARD, THE LOST ART OF DRAWING THE LINE: HOW FAIRNESS WENT TOO FAR 25 (New York: Random House, 2001). For evidence about malpractice premiums, see Eisler, Appleby & Kasindorf, *Hype*, at A3. For research on withdrawal from practice and defensive medicine, see KAGAN, ADVERSARIAL LEGALISM, 274 n. 28; Gary Schwartz, *Reality in the Economic Analysis of Tort Law: Does Tort Law Really Deter?*, 42 UCLA LAW REVIEW 377 (1994); BELL & O'CONNELL, ACCIDENTAL JUSTICE, 92–93; OFFICE OF TECHNOLOGY ASSESSMENT, DEFENSIVE MEDICINE AND MEDICAL MALPRACTICE 56, 71, 74, 103 (1994); Michelle M. Mello & Troyen A. Brennan, *Deterrence of Medical Errors: Theory and Evidence for Malpractice Reform*, 80 TEXAS LAW REVIEW 1595, 1606–9 (2002). For unsafe products, see BELL & O'CONNELL, ACCIDENTAL JUSTICE, 189; Andrew D. Dyer, Todd E. Hymstead & N. Craig Smith, *Dow Corning Corporation: Product Stewardship, in* CASES ON LEADERSHIP, ETHICS, AND ORGANIZATIONAL INTEGRITY: A STRATEGIC PERSPECTIVE 298 (Lynn Sharp Paine ed.) (New York: McGraw-Hill, 1996). For examples of positive effects, see NADER & SMITH, NO CONTEST, 315–17.

21. Daniel S. Bailis & Robert J. MacCoun, *Estimating Liability Risks with the Media as Your Guide: A Content Analysis of Media Coverage of Tort Litigation*, 20 LAW AND HUMAN BEHAVIOR 419, 426 (1996); Galanter, *The Regulatory Function of the Civil Jury*, 85; Amos Tversky & Daniel Kahneman, *Availability: Heuristic for Judging Frequency Probability*, 5 COGNITIVE PSYCHOLOGY 207 (1977); Donald R. Songer, *Tort Reform in South Carolina: The Effect of Empirical Research on Elite Perceptions Concerning Jury Verdicts*, 39 SOUTH CAROLINA LAW REVIEW 5, 85 (1988); Galanter, *The Regulatory Function of the Civil Jury*, 86; William Glaberson, *When the Verdict Is Just a Fantasy*, NEW YORK TIMES, June 6, 1999, at E1.

22. BURKE, LAWYERS, 194; KAGAN, ADVERSARIAL LEGALISM, 126–27, 137; Charles Silver, *Does Civil Justice Cost Too Much?*, 80 TEXAS LAW REVIEW 2073, 2099 (2002). Manhattan Institute, TRIAL LAWYERS INC. 4 (New York: Manhattan Institute, 2003). For plaintiff lawyers' fees, see Pamela Sherrid, *Lawyers on Trial*, U.S. NEWS & WORLD REPORT, December 17, 2001, at 34. In the Institute for Civil Justice Studies, plaintiffs in automobile accidents recovered 52 percent of total payouts; in nonautomobile tort litigation, plaintiffs recovered 43 percent. DEBORAH R. HENSLER, MARY E. BAIAN, JAMES S. KAKALIK & MARK A. PETERSON, TRENDS IN TORT LITIGATION: THE STORY BEHIND THE STATISTICS 2–3 (Santa Monica, Calif.: Rand Institute for Civil Justice, 1987). For Japan, see KAGAN, ADVERSARIAL LEGALISM, 136–37; Takao Tanase, *The Management of Disputes: Automobile Accident Compensation in Japan*, 24 LAW AND SOCIETY REVIEW 650, 660 (1990).

23. Brian Wolfman & Alan B. Morrison, *Representing the Unrepresented in Class Actions Seeking Monetary Relief*, 71 NEW YORK UNIVERSITY LAW REVIEW 439, 502–7; NADER & SMITH, NO CONTEST, 195; CRIER, THE CASE AGAINST LAWYERS, 194.

24. Dave Barry, *Lawyers Put the Bite on Denture-Adhesive Maker*, ORLANDO SENTINEL, November 23, 1993, at 22.

25. Herbert Kritzer, *The Wages of Risk: The Returns of Contingency Fee Legal Practice*, 47 DE PAUL LAW REVIEW 267, 302 (1998).

26. Alison Frankel, *Greedy, Greedy, Greedy*, AMERICAN LAWYER, November 1996, at 71.

27. For medical malpractice cases, see Peter W. Huber, *Easy Lawsuits Make Bad Medicine*, FORBES, April 21, 1997, at 166; KAGAN, ADVERSARIAL LEGALISM, 140; Mello & Brennan, *Deterrence of Medical Errors*, 1619. For other tort claims, see KAGAN, ADVERSARIAL LEGALISM, 146; and Silver, *Does Civil Justice Cost Too Much?*, 2076.

28. For inconsistencies, see KAGAN, ADVERSARIAL LEGALISM, 140–41; Daphne Eviator, *Is Litigation a Blight or Built In?*, NEW YORK TIMES, November 23, 2002, at A23; Joseph Sanders, *Adversarial Legalism and Civil Litigation: Prospects for Change*, 28 LAW AND SOCIAL INQUIRY 719 (2003); Cass R. Sunstein et al., *Assessing Punitive Damages (with Notes on Cognition and Valuation in Law)*, 107 YALE LAW JOURNAL 2071, 2094–2108 (1998). For regional variations, see OLSON, THE RULE OF LAWYERS, 209–36; Adam Liptak, *Playing the Angles in Class-Action Lawsuits*, NEW YORK TIMES, November 17, 2002, at A11; *Ten-Gallon Tort Reform*, at A10; Jim Copeland, *The Tort Tax*, WALL STREET JOURNAL, June 11, 2003, at A16. For aberrational damage verdicts, see *id.*; Adam Liptak, *Shot in the Arm for Tort Overhaul*, NEW YORK TIMES, November 17, 2002, at A10. For asbestos inconsis-

tencies, see Deborah R. Hensler, *As Time Goes By: Asbestos Litigation after Anchem and Ortiz*, 80 Texas Law Review 1899, 1923 (2002).

29. Kagan, Adversarial Legalism, 141–46; Schwartz, *Reality in Tort Law*, 377. For medical malpractice, see Mello & Brennan, *Deterrence of Medical Errors*, 1618–21. For other liability contexts, see Kagan, Adversarial Legalism, 141; George Eads & Peter Reuter, *Designing Safer Products: Corporate Response to Product Liability Law and Regulation*, 7 Journal Product Liability 263 (1984).

30. Robert J. Samuelson, *Delegating Democracy*, Newsweek, June 12, 2000, at 59; Marcia Coyle, *Bill Targets Class Action Fees, Sparked by Ire over Tobacco Money*, National Law Journal, May 19, 2003, at A1.

31. Burke, Lawyers, 7, 179; Kagan, Adversarial Legalism.

32. Sherrid, *Lawyers on Trial*, 34; Olson, The Rule of Lawyers, 18–71.

33. *See* Burke, Lawyers, 27–33; Class Action Fairness Act, H.R. 1115, 108th Cong. (2003); Justin Gest, *For Third Time House OKs Reforming Class-Action Suits*, Los Angeles Times, June 13, 2003, at A7; Rebecca Rodriguez, *Tort Reform Narrowly Approved*, San-Antonio Express-News, September 14, 2003, at A1; Bernard Wysocki, Jr., *Seeking a Cap for Malpractice*, Wall Street Journal, October 7, 2003, at A4. For loser pays, see Rhode, Interests of Justice, 129; Crier, The Case against Lawyers, 211.

34. Eisler, Appleby & Kasindorf, *Hype*, at A3; Court, *Damage Cap*, at A13.

35. Robert Kagan, *Do Lawyers Cause Adversarial Legalism?: A Preliminary Inquiry*, 9 Law and Society Review 1, 8 (1994). The Common Sense Legal Reform Act, H.R. 10, 104th Cong. (1995); The Attorney Accountability Act, H.R. 988, 104th Cong. (1995); Herbert M. Kritzer, Prepared Statement, *Attorney Accountability, Hearings before the Subcommittee on Courts and Intellectual Property of the Committee on the Judiciary*, House of Representatives, 104th Cong., 1st Session, February 6, 1995, 49–66; Thomas D. Rowe, Jr., Prepared Statement, in *id.*, 42–47. Werner Pfenningstorf & Donald G. Gifford, *Introduction*, in A Comparative Study of Liability Law and Compensation Schemes in Ten Countries and the United States (Donald G. Gifford & William M. Richman eds.) (Oak Brook, Ill.: Insurance Research Council, 1991).

36. Nader & Smith, No Contest, 299–300; Robert Gnaizda, *Secret Justice for the Privileged Few*, 66 Judicature 6, 11 (1987); Owen Fiss, *Against Settlement*, 93 Yale Law Journal 1073 (1984).

37. Deborah R. Hensler, *In Search of Good Mediation: Rhetoric, Practice and Empiricism*, in Handbook of Justice Research in Law (Joseph Sanders & V. Lee Hamilton eds.) (New York: Plenum, 2000).

38. Marc Galanter & Mia Cahill, *"Most Cases Settle": Judicial Promotion and Regulation of Settlements*, 46 Stanford Law Review 1339 (1994); Richard C. Reuben, *The Lawyer Turns Peacemaker*, ABA Journal, August, 5, 1996; Judith Resnik, *Failing Faith: Adjudicatory Procedure in Decline*, 53 University of Chicago Law Review 494, 553 (1986); E. Allan Lind & Tom R. Tyler, The Social Psychology of Procedural Justice 177 (New York: Plenum, 1988) (describing biases due to adversary strategies in arbitration). For imbalances, see Richard Delgado, *Fairness and Formality: Minimizing the Risk of Alternative Dispute Resolution*, Wisconsin Law Review 135 (1985). For a study finding no significant differences in federal cases, see James S. Kakalik et al., *An Evaluation of Mediation and Early*

Neutral Evaluation under the Civil Justice Reform Act: A Summary, DISPUTE RESO-
LUTION MAGAZINE 4–7 (Summer 1997). For mixed results, see studies cited in
Reuben, *Lawyer Turns Peacemaker*, 56–59; Deborah R. Hensler, *Puzzling over ADR:
Drawing Meaning from the RAND Report*, DISPUTE RESOLUTION MAGAZINE 8, 9
(Summer 1997).

39. Reuben, *Lawyer Turns Peacemaker*, 61; Jeffrey W. Stempel, *Reflections on Judicial ADR and the Multi-Door Courthouse at Twenty: Fait Accompli, Failed Overture,
or Fledgling Adulthood?*, 11 OHIO STATE JOURNAL ON DISPUTE RESOLUTION 297,
319, 339, 351 (1996); *see* Fiss, *Against Settlement*; David Luban, *Settlements and the
Public Realm*, 83 GEORGETOWN LAW REVIEW 2619 (1995); LIND & TYLER, SOCIAL
PSYCHOLOGY OF PROCEDURAL JUSTICE, 122.

40. Marc Galanter, *Why the Haves Come Out Ahead: Speculations on the Limits of
Legal Change*, 9 LAW AND SOCIETY REVIEW 95 (1974).

41. Frank E. A. Sander & Stephen B. Goldberg, *Fitting the Forum to the Fuss: A
User-Friendly Guide to Selecting an ADR Procedure*, 10 NEGOTIATION JOURNAL, 67
(1994). For standardized pain and suffering formulas, see KAGAN, ADVERSARIAL
LEGALISM, 137–39, 238, 275.

42. For other countries, see KAGAN, ADVERSARIAL LEGALISM, 137–39. For U.S.
compensation funds, see Burke, Law, Lawyers, and Legal Rights, 38–40. For
hospitals and insurers, see Eisler, Appleby & Kasindorf, *Hype*; Oppel, *Bush Enters Fray*, at A20; *Insurers, Hospitals Try Apologies for Errors*, USA TODAY, March 5,
2003, at 5B. For experts' proposals, see Mello & Brennan, *Deterrence of Medical
Errors*, 1623–29; Philip K. Howard, *Yes, It's a Mess—But Here's How to Fix It*,
TIME, June 9, 2003, at 58; Philip K. Howard, *Legal Malpractice*, WALL STREET
JOURNAL, January 27, 2003, at A16; Betsy McCaughey, *Medical Courts Would Heal
Infirmities of Legal System*, INVESTOR'S BUSINESS DAILY, July 17, 2003, at A15.

43. For no-fault studies, see KAGAN, ADVERSARIAL LEGALISM, 235–38. For
medical malpractice, see Mello & Brennan, *Deterrence of Medical Errors*, 1623–29.
For estimates of patient deaths, see National Academy of Sciences study discussed in Eisler, Appleby & Kasendorf, *Hype*, at A3.

44. For the need for better cross-cultural information, see *Review Symposium on
Kagan's Adversarial Legalism: The American Way of Law*, 28 LAW AND SOCIAL IN-
QUIRY 719–872 (2003). For individual preferences, see LIND & TAYLOR, SOCIAL
PSYCHOLOGY OF PROCEDURAL JUSTICE, 64–67, 102–4; Stempel, *Reflections on Judi-
cial ADR*, 353–54. For preferences concerning out-of-court dispute resolution,
see MICHAEL ZANDER, THE STATE OF JUSTICE 29–32 (London: Sweet & Maxwell,
2000); HAZEL G. GENN, PATHS TO JUSTICE: WHAT PEOPLE DO AND THINK ABOUT
GOING TO LAW 18 (Oxford: Hart Publishing, 1999).

45. Mello & Brennan, *Deterrence of Medical Errors*, 1623–30; Leslie Bernstein,
Why Wasn't He Stopped Sooner?, TIME, June 9, 2003, at 57.

46. For class action and contingent fees, see RHODE, INTERESTS OF JUSTICE,
174–82; *Giveback Time*, AMERICAN LAWYER, August 2003; Martha Neil, *Texas
Clips Coupons*, ABA JOURNAL REPORT, July 3, 2003; Coyle, *Class Action Fees*;
Peter Blumberg, *Keeping a Secret*, SAN FRANCISCO DAILY JOURNAL, September 13,
2003, at A1; Lester Brickman, *ABA Regulation of Contingency Fees: Money Talks,
Ethics Walks*, 65 FORDHAM LAW REVIEW 247, 305–8 (1996); LESTER BRICKMAN,
MICHAEL J. HOROWITZ & JEFFREY O'CONNELL, RETHINKING CONTINGENT FEES

(New York: Manhattan Institute, 1994). For bar discipline, see Monte Morin, *State Bar Suspends Attorneys over Suits*, Los Angeles Times, May 22, 2003, at B1, B10; see also Michael Hytha, *'People's Lawyer' Gets Mild Penalty from State Bar*, San Francisco Chronicle, August 8, 1997, at A19.

Chapter 3

1. For early American constitutional provisions, see Reginald Heber Smith, Justice and the Poor (Boston: Little Brown, 1911). For the English statute and practices, see 11 Hen. 7, ch. 12 (1495); 2 William S. Holdsworth, A History of English Law 478–79, 491 (London: Methuen, 3d ed. 1923); F. C. G. Gurney-Champion, Justice and the Poor in England 2 (London: George Routledge & Sons, 1926); David L. Shapiro, *The Enigma of the Lawyer's Duty to Serve*, 55 New York University Law Review 735, 740–42 (1980). For the Virginia statute, see Charles Warren, History of the American Bar 41 (Boston: Little Brown, 1911).

2. Lawrence M. Friedman, A History of American Law 81–84 (New York: Simon & Schuster, 2d ed. 1973); Daniel J. Boorstin, The Americans: The Colonial Experience 195–97 (New York: Random House, 1958); Warren, History of the American Bar, 5–13; Roscoe Pound, The Lawyer from Antiquity to Modern Times 137–43 (St. Paul, Minn.: West Pub. Co., 1953).

3. For the post-revolutionary period, see Warren, History of the American Bar, 212; Pound, Lawyer from Antiquity, 177–78; J. Willard Hurst, The Growth of American Law (Boston: Little Brown, 1950). For the laxity of admission procedures and rudimentary nature of legal education during the Jacksonian period, see Deborah L. Rhode & David Luban, Legal Ethics (New York: Foundation Press, 4th ed. 2004); Friedman, History of American Law, 264–79; Warren, History of the American Bar, 161–68; Barlow F. Christensen, *The Unauthorized Practice of Law: Do Good Fences Really Make Good Neighbors—Or Even Good Sense?*, 1980 American Bar Foundation Research Journal 159–61.

4. For the accessibility of law and legal procedure, see Friedman, History of American Law, 84–87; Warren, History of the American Bar, 5–8, 157–61. For the role of lay practitioners, see Warren, History of the American Bar, 5–8; Friedman, History of American Law, 84. For the abuses of such practitioners and prohibitions on their court appearances, see Anton-Hermann Chroust, The Rise of the Legal Profession in America 271–79, 300 (Norman: University of Oklahoma Press, 1965); Richard B. Bernstein & Kim S. Rice, Are We to be a Nation? 197 (Cambridge, Mass.: Harvard University Press, 1987); Bruce Green, *Lethal Fiction*, 78 Iowa Law Review 433, 463 n. 113, 466 n. 123 (1993).

5. Smith, Justice and the Poor, 11.

6. Earl Johnson, Jr., Justice and Reform: The Formative Years of the OEO Legal Services Program 3 (New York: Russell Sage Foundation, 1974); Statute of Henry VII, 1495, II Hen. VII, c.12; Theodore Plucknett, A Concise History of the Common Law 388 (London: Butterworths, 3d ed. 1940); Sir James F. Stephen, A History of the Criminal Law of England 260–61, 397

(London: MacMillan & Co., 1883); William M. Beaney, Jr., The Right to Counsel in American Courts 12–16 (1951) (unpublished dissertation, University of Michigan); Powell v. Alabama, 287 U.S. 45, 61 (1932).

7. Beaney, Right to Counsel, 14–18; THOMAS M. COOLEY, CONSTITUTIONAL LIMITATIONS 330–38 (Boston: Little Brown, 1st ed. 1868); STEPHEN, HISTORY OF THE CRIMINAL LAW, 424; HALSBURY LAWS OF ENGLAND, CRIMINAL LAW AND PROCEDURE Pt. V. and 684. For the tradition of dock briefs, see Shapiro, *Enigma,* 742. For barristers' willingness to take unpaid cases, see GURNEY-CHAMPION, JUSTICE AND THE POOR IN ENGLAND, 8; Richard Abel, *Law without Politics: Legal Aid under Advanced Capitalism,* 32 UCLA LAW REVIEW 474, 501 (1985).

8. For state constitutional provisions, see Powell v. Alabama, 287 U.S. 61–64; Beaney, Right to Counsel, 23–24; JULIUS GOEBEL & T. RAYMOND NAUGHTON, LAW ENFORCEMENT IN COLONIAL NEW YORK 574 (New York: Commonwealth Fund, 1944); ARTHUR SCOTT, CRIMINAL LAW IN COLONIAL VIRGINIA 76–80 (Chicago: University of Chicago Press, 1930). For the lack of research, see Alan Rogers, *"A Sacred Duty": Court-Appointed Attorneys in Massachusetts Capital Cases, 1780–1980,* 41 AMERICAN JOURNAL OF LEGAL HISTORY 441, 442 (1997).

9. Beaney, Right to Counsel, 42, 317; Green, *Lethal Fiction,* 463–65; Mindy D. Black, Note, *The Criminal Defendant's Sixth Amendment Right to Lay Representation,* 52 OHIO LAW REVIEW 460, 461 (1985); Note, *The Representation of Indigent Criminal Defendants in the Federal District Courts,* 76 HARVARD LAW REVIEW 579, 591, 599 (1963).

10. Beaney, Right to Counsel, 124–48; EMERY A. BROWNELL, LEGAL AID IN THE UNITED STATES 35 (Rochester, N.Y.: The Lawyers Co-operative Publishing Company, 1951); Patterson v. State, 25 So. 2d 713 (Florida 1947), *cert. denied,* 329 U.S. 789 (1948).

11. Beaney, Right to Counsel, 148–55; State v. Morton, 27 N.W.2d 158 (Minnesota 1947).

12. For the comparisons between small-town America and the needs of an urban industrialized nation, see SPECIAL COMMITTEE OF THE ASSOCIATION OF THE BAR OF THE CITY OF NEW YORK AND THE NATIONAL LEGAL AID AND DEFENDER ASSOCIATION, EQUAL JUSTICE FOR THE ACCUSED 46 (New York: Doubleday & Co., 1959); Gregg L. Barak, In Defense of the Poor: The Emergence of the Public Defender System in the United States 51 (1974) (unpublished dissertation, University of California–Berkeley). For the inadequacies of the assignment system, see SMITH, JUSTICE AND THE POOR 101, 103; Charles S. Potts, *Right to Counsel in Criminal Cases: Legal Aid or Public Defender,* 28 TEXAS LAW REVIEW 491, 503–8 (1949–50).

13. BROWNELL, LEGAL AID, 35, 84. For small towns, see Bertram F. Wilcox & Edward J. Bloustein, *Account of a Field Study in a Rural Area of the Representation of Indigents Accused of Crime,* 59 COLUMBIA LAW REVIEW 551, 567–69 (1959). For the Philadelphia figures, see Herman I. Pollock, *Equal Justice in Practice,* 45 MINNESOTA LAW REVIEW 737, 749 (1961). For the Illinois effort, see Charles J. Harrington & Gerald W. Getty, *The Public Defender: A Progressive Step towards Justice,* 42 ABA JOURNAL 1139 (1956). For the study of petty criminal courts, see Caleb Foote, *Vagrancy-Type Law and its Administration,* 104 UNIVERSITY OF PENNSYLVANIA LAW REVIEW 603 (1956).

14. For compensation, see Beaney, Right to Counsel, 197; Potts, *Right to Counsel*, 505; Brownell, Legal Aid, 124–25; Smith, Justice and the Poor, 112. For the inexperience and poor quality of assigned lawyers, see *id.*, 113–14; Beaney, Right to Counsel, 327; Wilcox & Bloustein, *Field Study*; Potts, *Right to Counsel*, 503–4.

15. Edward Lumbard, New England Conference on the Defense of Indigent Persons Accused of Crime, Cambridge, October 31, 1963, quoted in Anthony Lewis, Gideon's Trumpet 199–200 (New York: Random House, 1964). For jailhouse lawyers, see Smith, Justice and the Poor, 114; Clara Shortridge Foltz, *Public Defenders*, 34 American Law Review 396, 397 (1897); David Mars, *Public Defenders*, 46 Journal of Criminal Law, Criminology and Police Science 199, 207 (1955); Edward J. Dimock, *The Public Defender: A Step towards a Police State?*, 42 ABA Journal 219 (1956).

16. For other nations, see Barak, In Defense of the Poor, 54–55. For Foltz's views, see Foltz, *Public Defender*, 403. For other advocates, see Smith, Justice and the Poor, 123–27; Beaney, Right to Counsel, 310; Charles Mishkin, *The Public Defender*, 22 Journal of the American Institute of Criminal Law and Criminology 489, 503 (1931–32). For claims about "shifty" practitioners, see Barak, In Defense of the Poor, 185. For claims about the "tone" of the justice system, see Esther Lucile Brown, Lawyers and the Promotion of Justice 257 (New York: Russell Sage Foundation, 1938).

17. For concerns about coddling criminals, see Barak, In Defense of the Poor, 69, and Brownell, Legal Aid, 146. For the unseemliness of concentrating both prosecutorial and defense power in the same hands, see Harry E. Smoot, *The Public Defender: A Constructive Suggestion*, 10 Journal of the American Institute of Criminal Law and Criminology 617 (1920). For concerns about "socialization," see Dimock, *Public Defender*; Beaney, Right to Counsel, 308; Special Committee of the New York Bar, Equal Justice, 45. For other concerns, see Beaney, Right to Counsel, 308.

18. For the evidence on performance, see Beaney, Right to Counsel, 309 n.2; Lee Silverstein, Defense of the Poor in Criminal Cases in American State Courts (Chicago: American Bar Association, 1965); Brown, Lawyers and the Promotion of Justice, 258. For clients' views, see Jonathan D. Casper, *Did You Have a Lawyer When You Went to Court? No, I Had a Public Defender*, in Criminal Justice: Law and Politics (George F. Cole ed.) (Belmont, Calif.: Wadsworth Publishing Co., 1993).

19. Joel F. Handler, Ellen Jane Hollingsworth & Howard S. Erlanger, Lawyers and the Pursuit of Legal Rights 39 (New York: Academic Press, 1978).

20. Powell v. Alabama, 287 U.S. 45, 71 (1932).

21. Johnson v. Zerbst, 304 U.S. 458, 468 (1938); Betts v. Brady, 316 U.S. 455 (1942).

22. For the tabulation of decisions, see Beaney, Right to Counsel, 238. For the twenty factors, see Lewis, Gideon's Trumpet, 123. For the reversal rate, see *id.*, at 151. For state cases, see De Meerleer v. Michigan, 329 U.S. 663, 665 (1947); Commonwealth ex rel Sinnan v. Maroney, 176 A.2d 94, 96–97 (Pennsylvania 1961). For the appellate argument, see Abe Fortas, quoted in Lewis, Gideon's Trumpet, 172.

23. Gideon v. Wainwright, 372 U.S. 335, 344 (1963); Lewis, Gideon's Trumpet, 4–5, 37.

24. Gideon v. Wainwright, 372 U.S. at 337.

25. Argersinger v. Hamlin, 407 U.S. 25 (1972); Alabama v. Shelton, 535 U.S. 654 (2002).

26. SMITH, JUSTICE AND THE POOR, 135–43, 192; JEROLD S. AUERBACH, UNEQUAL JUSTICE 53–54 (New York: Oxford University Press, 1976); REGINALD HEBER SMITH & JOHN S. BRADWAY, GROWTH OF LEGAL AID WORK IN THE UNITED STATES, Bulletin No. 607 (Washington, D.C.: United States Bureau of Labor Statistics, 1926).

27. For social agitators and protection of workingmen, see Von Breisan, quoted in AUERBACH, UNEQUAL JUSTICE, 55. For Smith, see JUSTICE AND THE POOR, 13, 14, 10, 152. For Roosevelt, see AUERBACH, UNEQUAL JUSTICE, 55. For "public relations," see BROWNELL, LEGAL AID, 55 and BRYANT GARTH, NEIGHBORHOOD LAW FIRMS FOR THE POOR 32 (Rockville, Md.: Sijthoff & Noardhoff, 1980).

28. SMITH, JUSTICE AND THE POOR, 9.

29. For the ABA resolutions and lack of subsequent progress, see BROWNELL, LEGAL AID, 8, 9, 230. For the Chicago campaign, see AUERBACH, UNEQUAL JUSTICE, 57. For the New York effort, see MARTHA F. DAVIS, BRUTAL NEED: LAWYERS AND THE WELFARE RIGHTS MOVEMENT, 1960–1973 (New Haven, Conn.: Yale University Press, 1993). For the 1950 bar funding contributions, see GARTH, NEIGHBORHOOD LAW FIRMS, 19.

30. AUERBACH, UNEQUAL JUSTICE, 236 (quoting Harold Gallagher). See also Alan W. Houseman, Political Lessons: Legal Services for the Poor—A Commentary, 83 GEORGETOWN LAW JOURNAL 1669, 1678 (1995). For economic concerns, see GARTH, NEIGHBORHOOD LAW FIRMS, 86; Note, Neighborhood Law Offices, 80 HARVARD LAW REVIEW 805, 843–45 (1967).

31. AUERBACH, UNEQUAL JUSTICE, 62, 56 (quoting Von Breisen); BROWNELL, LEGAL AID, 72; SMITH, JUSTICE AND THE POOR, 167; Lee Silverstein, Eligibility for Free Legal Services in Civil Cases, 44 JOURNAL OF URBAN LAW 549, 555–56 (1967).

32. JACK KATZ, POOR PEOPLE'S LAWYERS IN TRANSITION 44 (New Brunswick, N.J.: Rutgers University Press, 1982); BROWNELL, LEGAL AID, 73; Silverstein, Eligibility for Free Legal Services, 549, 552, 576–77, 583; Harry P. Stumpf, Henry P. Schoerluke & Forest D. Dill, The Legal Profession and Legal Services: Exploration in Local Bar Politics, 6 LAW AND SOCIETY REVIEW 47, 49 (1971).

33. For the figures on programs, see Houseman, Political Lessons, 1670–71; GARTH, NEIGHBORHOOD LAW FIRMS, 20; JOHNSON, JUSTICE AND REFORM, 9. For the policies on appeals, appearances, and complicated matters, see id., 9; Houseman, Political Lessons, 1670–71; Silverstein, Eligibility for Free Legal Services; KATZ, POOR PEOPLE'S LAWYERS, 45. For the policies on compromise, see DAVIS, BRUTAL NEED, 13. For the lack of law reform and community outreach, see id.; GARTH, NEIGHBORHOOD LAW FIRMS, 20; and HANDLER, HOLLINGSWORTH & ERLANGER, LAWYERS AND THE PURSUIT OF LEGAL RIGHTS, 20. For the lack of Supreme Court cases, see JOHNSON, JUSTICE AND REFORM, 13–14. For the low pay and recruitment and retention difficulties, see HANDLER, HOLLINGSWORTH & ERLANGER, LAWYERS AND THE PURSUIT OF LEGAL RIGHTS, 20; RICHARD L. ABEL, AMERICAN LAWYERS 132 (New York: Oxford, 1989); BROWNELL, LEGAL AID, 4; AUERBACH, UNEQUAL JUSTICE, 58. For the Chicago example, see KATZ, POOR PEOPLE'S LAWYERS, 22.

34. GARTH, NEIGHBORHOOD LAW FIRMS, 27–34; Houseman, Political Lessons, 1673–75; JOHNSON, JUSTICE AND REFORM, 57.

35. *See* Johnson, Justice and Reform, 272; Auerbach, Unequal Justice, 274; Garth, Neighborhood Services, 33; Houseman, *Political Lessons*, 1678–79. For the hallway incident, see Stump, Schoerluke & Dill, *The Legal Profession and Legal Services*, 52.

36. For Judicare, see Johnson, Justice and Reform, 118–19, 225, 238; Garth, Neighborhood Law Firms, 34; Abel, American Lawyers, 134; Stumpf, Shroerlucke & Dill, *The Legal Profession and Legal Services*, 52–57. For the funding increase, see Garth, Neighborhood Law Firms, 31; Handler, Hollingsworth & Erlanger, Lawyers and the Pursuit of Legal Rights, 19. For legal education and the new breed of lawyers, see Garth, Neighborhood Law Firms, 34; Houseman, *Political Lessons*, 1683.

37. For the court victories, see Susan E. Lawrence, The Poor in Court — The Legal Services Program and Supreme Court Decision Making, Appendix A (Princeton, N.J.: Princeton University Press, 1990). For the proposed Murphy Amendment restricting suits against the government, see 113 Congressional Record 27, 155 (1967); Handler, Hollingsworth & Erlanger, Lawyers and the Pursuit of Legal Rights, 35; Garth, Neighborhood Law Firms, 36. For political opposition and the Nixon Era, see Johnson, Justice and Reform, 132–33; Handler, Hollingsworth, & Erlanger, Lawyers and the Pursuit of Legal Rights, 40–44.

38. For the Corporation charter, see 42 U.S.C. § 299 h. For the Reagan Administration's actions, see Loren Siegel & David Landau, No Justice for the Poor: How Cutbacks Are Destroying Legal Services (New York: American Civil Liberties Union, 1983).

39. Deborah L. Rhode, Pro Bono in Principle and in Practice, 2003, *available at* www.ssrn.com, excerpted at 54 Journal of Legal Education 413 (2003); Michael Millemann, *Mandatory Pro Bono in Civil Cases: A Partial Answer to the Right Question*, 49 Maryland Law Review 18, 33–35 (1990); Shapiro, *Enigma*, 739–40, 749–53; ABA Canons of Professional Ethics, Canon 12 (1908).

40. Mark J. Green, The Other Government: The Unseen Power of Washington Lawyers 264–65 (New York: Norton, 1976); Rhode, Pro Bono.

41. American Bar Association Code of Professional Responsibility, Ethical Consideration 2–25 (1970).

42. Newman Levy, *Lawyers and Money*, Harper's Magazine 293–94 (February 1927), quoted in Beaney, Right to Counsel, 102.

43. Auerbach, Unequal Justice, 282; Abel, American Lawyers, 130; Joel F. Handler, Ellen Jane Hollingsworth, Howard E. Erlanger & Jack Ladinsky, *The Public Interest Activities of Private Practice Lawyers*, 61 ABA Journal 1388, 1389 (1975); Philip Lochner, *The No-Fee and Low-Fee Legal Practice of Private Attorneys*, 9 Law and Society Review 431, 442–46 (1975).

44. Charles Kellogg, NAACP: A History of the National Association for the Advancement of Colored People (Baltimore: Johns Hopkins Press, 1967); Mark Tushnet, The NAACP's Legal Strategy against Segregated Education, 1925–1950 (Chapel Hill: University of North Carolina Press, 1987); Abel, American Lawyers, 135; Handler, Hollingsworth & Erlanger, Lawyers and the Pursuit of Legal Rights, 231.

45. By the close of the 1980s, some 150 statutes authorized fee awards. NAN
ARON, LIBERTY AND JUSTICE FOR ALL: PUBLIC INTEREST LAW IN THE 1980'S AND
BEYOND 55–56 (Boulder, Colo.: Westview Press, 1989); Serrano v. Priest, 182 Cal.
Rptr. 387 (1982).

46. ARON, LIBERTY AND JUSTICE, 4–5. For other definitions of public interest
law, see JEREMY COOPER, KEYGUIDE TO INFORMATION SOURCES ON PUBLIC INTER-
EST LAW 3–11 (New York: Mansell, 1991).

47. Roger K. Neuman, *Public Interest Firms Crop Up on the Right*, NATIONAL LAW
JOURNAL, August 26, 1996, at 1, 22; ARON, LIBERTY AND JUSTICE, 78; LEE EPSTEIN,
CONSERVATIVES IN COURT (Knoxville: University of Tennessee Press, 1985).

48. *See* RHODE & LUBAN, LEGAL ETHICS 729–34, 542–49; Nan Aron & Samuel S.
Jackson, Jr., *Non-Traditional Models for Legal Service Delivery, in* CIVIL JUSTICE: AN
AGENDA FOR THE 1990S 145–47 (Chicago: American Bar Association, 1989).

49. Gary Bellow, quoted in Comment, *The New Public Interest Lawyers*, 79 YALE
LAW JOURNAL 1069, 1077–78 (1970). *See* RHODE & LUBAN, LEGAL ETHICS; Aron &
Jackson, *Non-Traditional Models*.

50. For Roman practices, see WILLIAM FORSYTH, THE HISTORY OF LAWYERS 172
(New York: J. Cockcroft, 1875). For nineteenth-century American adversary
practices, see Lori B. Andrews, Birth of a Salesman: Lawyer Advertising and So-
licitation (Chicago: American Bar Association Press, 1981), and RHODE & LUBAN,
LEGAL ETHICS, 617. For early bans on solicitation, see 3 HOLDSWORTH, A HISTORY
OF ENGLISH LAW 395–99 (3d ed. 1924); Deborah L. Rhode, *Solicitation*, 36 JOUR-
NAL OF LEGAL EDUCATION 317, 318 (1986); Max Radin, *Maintenance by Champerty*,
24 CALIFORNIA LAW REVIEW 48, 48–57 (1935).

51. GEORGE SHARSWOOD, AN ESSAY ON PROFESSIONAL ETHICS (Philadelphia:
T & J Johnson, 1884); ABA OPINION OF THE COMMITTEE ON PROFESSIONAL
ETHICS AND GRIEVANCES, 71, 75 (1925).

52. ABEL, AMERICAN LAWYERS, 118; PHILIP M. STERN, LAWYERS ON TRIAL 55
(New York: Times Books, 1980). For the lack of attention to public interests, see
BARLOW F. CHRISTENSEN, LAWYERS FOR PEOPLE OF MODERATE MEANS 150 (Chi-
cago: American Bar Association, 1970).

53. AUERBACH, UNEQUAL JUSTICE, 41–48. For the study, see CRYSTAL EASTMAN,
WORK ACCIDENTS AND THE LAW (New York: Russell Sage Foundation, 1910).

54. For personal injury practices, see JEROME CARLIN, LAWYERS ON THEIR OWN
(San Francisco: Austin & Winfield, 1994); Rhode, *Solicitation*. For union referral
systems, see the cases discussed below. For public interest practice, see Rhode,
Solicitation, 325; *Twenty Years after Brown*, BALTIMORE SUN, May 17, 1974, at A14.
For the 1938 commentator, see Lloyd K. Garrison, The Legal Profession and the
Public, Address Delivered at the Second Annual Convention of the National
Lawyers' Guild (Washington, D.C., February 19, 1938), *reprinted in* the NATIONAL
LAWYERS' GUILD QUARTERLY, 127, 129.

55. For bar attitudes, see Henry Drinker, quoted in CHRISTENSEN, LAWYERS
FOR PEOPLE OF MODERATE MEANS, 154–55; HURST, GROWTH OF AMERICAN LAW,
331. For bar ethics committees, see Philip Shuchman, *Ethics and Legal Ethics: The
Propriety of the Canons as a Group Moral Code*, 37 GEORGE WASHINGTON LAW RE-
VIEW 244, 255–56 (1968). For committee decisions, see GEOFFREY C. HAZARD, JR.,

SUSAN P. KONIAK & ROGER C. CRAMTON, THE LAW AND ETHICS OF LAWYERING 1014 (New York: Foundation Press, 1999) (calendars); In re Maltby, 202 P.2d 902 (Arizona 1949) (matchbooks); ABA COMMITTEE ON PROFESSIONAL ETHICS, Formal Op. 309 (1963) (Christmas cards); HENRY S. DRINKER, LEGAL ETHICS 289 (New York: Columbia University Press, 1953) (size of sign); ABA COMMITTEE ON PROFESSIONAL ETHICS, Informal Op. C-747 (1964) (state bar jewelry); ABA COMMITTEE ON PROFESSIONAL ETHICS, Formal Op. 184 (1951).

56. Goldfarb v. Virginia State Bar, 421 U.S. 773, 787 (1975).

57. For the advertising cases, see Bates v. State Bar of Arizona, 433 U.S. 350 (1977); Zavderer v. Office Disciplinary Counsel, 471 U.S. 626 (1985) (illustration); Shapero v. Kentucky Bar Association, 486 U.S. 466 (1988) (mortgage). For solicitation cases, see In re Primis 436 U.S. 412 (1978) (public interest); Ohralik v. Ohio State Bar Association, 436 U.S. 447 (1978) (personal solicitation); Florida Bar v. Went For It, 515 U.S. 618 (1995) (accident victim mailing).

58. For early plans, see ALEC M. SCHWARTZ, A LAWYER'S GUIDE TO PREPAID LEGAL SERVICES: A HANDBOOK FOR THE SMALL FIRM (Chicago: American Bar Association, 1998); *Opening One More Door to Justice, in* CIVIL JUSTICE: AN AGENDA FOR THE 1990s (Esther F. Lardent ed.) (Chicago: American Bar Association, 1990). For ethical restrictions and court decisions, see ABA CANONS OF ETHICS, Canons 12, 34, 35, 47; BARLOW F. CHRISTENSEN, GROUP LEGAL SERVICES 41–48 (Chicago: American Bar Foundation, 1967); Peter L. Zumrah, *Group Legal Services and the Constitution,* 76 YALE LAW JOURNAL 966, 972 (1967).

59. Kristin Choo, *Linking Lawyers and Clients,* ABA JOURNAL 83 (February 2001); AMERICAN BAR ASSOCIATION STANDING COMMITTEE ON LAWYER REFERRAL AND INFORMATION SERVICE, REPORT TO THE HOUSE OF DELEGATES (Chicago: American Bar Association, 1993); ABA Model Lawyer Referral and Information Service Quality Assistance Act (1993); CHRISTENSEN, LAWYERS FOR PEOPLE OF MODERATE MEANS, 173; Linda Morton, *Finding a Suitable Lawyer: Why Consumers Can't Always Get What They Want and What the Legal Profession Should Do about It,* 25 UNIVERSITY OF CALIFORNIA AT DAVIS LAW REVIEW 283, 301–2 (1992).

60. NAACP v. Button, 371 U.S. 415 (1963); Brotherhood of Railroad Trainmen v. Virginia State Bar, 377 U.S. 1 (1964), *reh'g denied,* 377 U.S. 960 (1964); United Mine Workers Dist. 12 v. Illinois State Bar Association, 389 U.S. 217 (1967); United Transportation Union v. State Bar of Michigan, 401 U.S. 576, 585 (1971). For the bar opposition, see Judith Maute, *Pre-Paid and Group Legal Services: Thirty Years after the Storm,* 70 FORDHAM LAW REVIEW 915, 936 (2001).

61. For bar leaders' position, see ABA President John Satterfield, quoted in Deborah L. Rhode, *Policing the Professional Monopoly: An Empirical and Constitutional Analysis of Unauthorized Practice Prohibitions,* 34 STANFORD LAW REVIEW 1, 2 (1981). For early unauthorized practice enforcement, see *id.,* 7; ABEL, AMERICAN LAWYERS, 112–13; Christensen, *Unauthorized Practice,* 179–81; HURST, GROWTH OF AMERICAN LAW, 323.

62. For bar committees and statutory developments, see PROCEEDINGS OF THE FIFTY-THIRD ANNUAL MEETING OF THE ABA (Chicago: American Bar Association, 1930); ABEL, AMERICAN LAWYERS, 113; Rhode, *Professional Monopoly,* 8–9; Christensen, *Unauthorized Practice,* 191–92, 196, 203. For the ABA's claims, see Traverbridge Vonn Bauer quoted in Rhode, *Professional Monopoly,* 9. For histori-

ans' views, see Hurst, Growth of American Law, 323.

63. For ABA codes, see Model Code of Professional Responsibility, Ethical Consideration, 3–5 (1970); Model Rules of Professional Conduct, Rule 5.5, Comment (2002). For statutes, see Deborah L. Rhode, *The Delivery of Legal Services by Non-Lawyers*, 4 Georgetown Journal of Legal Ethics 209, 211 (1990).

64. Rhode, *Delivery of Legal Services*, 212; Alan Morrison, *Defining the Unauthorized Practice of Law: Some New Ways of Looking at an Old Question*, 4 Nova Law Journal 363, 370 (1980).

65. Abel, American Lawyers, 114; Christensen, *Unauthorized Practice*, 195–96, 200; Rhode, *Professional Monopoly*, 10.

66. Pound, Lawyer from Antiquity, 7. Russell Pearce, *Lawyers as America's Governing Class*, 8 University of Chicago Law School Roundtable 381 (2001).

Chapter 4

1. James Carter, Remarks at the 100th Anniversary Luncheon of the Los Angeles County Bar Association, May 4, 1978, *printed in* 64 ABA Journal 840, 842 (1978).

2. For unmet needs, see American Bar Association, Consortium on Legal Services and the Public, Legal Needs and Civil Justice: A Survey of Americans: Major Findings from the Comprehensive Legal Needs Study 3–10 (Chicago: American Bar Association, 1994); National Center for State Courts, Meeting the Needs of Self-Represented Litigants: A Consumer Based Approach, *available at* http://www.judgelink.org/a2j/proposal.html, accessed April 14, 2003; Janet Stidman Eveleth, *Is Middle Class America Denied Access to Justice?*, 29 Maryland Bar Journal 44, 45 (1996) (citing findings of the Maryland State Bar Association Moderate Income Access to Justice Advisory Task Force); Susan D. Carle, *Re-Valuing Lawyering for Middle-Income Clients*, 70 Fordham L. Review 719, 724 (2001). For reasons, see ABA Consortium, Legal Needs, 15–16.

3. ABA Consortium, Legal Needs, 7–19. For examples of poorer outcomes for individuals who lack lawyers, see Carol Seron, Gregg van Ryzin, Martin Frankel & Jean Kovath, *The Impact of Legal Counsel on Outcomes for Poor Tenants in New York City's Housing Court: Results of Random Experiment*, 35 Law & Society Review 426 (2001); Richard Zitrin & Carol M. Langford, The Moral Compass of the American Lawyers 129, 135 (New York: Ballantine, 1999); Russell Engler, *Out of Sight and Out of Line: The Need for Legal Regulation of Lawyers' Negotiations with Unrepresented Poor Persons*, 85 California Law Review 79, 107–8, 154–55 (1997); Deborah L. Rhode, *Access to Justice*, 69 Fordham Law Review 1785, 1793 (2001). For the couple's experience, see Amanda Ripley, *Who Needs Lawyers?*, Time, June 12, 2000, at 62.

4. For Americans' desires, see National Center of State Courts, A Market-Driven Approach to Civil Justice Reform, *available at* http://www.judgelink .org a2j/concept.html (last checked, April 13, 2003); George A. Reimer, *21st Century Mandatory State Bars: Change Agents in the Public Interest or State Sponsored Guilds?*, Professional Lawyer 125 (2002) (describing priorities of Citizens Justice Conference).

5. *See* Deborah L. Rhode, *The Delivery of Legal Services by Non-Lawyers,* 4 GEORGETOWN JOURNAL OF LEGAL ETHICS 199, 214–15 (1990); Deborah L. Rhode, *Policing the Professional Monopoly: A Constitutional and Empirical Analysis of Unauthorized Practice Prohibitions,* 34 STANFORD LAW REVIEW 1, 6–7 (1981).

6. Jennifer B. Lee, *Dot-Com, Esq.; Legal Guidance, Lawyer Optional,* NEW YORK TIMES, February 22, 2001, at G1; FreeAdvice Forum, *available at* http://forum .freeadvice.com; Robert J. Ambarogi, *The 10 Best Legal Sites on the Web,* L TECH. NEWS, July 23, 2001; *Express Divorce,* TIME, July 7, 2003, at 101; Johanna Bennett, *Plunging into Paperwork,* WALL STREET JOURNAL, June 9, 2003, at R3.

7. Rhode, *Delivery of Legal Services,* 213; JANA GOLDSCHMIDT, MEETING THE CHALLENGE OF PRO SE LITIGATION: A REPORT AND GUIDEBOOK FOR JUDGES AND COURT MANAGERS 10 (1998); Caitlin Liu, *Legal Answers Minus Lawyers,* LOS ANGELES TIMES, June 22, 2001, at A1; *Going Pro Se in Divorce Cases,* HALT: AMERICANS FOR LEGAL REFORM, THE LEGAL REFORMER NEWSLETTER 4 (Spring 2001); Engler, *Out of Sight,* 125.

8. Rhode, *Policing the Professional Monopoly,* 6–7; *see* Deborah L. Rhode, *Professionalism in Perspective: Alternative Approaches to Nonlawyer Practice,* 22 NEW YORK REVIEW OF LAW AND SOCIAL CHANGE 703, 705 (1996); and sources cited below in notes 21–22.

9. Tina L. Rasnow, *Traveling Justice: Providing Court-Based Pro Se Assistance to Limited Access Communities,* 29 FORDHAM URBAN LAW JOURNAL 1281, 1293 (2002); Personal correspondence with Bonnie Hough, Supervising Attorney, Equal Access Project, July 9, 2001, and Kathleen Sampson, American Judicature Society, January 7, 2002.

10. For clerks' attitudes toward domestic violence cases, *see* Deborah Epstein, *Effective Intervention in Domestic Violence Cases,* 11 YALE JOURNAL OF LAW AND FEMINISM 3, 33 (1999); Engler, *Out of Sight,* 126. For domestic violence studies, see Amy Farmer & Jill Tiefenthaler, *Explaining the Recent Decline in Domestic Violence,* 21 JOURNAL OF CONTEMPORARY ECONOMIC POLICY 158 (2003).

11. HALT, Americans for Legal Reform, Small Claims Reform Project and Small Claims Report Card, January 13, 2003, *available at* http://HALT.org./ smallclaims/screportcard.cfm; James C. Turner & Joyce A. McGee, *Small Claims Reforms: A Means of Expanding Access to the American Civil Justice System,* 5 UNIVERSITY OF THE DISTRICT OF COLUMBIA LAW REVIEW 177 (2000); statement of Thomas Gordon, HALT, *reprinted in* ABA STANDING COMMITTEE ON THE DELIVERY OF LEGAL SERVICES, REPORT ON THE PUBLIC HEARING ON ACCESS TO JUSTICE (Chicago: American Bar Association, August, 2003).

12. Epstein, *Effective Intervention,* 33; Margaret Martin Barry, *Access to Justice: On Dialogues with the Judiciary,* 29 FORDHAM URBAN LAW JOURNAL 1089, 1101 (2002); National Judicial Education Program, *available at* http://www.nowldef .org/html/njep/gendb.HTM; Engler, *Out of Sight.*

13. For the lack of policies, see Jona Goldschmidt, How Are Judges and Courts Coping with Pro Se Litigants? Report from a Survey of Judges and Court Managers (unpublished report, presented at the Law and Society Annual Meeting, St. Louis, Mo., 1997); Russell Engler, *And Justice for All—Including the Unrepresented Poor: Revisiting the Roles of the Judges, Mediators, and Clerks,* 67 FORDHAM LAW REVIEW 1987, 2013 (1999). For concerns about impartiality and opening the

floodgates, see Nancy McCarthy, *Plan to Help Unrepresented Litigants Sparks Board Debate*, CALIFORNIA BAR JOURNAL, January 2004, at 1, 18; Engler, *And Justice for All*, 2012–15; Goldschmidt, Pro Se Litigants, 19; Jacobsen v. Filler, 790 F.2d 1362 (9th Cir. 1986). For hostility, see Engler, *And Justice for All*, 2014–16; Barbara Bezdek, *Silence in the Court: Participation and Subordination of Poor Tenants' Voices in Legal Process*, 20 HOFSTRA LAW REVIEW 566, 574 (1992); Goldschmidt, Pro Se Litigants, 19; Barry, *Access to Justice*, 100. For domestic violence cases, see Epstein, *Effective Intervention*, 43.

14. Rasnow, *Traveling Justice*, 1295; Wendy Davis, *Special Problems for Special Courts*, ABA JOURNAL 32 (February 2003) (quoting Feinblatt); Paul von Zielbauer, *Court Treatment System Is Found to Help Drug Offenders Stay Clean*, NEW YORK TIMES, November 9, 2003, at 33, 35.

15. CALIFORNIA COMMISSION ON ACCESS TO JUSTICE, THE PATH TO EQUAL JUSTICE 21–24 (San Francisco, 2002); ABA Report on the Public Hearing; AMERICAN BAR ASSOCIATION AND NATIONAL LEGAL AID AND DEFENDER ASSOCIATION, SUPPORTING PARTNERS TO EQUAL ACCESS vii, 8 (Chicago: American Bar Association, 2002); Engler, *And Justice for All*, 2065–70; Rasnow, *Traveling Justice*, 1284–86, 1296, 1304; Goldschmidt, Pro Se Litigants, 19–22.

16. GREG BERMAN & JOHN FEINBLATT, PROBLEM SOLVING COURTS: A BRIEF PRIMER (New York: Center for Court Innovation, 2001); Davis, *Special Problems*, 32; Julia Weber, *Domestic Violence Courts*, 2 JOURNAL OF THE CENTER FOR FAMILIES, CHILDREN AND COURTS 23 (2000); Margot Lindsay & Mary K. Shitor, *The Public is Willing*, 29 FORDHAM URBAN LAW JOURNAL 1267, 1270 (2001); Nancy McCarthy, *Judge Focuses on Serving Families*, CALIFORNIA BAR JOURNAL 18 (February 2002); Anthony C. Thompson, *Courting Disorder: Some Thoughts on Community Courts*, 10 WASHINGTON UNIVERSITY JOURNAL OF LAW AND POLICY 63 (2002); Paul von Zielbauer, *Court Supervised Treatment*, at 35. For alternative dispute resolution, see DEBORAH L. RHODE, IN THE INTERESTS OF JUSTICE: REFORMING THE LEGAL PROFESSION 132–35 (New York: Oxford University Press, 2000).

17. *See* RHODE, IN THE INTERESTS OF JUSTICE, 132–33; Thompson, *Courting Disorder*; Davis, *Special Problems*, 32–33; Terry Carter, *Self Help Speeds Up*, ABA JOURNAL, July 2001; Engler, *And Justice for All*, 2045. For the absence of research, see Interview, Sampson.

18. Compulsory arbitration systems sponsored by employers who are repeat players often systematically disadvantage employees who are not. *See* Richard C. Reuben, *The Bias Factor*, CAL. LAW. 25 (November 1999); Katherine Van Wezel Stone, *Rustic Justice: Community and Coercion under the Federal Arbitration Act*, 77 NORTH CAROLINA L. REV. 931, 1015–17 (1999). For research on internal processes, see CHRISTINE PARKER, JUST LAWYERS 184–88 (Oxford: Oxford University Press, 1999). For preferences regarding dispute resolution, see MICHAEL ZANDER, THE QUALITY OF JUSTICE 29–32 (London: Sweet & Maxwell, 2000); and HAZEL G. GENN, PATHS TO JUSTICE: WHAT PEOPLE DO AND THINK ABOUT GOING TO LAW 217–18 (Portland, Ore.: Hart Publishing, 1999).

19. For definitions, see AMERICAN BAR ASSOCIATION, TASK FORCE ON THE MODEL DEFINITION OF THE PRACTICE OF LAW, REPORT TO THE HOUSE OF DELEGATES (Chicago: American Bar Association, 2003); Rhode, *Delivery of Legal Services*, 209, 211–12.

20. Michael Lewis, *Faking It*, NEW YORK TIMES MAGAZINE, July 15, 2001, at 32; Deborah L. Rhode, *Professionalism in Perspective: Alternative Approaches to Non-lawyer Practice*, 22 NEW YORK REVIEW OF LAW AND SOCIAL CHANGE 701 (1996).

21. For bar views, see Jonathan Rose, *Unauthorized Practice of Law in Arizona: A Legal and Political Problem that Won't Go Away*, 34 ARIZONA STATE LAW JOURNAL 585, 594 (2001) (quoting the State Bar of Arizona Consumer Protection Committee); James Podgers, *Legal Profession Faces Rising Tide of Nonlawyer Practice*, ABA JOURNAL, December 1993, at 51, 56; Alfred P. Carlton, Jr., Letter to the Editor, WALL STREET JOURNAL, April 28, 2003, at A13. For examples of unauthorized practice initiatives, see Rose, *supra; Illinois Lawyers Protect their Monopoly*, HALT, AMERICANS FOR LEGAL REFORM, THE LEGAL REFORMER NEWSLETTER 3 (Fall 2000); North Carolina State Bar Formal Ethics Op. 2002–09, January 24, 2003; *Governor Davis Signs Bar-Backed Bill to Crack Down on UPL*, CALIFORNIA LAWYER 1 (October 2002); WASHINGTON STATE BAR ASSOCIATION, COMMITTEE TO DEFINE THE PRACTICE OF LAW, FINAL REPORT (Seattle, Wash., 1999).

22. Bill Ibelle, *Controversial ABA 'Nonlawyer Practice' Report Due in August*, LAWYER WEEKLY USA July 3, section 13 (1995) (quoting Thomas Curtin); David Vladeck, Letter to Mary K. Ryan, Chair, Standing Committee on the Delivery of Legal Services, July 31, 2002, *reprinted in* ABA REPORT ON THE PUBLIC HEARINGS, Appendix H.

23. For consumer surveys, see BARBARA A. CURRAN, THE LEGAL NEEDS OF THE PUBLIC 231 (Chicago: American Bar Foundation, 1977); REPORT OF THE STATE BAR OF CALIFORNIA COMMISSION ON LEGAL TECHNICIANS 14 (San Francisco: State Bar of California Office of Professional Standards, 1990). For the realtors' case, see Rose, *Unauthorized Practice*, and State Bar v. Arizona Land Title & Trust, 366 P.2d 1, 14–15 (Ariz. 1961). For the Texas case, see Alan Morrison, *Defining the Unauthorized Practice of Law: Some Ways of Looking at an Old Question*, 4 NOVA LAW JOURNAL 363 (1980); Committee v. Parson Technology, 179 F.3d 956 (5th. Cir. 1999); Randall Samborn, *So What Is a Lawyer, Anyway?*, NATIONAL LAW JOURNAL, June 21, 1993, at 1, 12.

24. For other countries, see sources cited in RHODE, IN THE INTERESTS OF JUSTICE, 137; Deborah L. Rhode, *In the Interests of Justice: A Comparative Perspective on Access to Legal Services and Accountability of the Legal Profession*, MODERN LEGAL THOUGHT (2004). For this country, see Restatement (Third) of the Law Governing Lawyers § 4 Comment C (2001); HERBERT KRITZER, LEGAL ADVOCACY 193–203 (Ann Arbor: University of Michigan Press, 1998); Jean Braucher, *Counseling Consumer Debtors to Make Their Own Informed Choices—A Question of Professional Responsibility*, 5 AM. BANK. INST. L. REV. 165 (1997). For complaints, see STANDING COMMITTEE ON LAWYERS' RESPONSIBILITY FOR CLIENT PROTECTION OF THE AMERICAN BAR ASSOCIATION, 1994 SURVEY AND RELATED MATERIALS ON THE UNAUTHORIZED PRACTICE OF LAW: NONLAWYER PRACTICE xvii–iii (Chicago: American Bar Association, 1994); see also Rhode, *Policing the Professional Monopoly*. For lay performance generally, see Rhode, *Professionalism*, 709–10, Kritzer, LEGAL ADVOCACY.

25. *See* COMMISSION ON NONLAWYER PRACTICE, AMERICAN BAR ASSOCIATION, NONLAWYER PRACTICE IN THE UNITED STATES: SUMMARY OF THE FACTUAL RECORD BEFORE THE COMMISSION 18–19 (Chicago: American Bar Association,

1994); Alexandra A. Ashbrook, *The Unauthorized Practice of Law in Immigration: Examining the Propriety of Non-Lawyer Representation*, 5 Georgetown Journal of Legal Ethics 237, 249–51 (1991); Lucia Hwang, *The Fixers*, California Lawyer 20 (December 2002).

26. Debra Baker, *Is This Woman a Threat to Lawyers?*, ABA Journal, June 1999, at 57 (quoting Mary M. Johnstone, Delaware Chief Disciplinary Counsel); In re Arons, 756 A.2d 867 (Delaware 2000).

27. For examples of such proposals, see sources cited in Rhode, *Professionalism*, 715.

28. *See* Steven Brint, In an Age of Experts: The Changing Role of Professionalism in Politics and Public Life 76 (Princeton, N.J.: Princeton University Press, 1994) (discussing the unwarranted price increases due to restricted competition); Simon Domberger & Avrom Sherr, *The Impact of Competition on Pricing and Quality of Legal Services*, 9 International Review of Law and Economy 41, 55 (1989) (discussing Great Britain); George C. Leef, *Lawyer Fees Too High: The Case for Repealing Unauthorized Practice of Law Statutes*, Regulation 33, 34–35 (Winter 1997) (discussing Great Britain and Canada); Rhode, *Professionalism*, 712–13; American Bar Association, Commission on Multidisciplinary Practice, Report to the ABA House of Delegates, *reprinted in* 10 Professional Lawyer 1 (1999); Background Paper on Multidisciplinary Practice: Issues and Developments, *reprinted in* Professional Lawyer 10 (1998); Wayne Moore, *Improving the Delivery of Legal Services for the Elderly: A Comprehensive Approach*, 41 Emory Law Journal 849 (1972); Mark E. Doremus, *Wisconsin Elderlinks Initiative: Using Technology to Provide Legal Services to Older Persons*, 32 Wake Forest Law Review 545 (1997).

29. ABA Model Rules of Professional Conduct, Rules 5.4 and 5.7; ABA Model Code of Professional Responsibility, DR 3–102, DR 3–103, EC 3–8; ABA Committee on Professional Ethics, Formal Opinion 355 (1987).

30. John Gibeaut, *Squeeze Play*, ABA Journal, February 1998, at 42, 43; Cindy K. Goodman, *Line between Accounting, Law Professions May Soon Blur*, Miami Herald, March 1, 1999; for the lack of unauthorized practice enforcement, see Linda Galler, *Problems in Defining and Controlling the Unauthorized Practice of Law*, 42 Arizona Law Review 773, 779–80 (2002). For accountants' success, see Geoffrey Hazard, Jr., *Accountants vs. Lawyers: Let's Consider Facts*, National Law Journal, November 9, 1998, at A24.

31. For state bar actions, see Charles W. Wolfram, *Comparative Multidisciplinary Practice of Law Paths Taken and Not Taken*, 52 Case Western Law Review 961, 981 (2002); ABA Center for Professional Responsibility, Status of Multidisciplinary Practice Studies by State (and some local bars), *available at* http://www.abanet.org/cpr/ mdp-state_action.html. For overviews of the debate, see *id.*; *Symposium: The Brave New World of Multidisciplinary Practice*, 50 Journal of Legal Education 469 (2000); *Future of the Profession: A Symposium on Multidisciplinary Practice*, 84 Minn. L. Rev. 1083 (2000); Mary C. Daly, *Choosing Wise Men Wisely: The Risks and Rewards of Purchasing Legal Services from Lawyers in a Multidisciplinary Partnership*, 13 Geo. J. Legal Ethics 217 (2000). For a critique of the anticompetitive aspects of bar rules, see American Antitrust Institute,

CONVERGING PROFESSIONAL SERVICES: LAWYERS AGAINST THE MULTIDISCIPLINARY TIDE (Washington, D.C.: American Antitrust Institute, 2000).

32. For the lessons of Enron from opponents' perspective, see sources cited in Robert R. Keating, *Multidisciplinary Practice in a World of Invincible Ignorance: MDP, MJP, and Ancillary Business after Enron*, 44 ARIZONA LAW REVIEW 717, 718 (2002); Brenda Sandburg, *Enron Mess Gives a Boost to MDP Foes*, SAN FRANCISCO RECORDER, January 24, 2002, at 1; Steven C. Krane, *Rest in Peace, MDP: Let Lawyers Practice Law*, NATIONAL LAW JOURNAL, January 30, 2002, at A16.

33. For an overview of managed care and its lessons for lawyers, see George G. Harris & Derek F. Foran, *The Ethics of Middle Class Access to Legal Services and What We Can Learn from the Medical Profession's Shift to a Corporate Paradigm*, 70 FORDHAM LAW REVIEW 775, 807–70 (2001). For conflicts of interest, see *id.*; and Council on Ethical and Judicial Affairs, American Medical Association, *Ethical Issues in Managed Care*, 273 JOURNAL OF THE AMERICAN MEDICAL ASSOCIATION 330, 331 (1995).

34. For the lack of attention to clients' interests, see Keating, *Colorado and Denver in the House MDP Debate Declared Heresy by the ABA House of Delegates*, COLORADO LAWYER 48 (September 2000). For the lack of attention to societal interests, see David Luban, *Asking the Right Questions*, 72 TEMPLE LAW REVIEW 839 (1999).

35. For other conflicts of interest, see Keating, *Multidimensional Practice*, 720; Stephen Gillers, *The Anxiety of Influence*, 27 FLORIDA STATE UNIVERSITY LAW REVIEW 1123 (1999); Robert Gordon, Written Remarks to the Multidisciplinary Practice Commission, May 1999. For lawyers' conduct in Enron and other scandals, see Deborah L. Rhode & Paul Paton, *Lawyers, Ethics, and Enron*, 8 STANFORD JOURNAL OF LAW, BUSINESS, AND FINANCE 9 (2002); RHODE, IN THE INTERESTS OF JUSTICE, 108–9. For excerpts from the D.C. report, see *District of Columbia Bar Leadership Endorses Amending Rules to Allow MDPs*, 18 ABA/BNA LAWYERS' MANUAL ON PROFESSIONAL CONDUCT 383 (2002).

36. For quality studies, see Stephen R. Latham, *Regulation of Managed Care Incentive Payments to Physicians*, 22 AM. J. L. & MED. 399, 407 n. 84 (1995); Harris & Foran, *Middle Class Access*, 820. For malpractice, see *id.*, at 821–34.

37. ABA MULTIDISCIPLINARY PRACTICE COMMISSION, REPORT TO THE HOUSE OF DELEGATES; *D.C. Bar Leadership*, 380.

38. For lawyers' views, see Archer W. Honeycutt & Elizabeth A. Wibker, *Consumers' Perceptions of Selected Issues Relating to Advertising by Lawyers*, 7 JOURNAL OF PROFESSIONAL SERVICES MARKETING 119, 120 (1991) (finding that almost 90 percent of surveyed ABA members believe that advertising harms the profession's image); Mary Hladky, *High Court Case to Test Limits on Lawyer Ads*, LEGAL TIMES, January 9, 1995, at 1. For Burger's views, see David Margolick, *Burger Criticism Prompts Defense of Lawyer Ads*, NEW YORK TIMES, July 9, 1985, at A3; Warren E. Burger, *The Decline of Professionalism*, 63 FORDHAM LAW REVIEW 949, 953, 956 (1995). For consumer views, see William E. Hornsby, Jr., *Ad Rules Infinitum: The Need for Alternatives to State-Based Ethics Governing Legal Services Marketing*, 36 UNIVERSITY OF RICHMOND LAW REVIEW 49, 87–88 (2002); Milo Geyelin, *Debate Intensifies over State Regulations That Restrict TV Advertising by*

Lawyers, WALL STREET JOURNAL, August 31, 1992, at B1, B4; Diane B. MacDonald & Mary Anne Raymond, *Attorney Advertising: Do Attorneys Know their Clients?*, 7 JOURNAL OF PROFESSIONAL SERVICES MARKETING 99 (1991). For findings on public image, see Geoffrey C. Hazard, Jr., Susan P. Koniak & Roger C. Cramton, THE LAW AND ETHICS OF LAWYERING 1033 (New York: Foundation Press, 3d ed., 1999) ABA COMMISSION ON ADVERTISING, LAWYER ADVERTISING AT THE CROSSROADS: PROFESSIONAL POLICY CONSIDERATIONS (1995); Hornsby, *Ad Rules Infinitum*, 55; Richard J. Cebula, *Does Lawyer Advertising Adversely Influence the Image of Lawyers in the United States? An Alternative Perspective and New Empirical Evidence*, 27 JOURNAL OF LEGAL STUDIES 503 (1998); WIESE RESEARCH ASSOCIATES, ATTORNEY ADVERTISING PERCEPTION STUDY 10–11 (ABA, 1994).

39. *See* RHODE, IN THE INTERESTS OF JUSTICE, 148; PETER A. BELL & JEFFREY P. O'CONNELL, ACCIDENTAL JUSTICE: THE DILEMMA OF TORT LAW 165–66 (New Haven, Conn.: Yale University Press, 1997); ZITRIN & LONFORD, MORAL COMPASS OF THE AMERICAN LAWYER, 129, 135.

40. For cost as the major obstacle, see ABA CONSORTIUM, LEGAL NEEDS, 15–16. For individuals' preferred methods of finding lawyers, see Judith Maute, *Pre-Paid and Group Legal Services: Thirty Years after the Storm*, 70 FORDHAM LAW REVIEW 915, 936 (2001) (citing studies indicating that only a fifth of clients found lawyers through advertising or Yellow Page listings; most relied on recommendations from friends or other sources); Linda Morton, *Finding a Suitable Lawyer: Why Consumers Can't Always Get What They Want and What the Legal Profession Should Do about It*, 25 UNIVERSITY OF CALIFORNIA AT DAVIS LAW REVIEW 283, 287–88 (1992) (reporting studies indicating that consumers' primary concern in selecting lawyers is quality and that most rely on referrals from someone they know).

41. *See* Maute, *Group Services*, 916; DEBORAH L. RHODE & DAVID LUBAN, LEGAL ETHICS, 656–57 (New York: Foundation Press, 2000, 3d ed.); Alec M. Schwartz, A LAWYER'S GUIDE, PREPAID LEGAL SERVICES 131–32 (Chicago: American Bar Association, 1998). For costs, see Brian Heid & Eitan Misulovin, *The Group Legal Plan Revolution: Bright Horizon or Dark Future?*, 18 HOFSTRA LABOR AND EMPLOYMENT LAW JOURNAL 335 (2000).

42. For other nations' experience, see Francis Regan, *Whatever Happened to Legal Expense Insurance?*, 26 ALTERNATIVE LAW JOURNAL 293 (2001). For inadequate quality controls, see Heid & Misulovin, *Group Plan*, 345–46; Schwartz, PREPAID LEGAL SERVICES, 137. For consumers' reservations, see *id.* at 130–35. For concerns about overuse, see Heid & Misulovin, *Group Plan*, 346.

43. Heid & Misulovin, *Group Plan*, 361–62.

44. Steven K. Berenson, *Is It Time for Lawyer Profiles?*, 70 FORDHAM LAW REVIEW 645, 651–57, 680 (2001); RHODE, IN THE INTERESTS OF JUSTICE, 163–64.

45. Berenson, *Lawyer Profiles*, 680–81; RHODE, IN THE INTERESTS OF JUSTICE, 159–68.

46. Forrest S. Mosten, *Unbundling of Legal Services and the Family Lawyer*, 28 FAM. L.Q. 421 (1994); Fern Fisher-Brandveen & Rochelle Klempner, *Unbundled Legal Services: Untying the Bundle in New York State*, 29 FORDHAM URBAN LAW JOURNAL 1107, 1108 (2002). For a bibliography of materials, see http://www.abanet .org/legalservices/delunbund.html.

47. For lawyers' objections, see Fisher-Brandveen & Klempner, *Unbundled Legal Services*, 1114. For malpractice issues, see *id.*, 1114–16, Mosten, *Unbundling*, 434; ABA MODEL RULES OF PROFESSIONAL CONDUCT, Rule 1.2 Comment.

48. *See* sources cited in Jona Goldschmidt, *In Defense of Ghostwriting*, 29 FORDHAM URBAN LAW JOURNAL 1145, 1170–71 (2002); Fisher-Brandveen & Klempner, *Unbundled Legal Services*, 1117–22.

49. Fisher-Brandveen & Klempner, *Unbundled Legal Services*, 1121–24; Goldschmidt, *Ghostwriting*, 1167–68, 1188–92, 1207–8; ABA REPORT ON PUBLIC HEARING, 5–6.

50. Deborah Howard, *The Law School Consortium Project: Law Schools Supporting Graduates to Increase Access to Justice for Low and Moderate-Income Individuals and Communities*, 29 FORDHAM URBAN LAW JOURNAL 1245, 1246–47 n. 7, 1249, 1254 (2002).

51. AMERICAN BAR ASSOCIATION COMMISSION ON PROFESSIONALISM, "IN THE SPIRIT OF PUBLIC SERVICE"? A BLUEPRINT FOR THE REKINDLING OF LAWYER PROFESSIONALISM 51 (Chicago: American Bar Association, 1986).

Chapter 5

1. George W. Bush, quoted in LEGAL SERVICES CORPORATION, ANNUAL REPORT 2000–2001, PROGRESS IN THE NEW MILLENNIUM 11 (Washington, D.C.: Legal Services Corporation, 2001). For the legal needs studies, see *id.*, 6; Alan W. Houseman, *Civil Legal Assistance for Low-Income Persons: Looking Back and Looking Forward*, 29 FORDHAM URBAN LAW JOURNAL 1213, 1233 (2002); and the sources cited in chapter 1.

2. For public opinion surveys, see Mauricio Vivero, *From "Renegade" Agency to Institution of Justice: The Transformation of the Legal Services Corporation*, 29 FORDHAM URBAN LAW JOURNAL 1323, 1345 (2002); Deborah L. Rhode, *Access to Justice*, 69 FORDHAM LAW REVIEW 1785, 1791 (2001). For bar contributions, see Deborah L. Rhode, *Pro Bono in Principle and in Practice*, 54 JOURNAL OF LEGAL EDUCATION 413 (2003), *available at* http://www.ssrn.com; LSC Statistics: Private Attorney Involvement, All Programs, *available at* http://www.lsc.gov/pressr/pr_pai.htm.

3. Douglas Besharov, *Foreword*, *in* LEGAL SERVICES FOR THE POOR: TIME FOR REFORM ix (Douglas J. Besharov ed.) (Washington, D.C.: American Enterprise Institute Press, 1990) (quoting Jon Asher); BRENNAN CENTER FOR JUSTICE, ACCESS TO JUSTICE SERIES, AN UNSOLVED MYSTERY: WHY ARE ROGUE POLITICIANS TRYING TO KILL A PROGRAM THAT HELPS THEIR NEEDIEST CONSTITUENTS? 2 (1999) (quoting Burton). For similar assessments about the reluctance to engage in self-criticism, see Marc Feldman, *Political Lessons: Legal Services for the Poor*, 83 GEORGETOWN LAW JOURNAL 1529, 1534 (1995).

4. Legal Services Corporation Mission Statement, *available at* http://www.lsc.gov/welcome/wel._what.htr; 42 U.S.C. § 2996 (1994); Alan W. Houseman, *Competitive Funding for Legal Services*, in LEGAL SERVICES, 158, 161.

5. *See* Omnibus Consolidated Rescissions and Appropriations Act of 1996, Pub. L. 104–134, § 504, 110 Stat. 1321; 45 C.F.R. pt. 1610–42. For state restric-

tions, see Laura K. Abel & David S. Udell, *If You Gag the Lawyers Do You Choke the Courts? Some Implications for Judges When Funding Restrictions Curb Advocacy by Lawyers on Behalf of the Poor*, 29 FORDHAM URBAN LAW JOURNAL 873, 874–80 (2002); Alan W. Houseman, *Restrictions by Funders and the Ethical Practice of Law*, 67 FORDHAM LAW REVIEW 2187, 2196–97 (1999). For current rules, see ALAN W. HOUSEMAN & LINDA E. PERLE, WHAT CAN AND CANNOT BE DONE: REPRESENTATION OF CLIENTS BY LSC-FUNDED PROGRAMS (Washington, D.C.: Center for Law and Social Policy, 2001).

6. For the decline in funding, see LEGAL SERVICES CORPORATION, ANNUAL REPORT, 13; Houseman, *Civil Legal Assistance*, 1222. For per capita expenditures, see *id.*, and BRENNAN CENTER FOR JUSTICE, STRUGGLING TO MEET THE NEED: COMMUNITIES CONFRONT GAPS IN FEDERAL LEGAL AID 5 (New York: Brennan Center for Justice, 2003).

7. For a representative example of a carefully designed study, see AMERICAN BAR ASSOCIATION CONSORTIUM ON LEGAL SERVICES AND THE PUBLIC, LEGAL NEEDS AND CIVIL JUSTICE: COMPREHENSIVE LEGAL NEEDS SURVEY (Chicago: American Bar Association, 1994). Such surveys typically ask questions that do not necessarily require a characterization of the problem as legal: for example, "Did you experience unsafe or unhealthful conditions in a place you were renting such as the landlord frequently failing to provide heat, hot water, electricity, or working plumbing . . . ." *Id.*, note 26. *See also* Mitchell Zuckoff, *Uneven Justice: Limited Funds for Legal Aid Can Lead to Mismatches in Civil Cases*, BOSTON GLOBE, March 12, 2000, at A1.

8. For a ban on domestic relations, see Pamela A. MacLean, *Legal Disservices*, CALIFORNIA LAWYER, March, 1997, at 23 (discussing California Rural Legal Assistance policy). For descriptions of a two-and-a-half year waiting list, see LEGAL SERVICES PROJECT, FUNDING CIVIL LEGAL SERVICES FOR THE POOR: REPORT TO THE CHIEF JUDGE 5 (1998); Zuckoff, *Uneven Justice*, A1. For holistic services, see Tanya Neiman, *Reflections on Holistic Advocacy*, MANAGEMENT INFORMATION EXCHANGE JOURNAL, 34, 36–37 (Fall 1999); Stacey Brustin, *Legal Services Provision through MultiDisciplinary Practice—Encouraging Holistic Advocacy while Protecting Ethical Interests*, 73 UNIVERSITY OF COLORADO LAW REVIEW 787 (2002).

9. ABA CONSORTIUM, LEGAL NEEDS, 22; De Miller, *Copayments, Vouchers, and Judicare*, in LEGAL SERVICES FOR THE POOR: TIME FOR REFORM 197, 203 (Douglas J. Besharov ed.) (Washington, D.C.: American Enterprise Institute Press, 1990). For the special needs of rural poor, see Perry Wasserman, Delivering Long-Distance Justice, *available at* http://www.ejm.lsc.gov/EJMIssue3/LSCUpClose/lsc_up_close.htm; Tina Rasnow, *Traveling Justice: Providing Court Based Pro Se Assistance to Limited Access Communities*, 29 FORDHAM URBAN LAW JOURNAL 1281 (2002). For immigrant communities, see Robert L. Bach, *Building Community among Diversity: Legal Services for Impoverished Immigrants*, 27 UNIVERSITY OF MICHIGAN JOURNAL OF LAW REFORM 639, 643 (1994). For the reluctance of legal aid programs to engage in outreach, see Ingrid V. Eagly, *Community Education: Creating a New Vision of Legal Service Practice*, 4 CLINICAL LAW REVIEW 433, 441–42 (1998); Alan W. Houseman, *Political Lessons: Legal Services for the Poor— A Commentary*, 83 GEORGETOWN LAW JOURNAL 1669, 1696–97 (1995).

10. Besharov, *Foreword*, in Legal Services, 5; Feldman, *Political Lessons*, 1537–41.

11. 45 C.F.R. § 1620.2. For successes in priority setting, see Houseman, *Political Lessons*, 1702. For problems in priority setting, see Paul E. Lee & Mary M. Lee, *Reflections from the Bottom of the Well: Racial Bias in the Provision of Legal Services to the Poor*, 27 Clearinghouse Review 311, 315–16 (1993); Feldman, *Political Lessons*, 1537–41; Peter Margulies, *Representation of Domestic Violence Survivors as a New Paradigm of Poverty Law*, 63 George Washington Law Review 1071, 1090 (1995). For pressures to increase caseloads, see *id.*, Raymond H. Brescia, Robin Goldman, Robert A. Solomon, *Who's in Charge, Anyway? A Proposal for Community-Based Legal Services*, 25 Fordham Urban Law Journal 831, 835–38, 846 (1998). For McKay's statements, see Janet Elliott, *Repositioning Legal Aid: New Leader Hopes Battered Moms Can Rescue Poverty Law*, Texas Lawyer, March 16, 1998; and Houseman, *Civil Legal Assistance*, 1232.

12. For the characterizations of legal service programs, see Kenneth F. Boehm, *The Legal Services Program: Unaccountable, Political, Anti-Poor, beyond Reform, and Unnecessary*, 17 St. Louis University Public Law Review 321, 328 (1998). For taxpayers' funds, see Boehm, *Legal Services*, 327 (quoting William F. Harvey, former LSC Chair); Deborah M. Weissman, *Law as Largesse: Shifting Paradigms of Law for the Poor*, 44 William & Mary Law Review 737, 762 (2002) (quoting Congressman Taylor); *Accountability for Legal Services*, Wall Street Journal, September 13, 1995, at 12. For assertedly counterproductive cases, see *id.*, Boehm, *Legal Services*, 333–34, 340–51; Michael Horowitz, *Response to "Should the Government Fund Legal Services? If So, What Should the Lawyers Do?"* 2 Journal of the Institute for the Study of Legal Ethics 411, 412 (1999); Kenneth F. Boehm, Testimony before the Small Business, Government Programs, and Oversight Committee, U.S. House of Representatives, Federal Document Clearinghouse Congressional Testimony, March 18, 1998; Statement of Bob Barr, Subcommittee on Commercial and Administrative Law, House of Representatives, Committee on the Judiciary, Hearings February 28, 2002, at 3. For abstract compassion, see George Will, *Gladiators for Liberation: Fight for a Peculiar Public Interest*, Albany Times Union, May 7, 1995, at E5. For Bob Dole's statement, see 141 Congressional Record S 14605 (September 28, 1995).

13. For the lack of support for critics' claims, see Weissman, *Law as Largesse*, 763. For meritorious claims by the poor, see Steven Gunn, *Eviction Defense for Poor Tenants: Costly Comparison or Justice Served?*, 13 Yale Law and Policy Review 385, 386 (1995); Carol Seron, Gregg van Ryzin, Martin Frankel & Jean Kovath, *The Impact of Legal Counsel on Outcomes for Poor Tenants in New York City's Housing Courts: Results of a Randomized Experiment*, 35 Law & Society Review 419 (2001).

14. For claims about political bias and the lack of representation of schools or housing projects, see Boehm, *Legal Services*, 342–44; Boehm, Testimony, 15–18.

15. For the lack of training, see Houseman, *Political Lessons*, 1698; Michael Diamond, *Community Lawyering: Revisiting the Old Neighborhood*, 32 Columbia Human Rights Law Review 67 (2000). For the lack of inclination, see Feldman, *Political Lessons*; Gerald Lopez, Rebellious Lawyering: One Chicano's View of Progressive Law Practice (Boulder, Colo.: Westview Press, 1992); Anthony V. Alfieri, *Theories of Practice: The Integration of Progressive Thought and Action:*

Disabled Clients, Disabling Lawyers, 43 HASTINGS LAW JOURNAL 769 (1992); Lucie E. White, *To Learn and Teach: Lessons from Driefontein on Lawyering and Power*, 43 WISCONSIN LAW REVIEW 699 (1988). For prohibited activities, see 45 CFR §§ 1600–1644 (1998).

16. LOPEZ, REBELLIOUS LAWYERING; Eagly, *Community Education*, 444; Brescia, Goldman & Solomon, *Who's in Charge*, 842; Richard D. Marsico, *Working for Social Change and Preserving Client Autonomy: Is There a Role for "Facilitative" Lawyering?*, 1 CLINICAL LAW REVIEW 639, 650 (1995); Paul R. Tremblay, *Toward a Community-Based Ethic for Legal Services*, 37 UCLA LAW REVIEW 1101 (1990).

17. Vivero, *Renegade Agency*, 1343.

18. Camille D. Holmes, Linda E. Perle & Alan W. Houseman, *Race-Based Advocacy: The Role and Responsibility of LSC-Funded Programs*, JOURNAL OF POVERTY LAW AND POLICY 61 (May–June 2002); Alan W. Houseman, *Racial Justice: The Role of Civil Legal Assistance*, JOURNAL OF POVERTY LAW AND POLICY 5 (May–June 2002); Lee & Lee, *Bottom of the Well*; John A. Powell, *Race and Poverty: A New Focus for Legal Services*, 27 CLEARINGHOUSE REVIEW 299 (1993).

19. BRENNAN CENTER, STRUGGLING TO MEET THE NEED, 5; Houseman, *Civil Legal Assistance*, 1230. For state efforts, see SPAN (Supporting Partnerships to Expand Access to Justice), Report: Access to Justice Partnerships, State by State v, 33, 75, *available at* www.nlada.org/civil_SPAN/SPAN_Report; Associated Press Newswire, Attorneys Raise $13,065 for Legal Aid Fund, December 13, 2002. For the IOLTA decision, see Brown v. Legal Foundation of Washington, 538 U.S. 21 (2003). For California funding, see Kristina Horton Flaherty, *Supreme Court Rules IOLTA is Constitutional*, CALIFORNIA BAR JOURNAL 1, 7 (May 2003).

20. Margaret Graham Tebo, *Aiding Legal Aid*, ABA JOURNAL 28 (June 2002). For discussion of mandatory pro bono requirements, see Rhode, *Pro Bono in Principle*. For funding proposals, see Erik Cummins, *Novel Proposal Would Privatize Legal Services for Poor*, SAN FRANCISCO DAILY JOURNAL, August 22, 2001, at 1, 16 (describing proposal for 2 percent contribution of gross revenues by largest firms to support legal services); William Carlsen, *San Francisco Lawyer Proposes a Tax on Lawyers*, SAN FRANCISCO CHRONICLE, February 7, 1989, at A7 (describing proposal for 6 percent tax on fees by law firms taking in more than $500,000).

21. Legal Aid Society of Hawaii v. Legal Services Corporation, 145 F.3d 1017 (9th Cir. 1998), *cert. denied*, 525 U.S. 1015 (1998); Velazquez v. Legal Services Corporation, 164 F.3d 757 (2d Cir. 1999), *cert. granted*, 529 U.S. 1052 (2000); Legal Services Corporation v. Velazquez, 531 U.S. 533 (2001). For a critique of bar ethics committees' failure to condemn these restrictions, see David Luban, *Taking Out the Adversary: The Assault on Progressive Public Interest Lawyering*, 91 CALIFORNIA LAW REVIEW 209, 225–26 (2003).

22. Abel & Udell, *If You Gag the Lawyers*, 881; David S. Udell, *The Legal Services Restrictions: Lawyers in Florida, New York, Virginia and Oregon Describe the Costs*, 17 YALE LAW AND POLICY REVIEW 337 (1998).

23. For cases recognizing First Amendment interests, see Abel & Udell, *If You Gag the Lawyers*, 887–94; see NAACP v. Button, 371 U.S. 415; In re Primus, 436 U.S. 412 (1978). For the need for class actions, see BRENNAN CENTER FOR JUSTICE, LEFT OUT IN THE COLD: HOW CLIENTS ARE AFFECTED BY RESTRICTIONS ON THEIR LEGAL SERVICES LAWYERS (New York: Brennan Center for Justice, 2000).

For lawyers' ethical obligations, see ABA MODEL RULES OF PROFESSIONAL CONDUCT R. 1.1 (requiring competent representation); R. 5.4 (prohibiting a lawyer from permitting a person "who pays the lawyer to render services for another to direct or regulate the lawyer's professional judgment in rendering such services"); see Houseman, *Restrictions*, 2191; Samuel J. Levine, *Legal Services Lawyers and the Influence of Third Parties on the Lawyer–Client Relationship: Some Thoughts from Scholars, Practitioners, and Courts*, 67 FORDHAM LAW REVIEW 2319, 2330 (1999).

24. Abel & Udell, *If You Gag the Lawyers*, 887–94.

25. For discussion of the defenses of restrictions, see Alan Houseman, *Civil Legal Assistance*, 1230. For critiques, see Abel & Udell, *If You Gag the Lawyers*, 882–94; Luban, *Taking Out the Adversary*, 220–25.

26. Buckhannon Board and Care Home, Inc., v. West Virginia Department of Health and Human Resources, 532 U.S. 598, 605 (2001). For legislative history, see H.R. Rep. No. 94–1558, 7 (1976); S. Rep. 94–1011, 5 (1976); Weissman, *Law as Largesse*, 782. For legislative reform, see Margaret Graham Tebo, *Fee Shifting Fallout*, ABA JOURNAL, July 2003, at 54.

27. For the impact of funding restrictions, see Houseman, *Restrictions*, 2233. For prison abuse, see AMNESTY INTERNATIONAL, ABUSE OF WOMEN IN CUSTODY (New York: Amnesty International, 2001); HUMAN RIGHTS WATCH, ALL TOO FAMILIAR: SEXUAL ABUSE OF WOMEN IN U.S. STATE PRISON (New York: Human Rights Watch, 2001); HUMAN RIGHTS WATCH, NO ESCAPE: MALE RAPE IN U.S. PRISON (New York: Human Rights Watch, 2001). For the private bar's unwillingness to handle such litigation, see Margaret Graham Tebo, *The Closing Door: US Policies Leave Immigrants Separate and Unequal*, ABA JOURNAL, July 2001, at 42; Deborah L. Rhode, *Indifference Rules*, NATIONAL LAW JOURNAL, October 28, 2001, at A25.

28. For the invisibility of legal aid offices, see LEADERS FOR JUSTICE ADVISORY COUNCIL, NATIONAL ASSOCIATION OF LEGAL AID AND DEFENDER ASSOCIATION (NLADA), LEADERS FOR JUSTICE: A NATIONAL LEADERSHIP DEVELOPMENT INITIATIVE FOR THE LEGAL AID COMMUNITY AND THE EQUAL JUSTICE MOVEMENT 8 (Washington, D.C.: NLADA, 2002). For the need to engage in public education and efforts to do so, see *id.*, describing the Campaign for Equal Access: Bringing Justice Home. For examples, see BRENNAN CENTER FOR JUSTICE, LEGAL SERVICES CLIENTS TELL THEIR STORY 2 (New York: Brennan Center for Justice, 1999); BRENNAN CENTER, STRUGGLING TO MEET THE NEED, 6–8; Lynn M. Kelly, *Lawyering for Poor Communities on the Cusp of the Next Century*, 25 FORDHAM URBAN LAW JOURNAL 721, 722–23 (1998); Phyllis Coleman & Ronald A. Shallaw, *Ineffective Assistance of Counsel: A Call for a Stricter Test in Civil Commitments*, 27 JOURNAL OF THE LEGAL PROFESSION 37, 40 (2003).

29. For recommendations of broader coverage, see Lee Silverstein, *Full Legal Services*, 44 JOURNAL URBAN LAW 571 (1997); *Recommendations of the Conference on the Delivery of Legal Services to Low Income Persons*, 67 FORDHAM LAW REVIEW 1751, 1779–80 (1999); Besharov, *Introduction*, xvii, 21–22. For domestic violence victims' ineligibility for assistance despite their lack of access to resources, see Margulies, *Representation of Domestic Violence Survivors*, 1071, 1090; Margaret B.

Brown, *Domestic Violence Advocates' Exposure to Liability for Engaging in the Unauthorized Practice of Law*, 34 COLUMBIA JOURNAL OF LAW AND SOCIAL PROBLEMS 279, 282 (2001). For other nations, see CHRISTINE PARKER, JUST LAWYERS 33–36 (New York: Oxford University Press, 1999); Gary Bellow, *Legal Services in Comparative Perspective*, 5 MARYLAND JOURNAL OF CONTEMPORARY LEGAL ISSUES 371, 375–76 (1994).

30. *See* Jeffrey Selingo, *'President' Sheen Seeks Americorps Expansion*, CHRONICLE OF HIGHER EDUCATION, October 24, 2000, at A3.

31. For coordination, see Houseman, *Civil Legal Assistance*, 1234–36. For mobile units, see Rasnow, *Traveling Justice*, 1289–92. For technological innovation, see LSC Resource library, *available at* http://www.lri.lsc.gov. For Great Britain's centralized intake system, see Lord Chancellor's Department Community Legal Service Division, The Community Legal Service: A Consultation Paper (May 1999), *available at* http://www.lcd.gov.uk/comlegser/legcom.pdf. For hotlines, see Jan A. May, *Mapping a Labyrinth to Justice: Legal Service Methodologies Implemented in the District of Columbia*, UNIVERSITY OF THE DISTRICT OF COLUMBIA LAW REVIEW, 96, 98 (2000).

32. For client self-help, see LOPEZ, REBELLIOUS LAWYERING. For community empowerment, see Brescia, Goldman & Solomon, *Who's in Charge*, 857–58. For clients' volunteer services, see Edgar Cahn, *Coproducing Justice: The New Imperative*, 5 UNIVERSITY OF THE DISTRICT OF COLUMBIA LAW REVIEW 105, 109–10; 118–19 (2000); Jennifer Gordon, *We Make the Road by Walking: Immigrant Workers, the Workplace Project and the Struggle for Social Change*, 30 HARVARD CIVIL RIGHTS–CIVIL LIBERTIES LAW REVIEW 407 (1995). For lay volunteers, see John D. Asher, *Lay Volunteers*, in Besharov, LEGAL SERVICES, 106–7 and May, *Mapping a Labyrinth*, 102. For pro bono programs, see Rhode, *Pro Bono in Principle*.

33. For the needs of homeless clients, see Lucie White, *On Abolitionist Critiques, "Homeless Service" Programs, and Pragmatic Change*, 19 ST. LOUIS UNIVERSITY PUBLIC LAW REVIEW 475 (2000). For the needs of domestic violence clients, see Barbara J. Hart, Coordinated Community Approaches to Domestic Violence, Minnesota Center against Violence and Abuse, *available at* http://www.mincava.umn.edu/hart/nij.htm. For the value of collaboration in enhancing skills and policy work, see Stacy L. Brustin, *Legal Services Provision through Multidisciplinary Practice—Encouraging Holistic Advocacy while Protecting Ethical Interests*, 73 UNIVERSITY OF COLORADO LAW REVIEW 787, 801 (2002); J. Michael Norwood & Alan Peterson, *Problem Solving in a Multidisciplinary Environment? Must Ethics Get in the Way of Holistic Services?*, 9 CLINICAL LAW REVIEW 337, 364–66 (2002); Leigh Goodmark, *Can Poverty Lawyers Play Well with Others? Including Legal Services in Integrated, School-Based Service Delivery Programs*, 4 GEORGETOWN JOURNAL ON FIGHTING POVERTY 243 (1997); Louise G. Trubek & Jennifer J. Farnham, *Social Justice Collaboratives: Multidisciplinary Practices for People*, 7 CLINICAL LAW REVIEW 227 (2000).

34. For bar ethical rules, see ABA MODEL RULES OF PROFESSIONAL CONDUCT R. 5.4 (2002); ABA MODEL CODE OF PROFESSIONAL RESPONSIBILITY DR 3-102 (A). For bar opposition to multidisciplinary partnerships, see DEBORAH L. RHODE & GEOFFREY C. HAZARD, JR., PROFESSIONAL RESPONSIBILITY AND REGU-

LATION 183–88 (New York: Foundation Press, 2002). For a history of bar debates and a comprehensive collection of materials on multidisciplinary practice, see http://www.abanet.org/cpr/multicom.html.

35. For ways to address ethical issues, see Jacqueline St. Joan, *Building Bridges, Building Walls: Collaboration Between Lawyers and Social Workers in a Domestic Violence Clinic and Issues of Client Confidentiality*, 7 CLINICAL LAW REV. 403, 430–38 (2001). Norwood & Peterson, *Problem Solving*, 354–56. For example, see Stacy L. Brustein, *Legal Service Provision Through Multidisciplinary Practice— Encouraging Holistic Advocacy While Protecting Ethical Interests* 73 UNIVERSITY OF COLORADO LAW REVIEW 787 (2002).

36. Natalie Hanlon & Elizabeth Rada Carver, *Clayton/Mile High Family Futures Project*, COLO. LAW (July 1991). For the San Francisco program, see Alan W. Houseman, *Civil Legal Assistance for the Twenty-First Century: Achieving Equal Justice for All*, 17 YALE LAW AND POLICY REVIEW 369, 412 (1998). For a representative domestic violence program, see WEAVE, *available at* http://www .weaveincorp.org/about/programs.htm.

37. Holmes, Perle & Houseman, *Race-Based Advocacy*, 64–68.

38. For the need for more evaluation, research, and coordination and the obstacles to obtaining it, see LEADERS FOR JUSTICE, 17–22; Houseman, *Civil Legal Assistance for the Twenty-First Century*, 431; Houseman, *Political Lessons*, 1694; *Recommendations, supra* note 29, 1797–98. For technological innovations, see JULIA GORDON, PROJECT FOR THE FUTURE OF EQUAL JUSTICE, EQUAL JUSTICE AND THE DIGITAL REVOLUTION: USING TECHNOLOGY TO MEET THE LEGAL NEEDS OF LOW-INCOME PEOPLE (Washington, D.C.: Center for Law and Social Policy and National Legal Aid and Defender Association, 2002). For a well-designed program assessment, see CENTER FOR POLICY RESEARCH, THE HOTLINE OUTCOMES ASSESSMENT STUDY, FINAL REPORT (Denver: Center for Policy Research, 2002). For the barriers encountered by users of pro se clinics, see Elizabeth McCulloch, *Let Me Show You How: Pro Se Divorce Courses and Client Power*, 48 FLORIDA LAW REVIEW 481 (1996); Blue Ribbon Citizens' Committee on Slum Housing (Los Angeles, unpublished report) (finding that not a single unrepresented tenant in 150 sampled cases won a habitability case); EMPIRICAL RESEARCH GROUP OF UCLA SCHOOL OF LAW, EVALUATION OF THE VAN NUYS LEGAL SELF HELP CENTER, FINAL REPORT (Los Angeles: UCLA School of Law, 2001) (finding Center assistance improved pro se litigants' ability to complete marital dissolutions but did not improve their success rate in landlord–tenant cases).

Chapter 6

1. For the Georgia case, see *No Fair Trial unless You Can Buy One*, ATLANTA JOURNAL-CONSTITUTION, September 9, 2001, at 8D (quoting Paula McMichen). For the number of defendants who qualify as indigents, see DAVID COLE, NO EQUAL JUSTICE: RACE AND CLASS IN THE AMERICAN CRIMINAL JUSTICE SYSTEM 66 (New York: Free Press, 1999). *See also* CAROLINE WOLF HARLOW, DEFENSE COUNSEL IN CRIMINAL CASES (Washington, D.C.: United States Department of Justice, 2000) (court-appointed counsel represents four-fifths of defendants ac-

cused of felonies in the nation's seventy-five largest counties). For arrest rates, see BUREAU OF JUSTICE STATISTICS, SOURCEBOOK OF CRIMINAL JUSTICE STATISTICS (Washington, D.C.: Department of Justice, 2001).

2. AMERICAN BAR ASSOCIATION, PERCEPTIONS OF THE U.S. JUSTICE SYSTEM 65 (Chicago: American Bar Association, 2000).

3. For the decline in expenditures, see ROBERT A. KAGAN, ADVERSARIAL LEGALISM: THE AMERICAN WAY OF LAW 94 (Cambridge, Mass.: Harvard University Press, 2001). For national expenditures and disparities between defense and prosecution, see COLE, NO EQUAL JUSTICE, 64, 84; Douglas McCollum, *The Ghost of* Gideon, AMERICAN LAWYER, March 2003, at 63, 67; *State Should Pay for Indigent Defense*, ATLANTA JOURNAL-CONSTITUTION, Dec. 31, 2001, at A11 (eight to one disparity). For relatively well-funded programs, see Gideon's Legacy Debated, Letters to the Editor, NATIONAL LAW JOURNAL, April 28, 2003, at A13; Norman Lefstein, *Reform of Defense Representation in Capital Cases: The Indiana Experience and its Implications for the Nation*, 29 INDIANA LAW REVIEW 495 (1996).

4. The classic treatment is in MELVIN LERNER, THE BELIEF IN A JUST WORLD (New York: Plenum, 1980).

5. For public opinion, see ABA, PERCEPTIONS, 59; *Public Divided on Supreme Court Rulings*, UNITED PRESS INTERNATIONAL, July 30, 2003 (discussing Harris Interactive Poll). For Georgia expenditures, see *No Fair Trial*, at D8; *Presumed Innocent Doesn't Apply to All*, ATLANTA JOURNAL-CONSTITUTION, August 5, 2001, at F8.

6. For Georgia's system, see Bill Rankin, *Funding Focus of Georgia Indigent Defense Panel*, ATLANTA JOURNAL-CONSTITUTION, August 23, 2003, at 3E; Margaret L. Steiner, *Adequacy of Fact Investigation in Criminal Lawyer's Trial Preparation*, 1981 ARIZONA STATE LAW JOURNAL 523, 538 (1981); Mike McConville & Chester Mirsky, *Guilty Plea Courts: A Social Disciplinary Model of Criminal Justice*, 42 SOCIAL PROBLEMS 216 (1995).

7. RICHARD A. POSNER, THE PROBLEMATICS OF MORAL AND LEGAL THEORY 163–64 (Cambridge, Mass.: Harvard University Press, 1999); Rich Tucker, *Legal Defense Group Faces Another Fight for Survival*, FLORIDA TIMES UNION, April 14, 2003, at A1 (quoting Brad Thomas).

8. For DNA exonerations, see JIM DWYER, PETER NEUFELD, & BARRY SCHECK, ACTUAL INNOCENCE 187–88, 263 (New York: Doubleday, 2000). For the point about the worst lawyers, see Stephen Bright, *Counsel for the Poor: The Death Sentence Not for the Worst Crime but for the Worst Lawyer*, 103 YALE LAW JOURNAL 1835, 1850–54 (1994).

9. Amy Bach, *Justice on the Cheap*, THE NATION, May 21, 2001, at 25; *Contract Lawyer Can't Get the Job Done*, ATLANTA JOURNAL-CONSTITUTION, May 5, 2001, at F10; Martin Lasden, *For a Fistful of Dollars*, CALIFORNIA LAWYER (Nov. 2001), at 28.

10. *Contract Lawyer*, at F10; Henry Weinstein, *Georgia Fails its Poor Defendants, Report Says*, LOS ANGELES TIMES, December 13, 2002, at 38; *No English Translates into No Fairness*, ATLANTA JOURNAL-CONSTITUTION, October 23, 2001, at A12; COLE, NO EQUAL JUSTICE, 83–85.

11. McCollum, *The Ghost of* Gideon, 63, 67; Adam Liptak, *County Says It's Too Poor to Defend the Poor*, NEW YORK TIMES, April 15, 2003, at A1, A13 (quoting

Thomas Pearson). For an overview of problems in many states, see Bruce A. Green, *Criminal Neglect: Indigent Defense from a Legal Ethics Perspective*, 52 Emory Law Journal 1169, 1179–83 (2003).

12. Bach, *Justice on the Cheap*, 26; Heath v. State, 574 S.E.2d 852, 853–54, & note 6 (Ga. App. 2002) (finding ineffective assistance), *cert. granted*, 2003 Ga. Sup. Ct 323 (March 28, 2003).

13. For the lack of standards, see Adele Bernhard, *Take Courage: What the Courts Can Do to Improve the Delivery of Criminal Defense Services*, 63 University of Pittsburgh Law Review 293, 304–5 (2002). For fees and caseloads, see Green, *Criminal Neglect*, 1179–81; David Cole, *Still No Equal Justice for Poor*, LA Times, March 17, 2003, at A13; Jane Fritsch & David Rohde, *Caseloads Push System to Breaking Point*, New York Times, April 9, 2001, at A1; Catherine Greene Burnett, Michael K. Moore & Allan K. Butcher, *In Pursuit of Independent, Qualified, and Ethical Counsel: The Past and Future of Indigent Criminal Defense in Texas*, 42 South Texas Law Review 595, 609, 624, 648 (2001); Jane Fritsche & David Rohde, *On Appeal, the Poor Find Little Law*, New York Times, April 10, 2001, at A1; Robert Sherrill, *Death Trip: The American Way of Execution*, The Nation, January 8/15, 2001, at 20; Deborah L. Rhode, In the Interests of Justice (New York: Oxford University Press, 2000). For the same point about lineups, see Bach, *Justice on the Cheap*, 26.

14. Sara Rimer & Raymond Bonner, *Lawyer's Death Row Record a Concern*, New York Times, June 11, 2000, at A1, A22 (noting judges' preference for lawyers who "moved cases quickly"); McConville & Mirsky, *Guilty Plea Courts*, 216; Burnett, Moore & Butcher, *In Pursuit of Independent Counsel*, 620, 622; Sherrill, *Death Trip*, 26; Stephen B. Bright, *Testimony before the Senate Committee on the Judiciary*, Federal News Service, June 27, 2001, at 6.

15. Cole, No Equal Justice, 83; Green, *Criminal Neglect*, 1179–80, 1197; Bernhard, *Take Courage*, 308; Fritsch & Rohde, *Caseloads*, at A10; Bright, *Counsel for the Poor*, 1850–54; John Gibeaut, *Defense Warnings*, ABA Journal, December 2001, at 35, 39; Anthony Lewis, *The Silencing of Gideon's Trumpet*, New York Times Magazine, April 20, 2003, at 50, 51.

16. Burnett, Moore & Butcher, *In Pursuit of Independent Counsel*, 634–35, 639; Cole, No Equal Justice, 86; Stephen Bright, personal correspondence, May 7, 2003. For the need for holistic services, see Cait Clarke, *Problem Solving Defenders in the Community: Expanding the Conceptual and Institutional Boundaries of Providing Counsel to the Poor*, 14 Georgetown Journal of Legal Ethics 401 (2001).

17. Stephen Bright, *Keep the Dream Alive*, Yale Law Report 27 (Fall 1999); see Stephen J. Schulhofer, *Plea Bargaining as Disaster*, 101 Yale Law Journal 1979, 1988 (1992); Kenneth B. Mann, *The Trial as Text: Allegory, Myth, and Symbol in the Adversarial Criminal Process—A Critique of the Role of Public Defender and a Proposal for Reform*, 32 American Criminal Law Review 743, 803–812 (1995).

18. For racist comments, see Randall Kennedy, Race, Crime and the Law 285, 293–94 (New York: Pantheon, 1997). For other examples and the Ku Klux Klan assignment, see Sherrill, *Death Trip*, 21. For defendant's lack of choice, see Bach, *Justice on the Cheap*, 26 (quoting Hulane George). For denial of access to counsel, see Lewis, *Silencing of Gideon's Trumpet*, 52. For restrictions, see Neil A.

Lewis, *Rules Set Up for Terror Tribunals May Deter Some Defense Lawyers*, NEW YORK TIMES, July 13, 2003, at A1. For community reactions, see Gwen Filosa, *Death Row Takes a Toll on Lawyers*, THE TIMES-PICAYUNE, Aug. 20, 2001, *available at* http://www.nola.com/news/t-p/frontpage/index.ssf?/newsstory/death20 .html; Bruce A. Green, *Lethal Fiction: The Meaning of "Counsel" in the Sixth Amendment*, 78 IOWA LAW REVIEW 433, 494 (1993); Deborah L. Rhode, *Terrorists and their Lawyers*, NEW YORK TIMES, April 16, 2002, at A31; Personal Correspondence, Robert Held, April 16, 2002. For McVeigh's lawyer, see Richard M. Steingard, *Would You Defend Timothy McVeigh?*, CALIFORNIA BAR JOURNAL 12–13 (June 1995).

19. For standards, see INSTITUTE FOR LAW AND JUSTICE, BUREAU OF JUSTICE, ASSISTANCE, UNITED STATES DEPARTMENT OF JUSTICE, COMPENDIUM OF STANDARDS FOR INDIGENT DEFENSE SYSTEMS (Washington, D.C.: United States Department of Justice, 2000); AMERICAN BAR ASSOCIATION, GUIDELINES FOR THE APPOINTMENT AND PERFORMANCE OF DEFENSE COUNSEL IN DEATH PENALTY CASES 18–19 (Chicago: American Bar Association, revised ed. 2003); Bernhard, *Take Courage*, 318–19. For Georgia's standards, see Bach, *Justice on the Cheap*, 27; JAMES KELLEY, LAWYERS CROSSING LINES 173 (Durham, N.C.: Carolina Academic Press, 2001).

20. For unsuccessful challenges, see Olive v. Maas, 811 So. 2d 644 (Florida Sup. Ct. 2002); Miranda v. Clark County, Nevada, 319 F. 3d. 465 (9th Cir. 2003); Bernhard, *Take Courage*, 302–4; Andrew Harris, *Oregon Can't Afford Indigents' Right to Counsel*, NATIONAL LAW JOURNAL, March 17, 2003, at A7; F.T.C. v. Superior Court Trial Lawyers Assn. 493 U.S. 411 (1990). For successful challenges, see Bernhard, *Take Courage*, 310–18; New York County Lawyers' Association v. Pataki, 727 N.Y.S. 2d851 (N.Y. Sup. Ct. 2001). For the need for judicial intervention, see COLE, NO EQUAL JUSTICE, 42.

21. For disciplinary agencies, see Green, *Criminal Neglect*, 1196; Dennis E. Curtis & Judith Resnik, *Grieving Criminal Defense Lawyers*, 70 FORDHAM LAW REVIEW 1615, 1617–21 (2002); Meredith J. Duncan, *The (So Called) Liability of Criminal Defense Attorneys: A System in Need of Reform*, BRIGHAM YOUNG UNIVERSITY LAW REVIEW 1, 30 – 43 (2002). For malpractice, see *id.*, CHARLES W. WOLFRAM, MODERN LEGAL ETHICS 207–15 (St. Paul, Minn.: West, 1988); John Leubsdorf, *Legal Malpractice and Professional Responsibility*, 48 RUTGERS LAW REVIEW 101, 111–19 (1995); Wiley v. San Diego County, 966 P.2d 983 (Cal. 1998).

22. For the disincentives to bring claims, see Green, *Criminal Neglect*, 1186–87. For the lack of counsel, see Ross v. Moffitt, 417 U.S. 600 (1974) (finding no right to counsel in discretionary appeals); Pennsylvania v. Finley, 481 U.S. 551 (1987) (finding no right to counsel in post-conviction proceedings); Murray v. Giarratano, 492 U.S. 1 (1989) (finding no right to counsel in post-conviction capital proceedings).

23. For state statutes and decisions, see Letty S. Di Guilio, *Dying for the Right to Effective Assistance of Counsel in State Post-Conviction Proceedings: State Statutes and Due Process in Capital Cases*, 9 BOSTON UNIVERSITY PUBLIC INTEREST LAW JOURNAL 109, 116–21 (1999). For the survey on petitioners' success, see IRA R. ROBBINS, TOWARD A MORE JUST AND EFFECTIVE SYSTEM OF REVIEW IN STATE DEATH PENALTY CASES (Chicago: American Bar Association, 1990).

24. For the "farce and mockery" standard, Trapnell v. United States, 725 F.2d 149, 151–53 (2d Cir. 1983). For the *Gibson* case, see the transcript of the habeas proceeding in Gibson v. Turpin, quoted in COLE, NO EQUAL JUSTICE, 75.

25. For Tennessee requirements, see Tennessee Code Annotated 40 – 30 – 107 (1990); House v. State, S.W.2d 705, 707 (Tenn. 1995); Di Guilio, *Dying*, 109. For attorney errors, see Coleman v. Thompson, 501 U.S. 722 (1991).

26. Burke W. Kappler, *Small Favors: Chapter 154 of the Antiterrorism and Effective Death Penalty Act, the States, and the Right to Counsel*, 90 JOURNAL CRIMINAL LAW AND CRIMINOLOGY 469, 488–516, 578 (2000).

27. For the standard, see Strickland v. Washington, 466 U.S. 668, 689–96 (1984). *See also* Bell v. Cone, 535 U.S. 685 (2002); United States v. Cronic, 466 U.S. 648 (1984). For success rates, see COLE, NO EQUAL JUSTICE, 80; Victor E. Flango & Patricia McKenna, *Federal Habeas Corpus Review of State Court Convictions*, 31 CALIFORNIA WESTERN LAW REVIEW 237, 259–60 (1995). For plea bargains, see Steven Zeidman, *To Plead or Not to Plead: Effective Assistance and Client-Centered Counseling*, 39 BOSTON COLLEGE LAW REVIEW 841 (1998).

28. For examples, see COLE, NO EQUAL JUSTICE, 79, 87; Bright, *Testimony*, 22; Duncan, *Liability*, 8; Green, *Lethal Fiction*, 433, 499–501; Bell v. Cone, 535 U.S. 685 (2002). For battered women, see Sarah M. Buel, *Effective Assistance of Counsel for Battered Women Defendants: A Normative Construct*, 26 HARVARD WOMEN'S LAW JOURNAL 286 (2003). For the Texas judge, see Texas Defender Service Lethal Indifference, xii (December 2002), available at http://www.texasdefender.org.

29. Wiggins v. Smith, 539 U.S. 510 (2003). For guidelines, see ABA Guidelines for the Appointment and Performance of Defense Counsel. For the Capital Jury Project, see Alex Kotlowitz, *In the Face of Death*, NEW YORK TIMES MAGAZINE, July 1, 2003, at 32.

30. *See* Yarborough v. Gentry, 540 U.S. ___ (2003).Tippins v. Walker, 77 F.2d 682 (2d Cir. l996); Burdine v. Texas, 66 F. Supp. 2d 854 (S.D. Tex. 1999) *aff'd. sub nom.* Burdine v. Johnson, 362 F.3d 386 (5th Cir.), *cert. denied sub nom.* Cockrell v. Burdine, 121 S. Ct. 2347 (2002); Henry Weinstein, *Condemned Man Awaits Fate in Texas Case of Dozing Lawyer*, LOS ANGELES TIMES, June 6, 2000, at A1; McFarland v. State, 928 S.W. 2d 482, 506 n. 20; Bob Herbert, *Cheap Justice in America*, NEW YORK TIMES, March 1, 1998, at E15; Bruce Shapiro, *Sleeping Lawyer Syndrome*, THE NATION, April 7, 1997, at 27–29 (quoting Judge Doug Shaver).

31. KENNEDY, RACE, CRIME, AND THE LAW 292; STEPHEN B. BRIGHT, CAPITAL PUNISHMENT: ACCELERATING THE DANCE WITH DEATH IN THE REHNQUIST COURT: JUDICIAL ACTIVISM ON THE RIGHT 89–90 (New York: Hill & Wang, 2002) (quoting Ruth Bader Ginsberg). For exonerations, Death Penalty Information Center: Innocence and Death Penalty, *available at* http://www.deathpenaltyinfor.org/innoc.html (2003).

32. Stephen B. Bright, *Sleeping on the Job*, NATIONAL LAW JOURNAL, Dec. 4, 2000, at A26 (quoting Bush). Calvin Burdine was convicted in 1986; the Supreme Court upheld reversal of his conviction in 2002. *See also* Sherrill, *Death Trip*, 20 (discussing the case of Ricardo Guerra, who spent fourteen years on death row before being exonerated). For circumstances leading to exoneration, see Hugo Adam Bedau, Causes and Consequences of Wrongful Convictions: An Essay-Review, 86 JUDICATURE 115, 117 (2002). *Accord*, Lawrence C. Marshall, *Do Exonerations Prove*

That "the System Works?", JUDICATURE 86 83 (September/October 2002).

33. For the demands in capital cases, see ABA, Guidelines; Richard J. Wilson & Robert L. Spanenberg, *State-Postconviction Representation of Defendants Sentenced to Death*, 72 JUDICATURE 331, 336–37 (1989); Green, *Lethal Fiction*, 495–99. For the special risks of police and prosecutorial abuse, see DWYER, NEUFELD & SCHECK, ACTUAL INNOCENCE 172–81, 229, 246–59, 265; Sherrill, *Death Trip*. For racial discrimination, see Amnesty International, United States of America: Death by Discrimination—The Continuing Role of Race in Capital Cases (2002), *available at* http://www.amnestyusa.org/abolish/reports/dp_discrimination .html; Leadership Conference on Civil Rights, Justice on Trial: Racial Disparities in the American Criminal Justice System (2000); U.S. General Accounting Office, Death Penalty Sentencing: Research Indicates Pattern of Racial Disparities (1990) (twenty-eight studies that show a pattern of racial disparities in charging, sentencing, and imposition of the death penalty).

34. For funding, see ABA, Guidelines; Sara Rimer, *Questions of Death: Raw Justice for Poor People in Alabama*, NEW YORK TIMES, March 2000, at A1; Dick Johnson, *Poor Legal Work Common for Innocents on Death Row*, NEW YORK TIMES, Feb. 5, 2000, at A1; Stephen B. Bright, *Does the Bill of Rights Apply Here Anymore?*, *Evisceration of Habeas Corpus and Denial of Counsel to Those Under Sentence of Death*, CHAMPION, November 1996, at 27–28. For the Resource Centers, see *id.*, COLE, NO EQUAL JUSTICE, 93 (quoting Robert Inglis). For the ABA's project, see American Bar Association, Death Penalty Representation Project, ABA Network (2002), *available at* http://www.abanet.org/deathpenalty.

35. For suspended, disbarred, and convicted attorneys, see ABA, Standards, 55; STEPHEN B. BRIGHT, EQUAL JUSTICE UNDER LAW (New York: Open Society Institute Occasional Papers Series, 2002); Sherrill, *Death Trip*, 19, 21. For the Texas comparison, see BRIGHT, CAPITAL PUNISHMENT, 90; *Justice O'Connor Expresses New Doubts about Fairness of Capital Punishment*, BALTIMORE SUN, July 9, 2001, at A3. For the national survey, see James S. Liebman, *Rates of Reversible Error and the Risk of Wrongful Execution*, 86 JUDICATURE 78, 82 (2002).

36. For reversible error, see James S. Leibman, Jeffrey Fagan & Valerie West, A Broken System: Error Rates in Capital Cases, 1973–95; James Liebman, *The Overproduction of Death*, 100 COLUMBIA L. REVIEW 2030, 2102–8 (2000). For spectator representation, see KELLEY, LAWYERS CROSSING LINES, 170–73; KENNEDY, RACE, CRIME AND THE LAW, 293–94; Bright, *Testimony*; Ex Parte Rojas, Texas Crim. App. No. 39, 062–01 (Price, J., dissenting) (2003).

37. For examples, see COLE, NO EQUAL JUSTICE, 86–87; Bright, *Testimony*; BRIGHT, EQUAL JUSTICE UNDER LAW; Julie Kay, *Capital Calamity*, MIAMI DAILY BUSINESS REVIEW TODAY, April 30, 2003, at A1; Ex Parte Rojas, No. 39, 062–01 (Tex. Court of Criminal Appeals 2002) (Price, J., dissenting). For the Texas study, see Texas Defender Service, Lethal Indifference.

38. For estimates of costs and delay, see KAGAN, ADVERSARIAL LEGALISM, 66; Sherrill, *Death Trip*, 16, 18.

39. For calls for a moratorium, see AUSTIN SARAT, WHEN THE STATE KILLS 288–89 (Princeton: Princeton University Press, 2002). For public attitudes, see Texas Defender Service, Lethal Indifference, i; Martin Lasden, *Executioners' Swan Song?*, CALIFORNIA LAWYER, March 2003, 11.

40. For racial bias and police and prosecutorial abuse, see sources cited in note 33; Stephen B. Bright, *Race, Poverty, the Death Penalty, and the Responsibility of the Legal Profession*, 1 SEATTLE JOURNAL FOR SOCIAL JUSTICE 73 (2002); Leibman, Fagan & West, A Broken System; DWYER, NEUFELD & SCHECK, ACTUAL INNOCENCE. For other problems, see *id.*; KAGAN, ADVERSARIAL LEGALISM, 81; Adam Liptak, *You Think DNA Evidence Is Foolproof? Try Again*, NEW YORK TIMES, March 16, 2003, at E6; Robert K. Olson, *Miscarriage of Justice*, 86 JUDICATURE 74 (2002).

41. For standards, see ABA STANDARDS FOR CRIMINAL JUSTICE: PROVIDING DEFENSE SERVICES Standard 5 – 5.3 (3d ed. 1992); TEXAS BAR STANDARDS, Standard 3.2 and Objective 6; Burnett, Moore & Butcher, *In Pursuit of Independent Counsel*, 651–56. For state funding, see John Gibeaut, *Declaring Independence*, ABA JOURNAL 41 (December 2001).

42. For centralization and independence, see NATIONAL LEGAL AID AND DEFENDER ASSOCIATION, NATIONAL STUDY COMMISSION ON DEFENSE SERVICES, GUIDELINES FOR LEGAL DEFENSE SYSTEMS IN THE UNITED STATES FINAL REPORT (1976); ABA STANDARDS FOR CRIMINAL JUSTICE: PROVIDING DEFENSE SERVICES Standard 5 – 1.2(c) and comment (3d ed. 1992, black letter approved 1990, commentary completed 1992); NATIONAL LEGAL AID AND DEFENDER ASSOCIATION, THE 10 PRINCIPLES OF A PUBLIC DEFENSE DELIVERY SYSTEM Principle 1 (2000); Liptak, *County Says It's Too Poor*, at A14. For the Indiana system, see Gibeaut, *Declaring Independence*, 41.

43. For performance standards, see ABA STANDARDS, 35–41; ABA STANDARDS FOR CRIMINAL JUSTICE: DEFENSE FUNCTION Standard 4, *in* ABA STANDARDS FOR CRIMINAL JUSTICE: PROSECUTION FUNCTION AND DEFENSE FUNCTION (3d ed. 1993); NATIONAL LEGAL AID AND DEFENDER ASSOCIATION, PERFORMANCE GUIDELINES FOR CRIMINAL DEFENSE REPRESENTATION (1997); Burnett, Moore & Butcher, *In Pursuit of Independent Counsel*, 649–50; Green, *Lethal Fiction*, 509–13. For removal, see ABA STANDARDS, 44–45; ABA STANDARDS FOR CRIMINAL JUSTICE: PROVIDING DEFENSE SERVICES Standard 5 – 2.3 (3d ed. 1992). For public defender evaluation procedures, see Kim Taylor-Thompson, *Tuning Up Gideon's Trumpet*, 71 FORDHAM LAW REVIEW 1461, 1498–1511 (2003); James R. Neuhard, *Lessons from the Public Defenders*, *in* LEGAL SERVICES FOR THE POOR: TIME FOR REFORM 140, 143–45 (Douglas J. Besharov ed.) (Washington, D.C.: American Enterprise Institute, 1990). For disciplinary agencies, see Green, *Criminal Neglect*, 1198; Curtis & Resnik, *Grieving Lawyers*, 1626.

44. For the need for data, see Burnett, Moore & Butcher, *In Pursuit of Independent Counsel*, 652; Texas Bar Standards, Standard 8.1. For the need for research concerning race, see Leadership Conference, JUSTICE ON TRIAL, 54.

Chapter 7

1. An expanded version of this chapter appears in Deborah L. Rhode, *Pro Bono in Principle and in Practice*, 54 JOURNAL OF LEGAL EDUCATION 413 (2003). The full version is available at http://www.ssrn.com and in a forthcoming book published by the Stanford University Press. Funding for the empirical survey was provided through the efforts of my Stanford colleagues Joseph Grundfest and David Mills, and by the Roberts Program in Law and Corporate Governance

at Stanford Law School. Assistance with the empirical design and analysis was provided by Barbara Curran of the American Bar Foundation, by Stanford colleagues John Donohue and Deborah Hensler, and by statistician Elizabeth Cameron. I am grateful to all the students who helped in compiling survey data, particularly Nathan Doty, Carolyn Janiak, Jonathan Sanders, and Angie Schwartz. For *lawyer* contributions see notes 17 and 18 *infra*.

2. *See* research summarized in ALAN LUKS, WITH PEGGY PAYNE, THE HEALING POWER OF DOING GOOD, xi–xii, 17–18, 45–54, 118–19 (iUniverse.com, 2d ed. 2001); John Wilson & Marc Musick, *The Effects of Volunteering on the Volunteer*, 62 LAW AND CONTEMPORARY PROBLEMS 141, 150–59 (1999); Marc A. Musick, A. Regula Herzog & James S. House, *Volunteering and Mortality among Older Adults: Findings from a National Sample*, 548 JOURNAL OF GERONTOLOGY S173, S178 (1999); ROBERT D. PUTNAM, BOWLING ALONE 333 (New York: Simon & Schuster, 2000); John M. Darley, *Altruism and Prosocial Behavior Research: Reflections and Prospects, in* PROSOCIAL BEHAVIOR 312–27 (Margaret S. Clark ed.) (Newbury Park, Calif.: Sage, 1991).

3. Daniel Becker, *The Many Faces of Pro Bono*, WASHINGTON LAWYER 22, 30 (May 2001); Cynthia Fuchs Epstein, *Stricture and Structure: The Social and Cultural Context of Pro Bono Work in Wall Street Firms*, 70 FORDHAM L. REV. 1689, 1693–94 (2002); ABA YOUNG LAWYERS DIVISION, CAREER SATISFACTION SURVEY 28 (Chicago: American Bar Association, 2000); ABA YOUNG LAWYERS DIVISION, CAREER SATISFACTION SURVEY 11 (Chicago: American Bar Association, 1995).

4. Jack W. Londen, *The Impact of Pro Bono Work on Law Firm Economics*, 9 GEORGETOWN JOURNAL OF LEGAL ETHICS 925 (1996); PETER D. HART RESEARCH ASSOCIATES, INC., A SURVEY OF ATTITUDES NATIONWIDE TOWARD LAWYERS AND THE LEGAL SYSTEM 18 (1993).

5. Tigran W. Eldred & Thomas Schoenherr, *The Lawyer's Duty of Public Service: More Than Charity?*, 96 WEST VIRGINIA LAW REVIEW 367, 390 and n. 94 (1994); sources cited in Reed Elizabeth Loder, *Tending the Generous Heart: Mandatory Pro Bono and Moral Development*, 14 GEORGETOWN JOURNAL OF LEGAL ETHICS 459 (2001); Deborah L. Rhode, *Cultures of Commitment: Pro Bono for Lawyers and Law Students*, 67 FORDHAM LAW REVIEW 2415, 2419 (1999).

6. Final Report to the Chief Judge of New York, *reprinted in* 19 HOFSTRA L. REV. 755, 782 (1991).

7. For objections, see Loder, *Mandatory Pro Bono*, 471–74; sources cited in Deborah L. Rhode, *Ethical Perspectives on Legal Practice*, 37 STANFORD LAW REVIEW 589, 610 (1985) (discussing "fascism" and "indentured servitude"); Eldred & Schoenherr, *The Lawyer's Duty*, 391 n. 97 (discussing references to "Big Brother" and the Soviet Union). For research on helping behavior and public interest commitments, see sources cited in Loder, *Mandatory Pro Bono*, 474, and Mark Sobus, *Mandating Community Service: Psychological Implications of Requiring Prosocial Behavior*, 19 LAW AND PSYCHOLOGY REVIEW 153, 163–65 (1995).

8. Esther F. Lardent, *Structuring Law Firm Pro Bono Programs: A Community Service Typology, in* THE LAW FIRM AND THE PUBLIC GOOD 83–84 (Robert A. Katzman ed.) (Washington, D.C.: Brookings Institution, 1995) (noting absence of research). *See* Michael Millemann, *Mandatory Pro Bono in Civil Cases: A Partial Answer to the Right Question*, 49 MARYLAND LAW REVIEW 18, 49, 64 (1990) (noting experience with Maryland bar that casts doubt on the assumption that

contributions would decline); David Luban, *A Workable (and Moral) Plan*, 64 MICHIGAN BAR JOURNAL 280, 283 (1986).

9. Philip R. Lochner, Jr., *The No Fee and Low Fee Legal Practice of Private Attorneys*, 9 LAW AND SOCIETY REVIEW 431, 442–46 (1975); Esther F. Lardent, *Pro Bono in the 1990s*, *in* AMERICAN BAR ASSOCIATION, CIVIL JUSTICE: AN AGENDA FOR THE 1990s 423, 434 (Esther F. Lardent ed.) (Chicago: American Bar Association, 1989).

10. For performance and bureaucracy concerns, see Ted R. Marcus, Letter to the Editor, CALIFORNIA LAWYER, August 1993, at 12; Roger C. Cramton, *Mandatory Pro Bono*, 19 HOFSTRA LAW REVIEW 1113, 1137 (1991); Esther F. Lardent, *Mandatory Pro Bono in Civil Cases: The Wrong Answer to the Right Question*, 49 MARYLAND LAW REVIEW 78, 99 (1990). For attorneys' reactions to pro bono cases and clients, see Lori Tripoli, *The Hypocritical Oath? Why Some Associates Opt Out of Pro Bono*, OF COUNSEL, May 17, 1999, at 1, 10, 11.

11. Millemann, *Mandatory Pro Bono*, 62.

12. For data on law firm and corporate employer contributions, see the text at notes 17 and 18 *infra*. For reporting requirements, see the text at note 38.

13. *Text of Initial Draft of Ethics Code Rewrite Committee*, LEGAL TIMES OF WASHINGTON, August 27, 1979, at 26, 45, col. 4; *Law Poll: Public Interest Legal Services*, 68 ABA JOURNAL 912 (1982). ABA MODEL RULES OF PROFESSIONAL CONDUCT R. 6.1 (1983).

14. ABA MODEL RULES OF PROFESSIONAL CONDUCT R. 6.1 (2002).

15. For state rules, see Judith L. Maute, *Pro Bono Publico in Oklahoma: Time for Change*, 53 OKLAHOMA LAW REVIEW 527, 572 (2000); ABA CENTER FOR PRO BONO, STATE PRO BONO SERVICE RULES. For requirements, see Amendments to Rule 4–6.1 of the Rules Regulating the Florida Bar Pro Bono Public Service, 696 So. 2d 734, 735 (Fla. 1997); Maryland Rules of Procedure 16–903 (2002); Madden v. Township of Delran, 601 A.2d 211 (N.J. 1992); *Revised Exemptions from Madden v. Delran Pro Bono Counsel Assignments for 2002*, NEW JERSEY LAW JOURNAL, March 11, 2002, at 1.

16. DEBORAH L. RHODE & DAVID LUBAN, LEGAL ETHICS (New York: Foundation Press, 3d ed. 2001). For lawyers' objections, see Millemann, *Mandatory Pro Bono*, 18, 65. For involuntary servitude claims, see Rhode, *Ethical Perspectives*, at 610; United States v. Kozminski, 487 U.S. 931, 952 (1988); Family Division of Trial Lawyers v. Moultrie, 725 F.2d 695 (D.C. Cir. 1984). For takings claims, see CHARLES W. WOLFRAM, MODERN LEGAL ETHICS 952 n. 26 (Minneapolis: West Publishing, 1986); Hurtado v. United States, 410 U.S. 578, 588 (1973); United States v. Dillon, 346 F.2d 633 (9th Cir. 1965), *cert. denied*, 382 U.S. 978 (1966). Although the Supreme Court has never ruled directly on the scope of judicial authority to compel uncompensated assistance, its dicta and summary dismissal of one challenge suggest that such authority is constitutional. Sparks v. Parker, 368 So. 2d 528 (Ala.), appeal dismissed, 444 U.S. 803 (1979); Powell v. Alabama, 287 U.S. 45, 73 (1932) (dicta).

17. For lawyers' expansive definitions, see CARROLL SERON, THE BUSINESS OF PRACTICING LAW 129–33 (Philadelphia: Temple University Press, 1996); Rhode, *Cultures of Commitment*, 2415, 2423; Gary Spencer, *Pro Bono Data Show Little Improvement*, NEW YORK LAW JOURNAL, March 5, 1999, at 1; Maute, *Pro Bono*, 562.

18. For contributions of time, see Judith S. Kaye & Jonathan Lippman, Report on the Pro Bono Activities of the New York State Bar 12 (Albany, N.Y.: New York State Unified Court System, 1999), *available at* http://www.courts.state.ny.us/probono/pbrpt.htm; Texas State Bar, Civil Legal Services to the Poor in Texas, Report to the Supreme Court of Texas 200 (2000), *available at* http://www.texasbar.com/attyinfo/probono/legpoor.htm; LSC Statistics: Private Attorney Involvement, All Programs, *available at* http://www.lsc.gov/pressr/pr_pai.htm; Corporate Pro Bono Org., *available at* http://corporateprobono.org/forms/news_full_record.cfm?newsID-1065 (last visited January 10, 2003). For financial contributions, see Kaye & Lippman, Report; FLORIDA BAR STANDING COMMITTEE ON PRO BONO SERVICES, REPORT TO THE SUPREME COURT OF FLORIDA (Tallahassee, Fla.: Florida Bar Association, 2001); telephone interview with Michael A. Tartaglia (November 7, 2002).

19. Interview with Esther Lardent, Pro Bono Institute (2002); Aric Press, *Eight Minutes*, AMERICAN LAWYER, July 2000, at 13; Jack Wax, *No More Lawyer Jokes*, NATIONAL LAW JOURNAL, December 23–30, 2002, at A17; Cameron Stracher, *Go Go Bono*, AMERICAN LAWYER, December 2000, at 51. For post-9/11 trends, see Dee McAree, *Pro Bono Mini Boom*, NATIONAL LAW JOURNAL, January 5, 2004, at 1, 23. Elizabeth Preis, *A Small Gain*, AMERICAN LAWYER 119 (July 2002); Susan Saulny, *Volunteerism among Lawyers Surges, Encouraged by the Slumping Economy*, NEW YORK TIMES, February 19, 2003, at A27.

20. *See The AmLaw 200: Gauging Pro Bono Commitment*, AMERICAN LAWYER, August 2002, at 113; Marc Galanter & Thomas Palay, *Public Service Implications of Evolving Law Firm Size and Structure*, in THE LAW FIRM AND THE PUBLIC GOOD 19, 41–47 (Robert A. Katzman ed.) (Washington, D.C.: Brookings Institution, 1995); Esther Lardent, *Pro Bono Work Is Good for Business*, NATIONAL LAW JOURNAL, February 19, 2001, at B20. Stanford Law Student Jacqueline Fink analyzed the correlation of pro bono work with profitability for the twenty-five most profitable firms according to 2000 American Lawyer data (unpublished paper, 2001). Three of the firms were at the top of the list and none were at the bottom.

21. *See* SPAN (State Planning Assistance Network), SUPPORTING PARTNERSHIPS TO EXPAND ACCESS TO JUSTICE REPORT: ACCESS TO JUSTICE PARTNERSHIPS, STATE BY STATE (March 2002); Orange County, Florida Bar Association, By-Laws, *available at* http://ocbanet.org (last visited December 3, 2001); Robert A. Stein, *Leader of the Pro Bono Pack*, ABA JOURNAL, October 1997, at 108; *Pro Bono NLJ Awards*, NATIONAL LAW JOURNAL, January 5, 2004, at 18–33; *The Pro Bono Honor Roll*, AMERICAN LAWYER, December 2001, at 80, 81.

22. For a historical overview, see CYNTHIA F. ADCOCK AND ALISON M. KEEGAN, A HANDBOOK ON LAW SCHOOL PRO BONO PROGRAMS: THE AALS PRO BONO PROJECT 7 (Washington, D.C.: Association of American Law Schools, June 2001). For ABA standards, see RECODIFICATION OF ABA ACCREDITATION STANDARDS Standard 302(e) (Curriculum), Standard 404 (faculty). For the AALS Commission and Project, see ABA Commission on Pro Bono and Public Service Opportunities in Law Schools, Learning to Serve: The Findings and Proposals of the AALS Commission on Pro Bono and Public Services Opportunities (1999), *available at* www.aals.org/probono/report.html (last visited October 31, 2002). For

law school programs, see Cynthia Adcock, Law School Pro Bono Programs, Fact Sheet (Washington, D.C.: Association of American Law Schools, 2003), *available at* http://www.abanet.org/legalservices/probono/lawschools; AALS Learning to Serve, 7; and Adcock & Keegan, Handbook, 11–12, 23–30. In the interests of full disclosure, I should note that the Commission was the presidential initiative that I created during my term as president of the Association of American Law Schools and that I helped secure funding for its work and for the subsequent follow-up project from the Open Society Institute.

23. AALS Learning to Serve, 4, 7; Notes of Focus Group Interviews conducted by the Association of American Law School's Commission on Pro Bono and Public Service Opportunities in Law schools (1998) (on file with author).

24. For faculty participation, see AALS Learning to Serve, 10, 17; Notes of Focus Group Interviews. For deans' satisfaction, see AALS Learning to Serve, 17.

25. AALS Learning to Serve, 3, 17; John Kramer, *Mandatory Pro Bono at Tulane Law School*, National Association for Public Interest Law, Connection Closeup Newsletter, September 30, 1991, at 1–2.

26. For service learning, see Lori J. Vogelgesang & Alexander W. Astin, *Comparing the Effects of Community Service and Service-Learning*, 7 Michigan Journal of Community Service and Service Learning 23, 34 (2000), and research summarized in Rhode, Pro Bono in Principle. For law students, see Committee on Legal Assistance, *Mandatory Law School Pro Bono Programs: Preparing Students to Meet their Ethical Obligations*, 50 The Record 170, 176 (1995); AALS Focus Group Interviews.

27. For experiential learning, see Deborah Maranville, *Infusing Passion and Context into the Traditional Law Curriculum through Experiential Learning*, 51 Journal of Legal Education 51, 56 (2001); Paula Lustbader, *Teach in Context*, 48 Journal of Legal Education 402 (1998). For pro bono experiences, see Kramer, *Mandatory Pro Bono*, 2; AALS Focus Group Interviews. For the lack of information or concern among law students, see the survey findings discussed in section 7.4 *infra*.

28. AALS Learning to Serve, 5–6.

29. Lucy E.White, *Pro Bono or Partnership?: Rethinking Lawyers' Public Service Obligations for a New Millennium*, 50 Journal of Legal Education 134, 142–45 (2000); Susan Bryant, *The Five Habits: Building Cross-Cultural Competence in Lawyers*, 8 Clinical Law Review 33 (2001); Michelle S. Jacobs, *Full Legal Representation for the Poor: The Clash between Lawyer Values and Client Worthiness*, 44 Howard Law Journal 257, 258–59 (2001).

30. Kimberly M. Allen, University of Pennsylvania Public Service Program Alumni Survey, 3–4 (1994) (unpublished survey, on file with the author); Pamela DeFanti Robinson, *Insurmountable Opportunities or Innovative Choices: The Pro Bono Experience at the University of South Carolina School of Law*, 42 South Carolina Law Review 959, 969–70 (1991).

31. For example, a recent widely reported study by Catalyst also reported a 28 percent response rate. Catalyst, Women in Law: Making the Case (New York: Catalyst, 2001).

32. For a full profile of the responding lawyers and a comparison with the profession as a whole, see Rhode, *Pro Bono in Principle*.

33. For a full explanation of survey methodology and results, as well as sources for the comments quoted, see Rhode, *Pro Bono in Principle*.

34. For research on altruistic behavior, see RICHARD BENTLEY & LUANA G. NISSAN, ROOTS OF GIVING AND SERVING 9 (Indianapolis: Center on Philanthropy, 1996); ANNE COLBY & WILLIAM DAMON, SOME DO CARE: CONTEMPORARY LIVES OF MORAL COMMITMENT (New York: Free Press, 1992); ROBERT COLES, THE CALL OF SERVICE: A WITNESS TO IDEALISM 91–94 (Boston: Houghton Mifflin, 1993); EVA FOGELMAN, CONSCIENCE AND COURAGE: RESCUERS OF JEWS DURING THE HOLOCAUST 155–160 (New York: Anchor Books, 1994); ALFIE KOHN, THE BRIGHTER SIDE OF HUMAN NATURE: ALTRUISM AND EMPATHY IN EVERYDAY LIFE 85–97, 284–85 (New York: Basic Books, 1990); Martin L. Hoffman, *Empathy and Prosocial Activism, in* SOCIAL AND MORAL VALUES: INDIVIDUAL AND SOCIETAL PERSPECTIVES 65–85 (Nancy Eisenberg, Janusz Reykowski & Ervin Staub ed.) (Hillsdale, N.J.: Lawrence Erlbaum, 1989); David Horton Smith, *Determinants of Voluntary Association Participation and Volunteering: A Literature Review,* 23 NONPROFIT AND VOLUNTARY SECTION QUARTERLY 243, 251–52 (1994).

35. Jane Mansbridge, *The Relation of Altruism and Self-Interest, in* BEYOND SELF-INTEREST (Jane J. Mansbridge ed.) (Chicago: University of Chicago Press, 1990); BENTLEY & NISSAN, ROOTS OF GIVING AND SERVING, 8–9; Smith, *Voluntary Associations,* 251.

36. For data on the lack of correlation between economic capacity and charitable giving, see INDEPENDENT SECTOR, GIVING AND VOLUNTEERING IN THE UNITED STATES: KEY FINDINGS 18, 36–37 (2001); Albert R. Hunt, *Charitable Giving: Good But We Can Do Better,* WALL STREET JOURNAL, December 21, 2000, at A19.

37. In an American Lawyer survey, only 28 percent of respondents' firms credited time on pro bono activities toward minimum billable hour requirements. *Commission AmLaw 100 and Law Firm Questionnaires,* AMERICAN LAWYER, August 2002, at 52.

38. For Florida's record, see Talbot D'Alembert, *Tributaries of Justice: The Search for Full Access,* 25 FLORIDA STATE UNIVERSITY LAW REVIEW 631, 633 (1998). For diversity examples, see LAWYERS FOR ONE AMERICA, BAR NONE: REPORT TO THE PRESIDENT OF THE UNITED STATES ON THE STATUS OF PEOPLE OF COLOR AND PRO BONO SERVICES IN THE LEGAL PROFESSION 30–31, 45–46 (San Francisco: Lawyers for One America, 2000); BAR ASSOCIATION OF SAN FRANCISCO, GOALS AND TIMETABLES FOR MINORITY HIRING AND ADVANCEMENT (San Francisco: Bar Association of San Francisco, 2000). For California legislation, see Assembly Bill 913, May 2, 2002; AB913, amending Section 6072 of the California Business and Professions Code; Shannon Lafferty, *Santa Clara to Require Pro Bono from Firms,* SAN FRANCISCO RECORDER, April 11, 2002, at 2.

39. Lauren Hallinan, *What Judges Can Do to Increase Equal Access to the Courts,* JUDGES JOURNAL 6 (Winter 2001). Susan J. Curry, *Meeting the Need: Minnesota's Collaborative Model to Deliver Law Student Public Service,* 28 WILLIAM MITCHELL LAW REVIEW 347 (2001); Thomas Adcock, *After Sept. 11, Record Number of Lawyers Answer the Call to Take on Pro Bono,* NEW YORK LAW JOURNAL, July 11, 2002, at 1.

40. Power of Attorney, http://www.powerofattorney.org; Vivia Chen, *Going Corporate,* AMERICAN LAWYER 94 (September 2003); Nathan Koppel, *American Export,* AMERICAN LAWYER 92 (September 2003). James Feroli, *When Pro Bono*

Work Is a Crime: The Government Lawyer and 18 USC § 205, ABA GOVERNMENT AND PUBLIC SECTOR LAWYERS DIVISION NEWSLETTER, THE PUBLIC LAWYER 2 (Winter 2001), in LAWYERS FOR ONE AMERICA, BAR NONE, 64–65; Marc Galanter, *'Old and in the Way': The Coming Demographic Transformation of the Legal Profession and Its Implications for the Provision of Legal Services*, 1999 WISCONSIN LAW REVIEW 1081 (2000); Beth Slater, *A New Firm Niche: Part-Time Pro Bono*, NATIONAL LAW JOURNAL, August 2, 1999, at A13; Terry Carter, *Taking Up the Slack*, ABA JOURNAL, October 2001, at 22.

41. *See* http://www.probono.net; Elizabeth Amon, *Corporate Pro Bono Gets Boost: In House Counsel Group Uses Web in Outreach to Members*, NATIONAL LAW JOURNAL, September 11, 2000, at A1; Hallinan, *What Judges Can Do*, 9.

42. *See* A. J. Noble, *Greenberg's Pro Bono Patrol*, AMERICAN LAWYER 20 (March 1999); Kenneth L. Jacobs, *How to Institutionalize Pro Bono at your Office*, MICHIGAN BAR JOURNAL 52, 56 (January/February 1999); William Carlsen, *San Francisco Lawyer Proposes a Tax on Lawyers*, SAN FRANCISCO CHRONICLE, February 7, 1989, at A7; and legal aid funding proposals discussed in chapters 5 and 6.

Chapter 8

1. Richard W. Stevenson, *The Struggle for Iraq: U.S. Budget*, NEW YORK TIMES, Sept 9, 2003, at A12; David Firestone, *The Struggle for Iraq: The Occupation; Lawmakers Back Request by Bush on Funds for Iraq*, NEW YORK TIMES, October 18, 2003, at A1.

2. ASSOCIATION OF AMERICAN LAW SCHOOLS (AALS), EQUAL JUSTICE PROJECT, PURSUING EQUAL JUSTICE: LAW SCHOOLS AND THE PROVISION OF LEGAL SERVICES (Washington, D.C.: AALS, 2002); CYNTHIA F. ADCOCK & ALISON M. KEEGAN, A HANDBOOK ON LAW SCHOOL PRO BONO PROGRAMS: THE AALS PRO BONO PROJECT (Washington, D.C., 2001).

3. For public opinion, see AMERICAN BAR ASSOCIATION, PERCEPTIONS OF THE UNITED STATES JUSTICE SYSTEM 59–61 (Chicago: American Bar Association, 1999). For public ignorance, see ROBERT A. KAGAN, ADVERSARIAL LEGALISM: THE AMERICAN WAY OF LAW 167, 248–51 (Cambridge, Mass.: Harvard University Press, 2001). HALT figures come from a personal interview, James Turner, Director HALT, February 2002. For the ABA figures, see http://www.abanet/name.html.

4. AMERICAN BAR ASSOCIATION AND NATIONAL LEGAL AID AND DEFENDER ASSOCIATION, SPAN, SUPPORTING PARTNERSHIPS TO EXPAND ACCESS TO JUSTICE, TWELVE LESSONS FROM SUCCESSFUL STATE ACCESS TO JUSTICE EFFORTS (Chicago: American Bar Association, 2003).

≗ INDEX ≗

American Bar Association (continued)
    Public Hearing on Access to Justice,
        88–89
American Bar Association Journal, 54
American Civil Liberties Union, 66
American Law Institute, 89
American Lawyer (magazine), 35, 161
American Medical Association, 62
American Tort Reform Association, 29
Americorps, 117
anticompetitive bar policies, 15, 69–78,
        96–97, 148, 190
    policing of, 87–91
Antiterrorism and Effective Death
        Penalty Act, 135
antitrust laws, 72, 77, 88
Arnold, Marcus, 87–88
Arons, Marilyn, 90
asbestos cases, 34, 36
Association of American Law Schools,
        156–57, 161, 180, 181, 189, 192
    Commission on Pro Bono and Public
        Service Opportunities in Law
        Schools, 156–57, 161, 180
attorney–client privilege, 95, 98, 114
attorneys. See lawyers; legal fees
Australia, 29, 86–87, 186

bankruptcy cases, 14, 61, 82, 85, 107
bar associations
    accountability and, 191
    admission standards and, 48, 49
    anticompetitive policies of, 15,
        69–71, 73–77, 87–91, 97, 148, 190
    disciplinary action by, 13
    effective representation guidelines
        of, 131
    legal aid and, 59–60, 103–104, 106,
        112, 116
    legal challenges to restrictive prac-
        tices of, 73–74
    multidisciplinary partnerships
        objections of, 91–96
    nonlawyer services and, 74–77,
        82–83, 88–89, 148
    poverty programs and, 62–63
    pro bono work and, 65, 145, 149,
        152–56, 184, 188
    referral systems and, 73, 99
    tort reform and, 27–28
    See also American Bar Association

barratry, 69
Barry, Dave, 34–35
Bates v. State Bar of Arizona (1977), 72
battered women. See domestic violence
        victims
Bellow, Gary, 68
benzene, 34–35
Betts v. Brady (1942), 56
bias, 61, 107, 122–44, 159. See also racial
        bias
Bread for the City (D.C.), 120
Bright, Stephen, 128
British law, 47–48, 49–50, 65
Brookings Institution, 32
Brown v. Board of Education (1954), 67,
        70
Buckhannan Board and Care Home Inc. v.
        West Virginia Department of Health
        and Human Resources (2001), 115
Burger, Warren, 97
Bush, George H. W., 26
Bush, George W., 26–27, 103, 138
Bush, Jeb, 125
business liability claims, 32, 34–36

California, 31, 45–46, 113, 138, 180
Canada, 7, 29, 112, 186
Canons of Professional Ethics (ABA,
        1908), 65, 69–70
capital cases. See death penalty
Capital Jury Project, 136
Carter, Jimmy, 79
case-processing systems, 76
Center for Court Innovation (N.Y.C.),
        85
certification, 21
champerty, 69
charity
    legal aid as, 58–59, 64
    pro bono services as, 19, 66, 145–49,
        154, 167–68
    public defender control by, 55
Chicago Bar Association, 75
Chicago legal aid organizations, 58–59,
        60, 62
Chicago Women's Club, 58
Child Advocacy Clinic (University of
        Mexico), 120
children, 5, 58, 90, 91, 104
Citizen Advice Bureaus (Britain),
        117

holistic assistance provision for, 120
lack of remedies for, 5, 9, 30, 83, 85
Legal Aid society services for, 61
multidisciplinary partnerships and, 91
poverty law offices and, 107
self-representation by, 82, 83, 84
Drinker, Henry, 71
due process, 8, 53, 56-57, 186
civil cases and, 9, 113, 192
criminal cases and, 124, 125-30

elderly individuals, 5, 91, 104, 118, 119
England. *See* Great Britain
environmental quality, 7, 8, 67
"Equal Justice" Project (AALS), 192
Essay on Professional Ethics (Sharswood), 69
ethical codes, 65-66, 69-70, 75, 95
accountability and, 191
group legal services and, 73, 98-99
lawyer-nonlawyer relationships and, 91-92
lawyer's professional image and, 71
lay assistance prohibitions and, 15
nonlawyer legal services and, 74, 87, 91, 95, 119, 190
pro bono work and, 16, 17, 65, 145, 149, 152-53
professional solicitation bans by, 69-70, 71, 77
unbundled services and, 100, 101
Ethical Cultural Society (Chicago), 59
ethnic bias, 123, 130, 142
Europe
death penalty abolishment in, 141
government per capita legal aid spending in, 112
group legal services in, 98
legal aid availability in, 7, 21, 104, 186
legal aid funding in, 187
litigation rates in, 29
multidisciplinary partnerships in, 191
no-fault systems in, 34, 38
public defender system in, 54
Every Man His Own Lawyer (manual), 81

federal funding. *See* government
Federal Trade Commission, 88
fees. *See* legal fees

fee-shifting initiatives, 40-41, 115
fee splitting, 91
Feinblatt, John, 85
felony cases
court-appointed counsel for, 11-12, 51, 122, 126, 128
English restraints on counsel for, 49-50
lack of representation in, 53
right to counsel ruling on, 56, 57
Findlaw (website), 92
First Amendment, 72, 113, 114
Florida, 41, 57, 125, 153, 154, 179
Foltz, Clara Shortridge, 54
Fordham University Law School, pro bono program, 161, 176
foundations, 62, 67, 102
Fourteenth Amendment, 56
freedom of speech, 8, 72
Friedman, Lawrence, 8
frivolous suits, 24-29, 33, 194
differing interpretations of, 26, 28
discouragement of, 39, 40-41, 45-46, 191

Galanter, Marc, 43
Georgia, 52, 124, 126, 131, 133-34
"ghostwritten" legal documents, 101
Gideon, Earl, 57
Gideon v. Wainwright (1963), 57, 113
Ginsburg, Ruth Bader, 137-38
global legal market, 92, 191
Goldfarb, Lewis and Ruth, 71-72
government
Americans' wariness of, 7, 38, 108
legal aid funding proposals for, 187-88
legal aid subsidy by, 3-4, 7, 10, 13, 19, 54, 55, 60, 62, 64, 65, 77, 103-21, 139, 186-88, 191-92
Legal Services Corporation and, 63-64, 103, 104, 105-16
regulation by, 35, 37
See also federal funding; public defender system; states
grassroots organization. *See* community services
Great Britain, 7, 29, 51, 69, 117, 186, 187
legal precedents from, 47-48, 49-50, 65
per capita legal aid spending in, 112

multidisciplinary legal practice and,
91
pro bono services for, 66
self-representation by, 82
unmet legal needs of, 3, 4, 79, 80,
103, 192
Millemann, Michael, 150
misdemeanor cases, 82, 86, 126
English precedent, 50
right to counsel for, 58, 122
Mississippi, 129
Model Rules of Professional Conduct
(ABA), 91–92, 100–101, 155, 181
moderate-income individuals. *See*
middle-income individuals
monopoly. *See* anticompetitive bar
policies
multidisciplinary partnerships, 91–96,
112, 190–91
collaborative relationships and,
119–20
Multidisciplinary Practice Commission
(ABA), 94, 95
"multidoor courthouses," 43

NAACP v. Button (1963), 73
National Association for Law Place-
ment, 180
National Association for the Advance-
ment of Colored People, 66–67,
73
National Lawyers Guild, 67, 71
National Legal Aid and Defender
Association, 126, 143
National Legal Service Corps, 117
national service volunteers, 117
Netherlands, 34
New Jersey, 88, 153
New York, 128, 148
Center for Court Innovation, 85
pro bono work, 154
New York Bar Association, 75
New York Legal Aid Society, 58, 59, 60
New York Times, 128
New Zealand, 7, 29, 112
Nixon Administration, 63
no-fault compensation systems, 34, 38,
43–46, 190
nonlawyer practice, 14–16, 20–21,
74–77, 81–91
ABA model definition of, 88

accounting firms and, 92–93
bar opposition to, 74–77, 82–83,
88–90, 148
do-it-yourself materials and, 19–20,
76, 81–82, 85, 89
ethical standards and, 15, 74, 87, 91,
95, 119, 190
historical precedents for, 48–49
multidisciplinary partnerships and,
91–96, 119
regulatory structure for, 20–21,
90–91
"routine tasks" exception and, 76,
87, 190
See also self-representation
Northwestern Law School, pro bono
program, 161, 176

Office of Economic Opportunity,
62–63
Office of Technology Assessment, 33
Oklahoma City bombing, 130
Oklahoma pro bono survey, 154
one-stop shopping. *See* multidiscipli-
nary partnerships
One Stop Women's Clinic, 120

Pacific Legal Foundation, 67
"pain and suffering" caps, 32, 40, 43
suggested standardized formula for,
43
paralegals, 15, 76
See also nonlawyer practice
Parent Information Center, 90
personal injury suits. *See* tort system
"plaintiff-friendly" venue, 36, 40
plea bargains, 12, 125, 129–30
politics
death penalty and, 135
judicial appointments and, 36, 128
Legal Service Corporation and, 105,
108–12
opposition to legal services and,
10–11
poor, "worthy" vs. "unworthy," 3–4,
109. *See also* low-income individuals, poverty law programs
Poor Persons Defense Act of 1903
(Britain), 50
Posner, Richard, 125
Pound, Roscoe, 77